CHILDREN, CINEMA
AND CENSORSHIP

Turner Classic Movies British Film Guides
General Editor: Jeffrey Richards

Cinema and Society Series
General Editor: Jeffrey Richards

Film and Community in Britain and France: From La Règle du Jeu *to* Room at the Top
Margaret Butler

Film Propaganda: Soviet Russia and Nazi Germany
Richard Taylor

Hollywood Genres and Post-War America: Masculinity, Family and Nation in Popular Movies and Film Noir
Mike Chopra-Gant

Hollywood's History Films
David Eldridge

Licence to Thrill: A Cultural History of the James Bond Films
James Chapman

From Moscow to Madrid: Postmodern Cities, European Cinema
Ewa Mazierska & Laura Rascaroli

Past and Present: National Identity and the British Historical Film
James Chapman

Powell and Pressburger: A Cinema of Magic Spaces
Andrew Moor

Propaganda and the German Cinema, 1933–1945
David Welch

Somewhere in England: British Cinema and Exile
Kevin Gough-Yates

Spaghetti Westerns: Cowboys and Europeans from Karl May to Sergio Leone
Christopher Frayling

Spectacular Narratives: Hollywood in the Age of the Blockbuster
Geoff King

Typical Men: The Representation of Masculinity in the Popular British Cinema
Andrew Spicer

The Unknown 1930s: An Alternative History of the British Cinema, 1929–1939
Edited by Jeffrey Richards

CHILDREN, CINEMA AND CENSORSHIP
From Dracula to the Dead End Kids

Sarah J. Smith

I.B. TAURIS

LONDON · NEW YORK

Published in 2005 by I.B. Tauris & Co Ltd
6 Salem Road, London W2 4BU
175 Fifth Avenue, New York NY 10010
www.ibtauris.com

In the United States and Canada distributed by Palgrave Macmillan, a division of St. Martin's Press, 175 Fifth Avenue, New York NY 10010

ISBN 1 85043 812 9 (hardback)
EAN 978 1 85043 812 0 (hardback)
ISBN 1 85043 813 7 (paperback)
EAN 978 1 85043 813 7 (paperback)

A full CIP record for this book is available from the British Library
A full CIP record for this book is available from the Library of Congress

Library of Congress catalog card: available

Project management by M&M Publishing Services
Typeset by FiSH Books, London
Printed and bound in Great Britain by MPG Books Ltd, Bodmin

For my Mum,
Jill Stidwell
(1932–2004)

Contents

Tables and Figures

Illustrations

Abbreviations

BBFC	British Board of Film Censors
BCEC	Birmingham Cinema Enquiry Committee
BFI	British Film Institute
BVC	Birkenhead Vigilance Committee
CEA	Cinematograph Exhibitors' Association
CEF	Children's Educational Films
CFD	Children's Film Department
ECEC	Edinburgh Cinema Enquiry Committee
FCCC	Film Censorship Consultative Committee
GBI	Gaumont British Instructional
LCC	London County Council
MPPDA	Motion Picture Producers and Distributors of America
PCA	Production Code Administration ('The Hays Office')
PFS	Payne Fund Studies
PRO	Public Record Office

General Editor's Introduction

Children were amongst the most regular and habitual filmgoers in the heyday of the cinema. It was generally agreed that their experience of film-watching was more intense than that of adults, owing to the visual impact of the medium and their emotional involvement with the stories. The cinema's influence on children greatly preoccupied society's cultural and educational elites. Few of the concerned groups would have dissented from the view expressed by Dr John Mackie, who edited the report of the Edinburgh Cinema Enquiry in 1933: 'The public...should realise the importance that the cinema has assumed in the lives of the children. Seven children out of every ten go to the pictures at least once a week. Most children spend longer at the cinema than they do at many school subjects. Here is an influence of first importance.'

Commentators on the cinema have frequently referred to adults' 'moral panic' about the influence of films on children. But in what is the most thorough, thoughtful and illuminating study yet of children's cinema-going experience in inter-war Britain, Sarah Smith qualifies and nuances that view. She concludes that there was not a 'moral panic' so much as a thoroughgoing and wide-ranging debate on the subject.

She argues convincingly for the interaction of the regulation of children's viewing from above and below; she traces the development of official film censorship and its application to children; she analyses the debates and conclusions of the four major local cinema enquiries in the 1930s (London, Birmingham, Edinburgh and Birkenhead); and she assesses the effectiveness or otherwise of particular regulatory restraints. There was, for example, the A certificate, which only permitted children to enter cinemas accompanied by an adult. Sarah Smith finds that some cinemas blatantly ignored the requirement and that children themselves asked adult strangers to take them in. I myself can recall that in the 1950s, when I was still a teenager, a cinema manager asked me to take a group of unaccompanied children into an A film. Then there was parental authority and self-regulation by the children – both of which had variable results.

Finally, drawing extensively on oral evidence, she vividly recreates the children's interaction with the films – their involvement in Saturday matinees and cinema clubs, their behaviour in the auditorium, their imitation of the dress, speech and behaviour observed in the film. The whole study adds up to a major and welcome contribution to our understanding of the role of cinema in the lives of 1930s children.

Jeffrey Richards

Acknowledgements

Much of the research for this book has drawn on archived interviews and correspondence with those who experienced cinema first hand in the 1930s. I have benefited enormously from listening to taped interviews and reading the files of over 300 such individuals, virtually none of whom I have met. I am therefore very grateful for their invaluable contribution to this work. My first thanks go to them and to those who conducted the original research projects.

I would like to thank those who facilitated my archive research, including Barbara Hall and the staff of the Margaret Herrick Library, Beverly Hills; Janet McBain, Curator of the Scottish Film Archive; Nick White in Special Collections at the British Film Institute; Andrew Martin, for access to the Going to the Pictures project in the Scottish Life Archive of the National Museums of Scotland; and particularly Annette Kuhn, not only for offering generous early access to the archives of the Cinema Culture in 1930s Britain project, but also for her interest and support for this work over the years.

Thanks to colleagues from the University of Reading, the University of Strathclyde (particularly my PhD supervisor, Callum Brown), the Social History Society, the Film History Seminar at the Institute of Historical Research, London, the Scottish Women's History Network, and all those who helped in many ways at different stages of this project.

I am also grateful to the Economic and Social Research Council, which provided generous funding support for my research.

Finally, thanks to my family and friends. You are too many to name, but you know who you are. Without your support I could not have started, maintained or finished this project, so ... thank you.

1

The Doom of a Generation?

Unless it is cleaned up within this generation,
[cinema] will undermine every existing agency for
decency and public order.

R.G. Burnett and E.D. Martell,
The Devil's Camera (1932)

In 1937, a new American film was passed with an A certificate by the
British Board of Film Censors (BBFC) for distribution in the UK.
This certificate, given the previous year to horror films such as *The
Walking Dead* (1936) and *Dracula's Daughter* (1936), informed
cinema managers and patrons that the film was not considered suitable
for children under 16 years old, unless they were accompanied by a
parent or *bona fide* adult guardian. The new film in question was Walt
Disney's *Snow White and the Seven Dwarfs* (1937). Thousands of
children would flock to see it on its first release in Britain and, as will
become apparent, the majority were probably quite undeterred by the
BBFC's attempts at regulation.

During the 1930s, authorities in Britain and across the world
struggled with the issue of children's cinema-going. At one extreme,
moral watch-dogs prophesied the doom of a generation corrupted by
the influence of the silver screen. At the other, champions of the
cinema declared its positive educational and social value to young
people. Meanwhile, children became one of the largest audience
segments in cinemas worldwide.

The debate surrounding children and film did not exist in isolation – it simply represented a peak in longstanding controversies over children and leisure which had been endemic across Europe and the USA for hundreds of years. Some argue that this debate might date back over 2,000 years to Plato, who suggested that poets should be banned from his ideal Republic, so that their stories about the questionable behaviour of the gods would not damage the vulnerable minds of children.[1]

Certainly, since at least the eighteenth century, a cavalcade of pastimes and technologies have been deemed undesirable – if not dangerous – for children, including penny magazines, playing in the street, fighting, dancing, gambling, sex, radio, cinema, television, comic books, rock music, videos and computer games. All have been cited as threats to children's safety, health, morality and literacy and have been blamed for increases in juvenile delinquency. And the debate continues: current targets include mobile phones, gangsta rap and the Internet and it can safely be predicted that Virtual Reality will be targeted in the near future.

Fears about the social effects of new media have therefore recurred for over two centuries and the debates they generate nearly always primarily revolve around the potential impact of these media on children. Despite thousands of research projects, conferences and other enquiries (most of which find the medium in question to be intrinsically benign), these issues refuse to be resolved. And whenever a shocking incident occurs involving young people, the immediate reaction is often to blame popular culture, however tenuous the link might be – as in the bogus scapegoating of *Child's Play 3* during the James Bulger murder case, or neo-Nazi websites, television, film and the music of 'shock rocker' Marilyn Manson after the Columbine High School Massacre.[2]

In his study 'Reservoirs of Dogma: An Archaeology of Popular Anxieties', Graham Murdock calls for more detailed historical research into these fears and their associated debates:

> If we are to develop a more comprehensive analysis of the interplay between popular media and everyday thinking, feeling and behaviour, and to argue convincingly for expressive diversity in film, television and the new media, we need to challenge popular fears. Retracing the intellectual and political history that has formed them is a necessary first step.[3]

As part of the 'first step', this book seeks to contribute to an understanding of the nature and impact of recurring debates surrounding children and media usage, by exploring one key example – the controversy surrounding children and cinema in the 1930s.

Although the field of film and cinema history is large and growing, surprisingly little has been written about the debate over children and cinema in 1930s Britain and only a few books explore the topic at any length. The most recent is Annette Kuhn's *An Everyday Magic*, a fascinating ethno-historical study of film reception during the 1930s, which often focuses on the cinema-going of children, owing to the nature of some of the primary sources involved.[4] Meanwhile, an overview of controversies surrounding children and leisure between around 1830 and 1996 is presented in John Springhall's *Youth, Popular Culture and Moral Panics*, which includes a concise yet detailed study of anxieties that arose around gangster films and child viewers in Britain and America during the 1930s. Terry Staples' *All Pals Together* also provides a narrative and nostalgic look at children and cinema in Britain between around 1900 and 1987, including some very interesting material on the 1930s.

Jeffrey Richards' valuable and perceptive exploration of cinema-going in Britain during the 1930s, *The Age of the Dream Palace*, outlines the debate over children and cinema and considers, among other things, the extent to which it may have reflected middle class attempts to control working class leisure and promote hegemony. In a similar vein, Stephen Humphries analyses debates over children and leisure (including cinema) in his work *Hooligans or Rebels?*, strongly arguing that class, rather than age, was the key factor in perceptions of juvenile delinquency. While social class was undoubtedly a factor in debates over children's cinema-going, I would suggest that it was by no means the most significant factor. Nevertheless, Humphries' emphasis on resistance, and his insistence that working class children were not simply the passive recipients of social control, are critical issues that will be explored in some detail in the chapters that follow.

No other works have directly tackled the subject of British children and cinema in the 1930s, although earlier periods and older age groups have received a little attention.[5] English language studies of the debate in other nations are also scarce. Anton Kaes, David Welch and Gary D. Stark have all assessed the general cinema debate of the 1920s and 1930s in Germany, but none of these authors are more than marginally interested in issues relating to children.[6] Meanwhile, Richard Stites' work on the history of Russian popular culture only mentions the subject of children and cinema in passing.[7]

More has been published on the subject in America, particularly concerning the major research project that dominated the American debate in the 1930s: the Payne Fund Studies. The key text in this field is the collaboration of Garth Jowett, Ian Jarvie and Kathryn Fuller, *Children and the Movies*.[8] However, even this volume is not directly concerned with the history of childhood, as its stated aim is to research the Payne Fund Studies themselves, in order to 'restore [them] to a place of honor in the history of communications research'.[9]

It is understandable but regrettable that there are also, as yet, no studies of this topic as an international phenomenon. Cinema was undoubtedly international from the outset, with inventors, financiers, producers, casts, crews, distribution networks and audiences ranging and mixing across the globe. There was also something of an international consensus regarding concerns over children and cinema in the 1930s. Common anxieties (along with opposing views of the educational potential of cinema) recurred across the board in nations with otherwise starkly different ideologies, from Britain and America to Nazi Germany and Communist Russia. For example, theories regarding the power of cinema to imbue children with a sense of political and national identity caused Americans to rail against the fascist and communist influences in European films of the 1930s, while Europeans of all political hues protested at length about the Americanising impact of Hollywood on their children. However, no work has yet been published that considers the international dimension of the debate over children and film, and sadly this book will do little to remedy the situation, although references to the international context have been made where possible.

Quite rightly, therefore, in his article on children and cinema in the 1910s and 1920s in America, Richard deCordova bemoans the dearth of literature in this field. 'It seems odd', he suggests, 'that...film history has so completely ignored the obsession with the child audience, particularly if we admit that it was the dominant feature of critical approaches to the cinema at the time.'[10] Certainly, although the debates have been outlined to some extent, little has been done to investigate the motivation and mechanisms that lay *behind* attempts to control children's viewing in the 1930s, or to place these attempts in their historical context regarding children, leisure and media. That is therefore a central aim of this book – to explore not only what happened, but how and why it happened.

In doing so, this book is a response to research in media and communications studies regarding controversies over children and television. For in this field, although scholars have increasingly come to recognise the cyclical nature of the debate surrounding children and leisure and, therefore, the need for historical research, little has yet been done.[11] As David Buckingham argues, the key to understanding the recurring debate about children and media influence of all kinds may lie not so much in analysing the *results* of the empirical research, but in examining its *context*. Thus, he argues, research into children and television may

> reveal as much about the tensions and contradictions within society as it does about either children or television. In this respect, it is important to locate the concern about the area historically, in the context both of evolving definitions of childhood and of recurrent responses to the perceived impact of new cultural forms and communications technologies.[12]

This book therefore aims to provide some historical background, in order to contribute to an understanding of ongoing debates regarding children and media. So far, scholars in media studies have mapped some of the historical landmarks of the debate from the air.[13] Now I will explore one of those historical landmarks from the ground, by providing an extended, detailed case study of the controversy over children and film in 1930s Britain.

First, though, two fundamental questions need to be addressed. Why has the decade of the 1930s been chosen? And how are children to be defined?

Moving pictures were introduced to the British public in 1896 and the first purpose-built cinema in Britain was erected ten years later. Thereafter, rapid growth occurred; by 1907 there were around 250 picture palaces in Britain, after which the number virtually doubled annually, rising to 1,600 by 1910 and nearly 4,000 in 1911. British cinemas continued to expand in both numbers and size, so that by 1939 the country had over 5,000 cinemas that attracted an attendance of approximately 20 million per week.[14] Cinema had become the first mass medium to be distributed simultaneously to audiences of millions and it therefore provoked much debate.

From the outset, defenders of cinema insisted that this was a highly promising form of self-improving education; an influential force of socialisation, with powerful potential for good. However, in reality, film quickly became established as an extremely popular form of entertainment rather than education, associated from the beginning with alcohol consumption, with early venues for film including travelling fairs, music halls and vaudevilles, most of which served alcohol. Furthermore, as the medium developed, its content was largely derived from the sensational narratives of melodrama and cheap literature, rather than worthy literary or educational alternatives. It was of great significance, therefore, that film became a cheap and massively attended source of entertainment, rather than improvement. Moreover, it was largely frequented by the urban working classes and, despite concerted efforts to the contrary, it was a medium principally driven by commercial interests, rather than religious, educational, or otherwise 'improving' ones.

Consequently, the cinema had numerous critics, mainly from middle class educational, religious and social welfare groups, who insisted that it represented a threat to society. Vulnerable, uneducated or uncontrollable viewers were considered especially at risk – namely, cinema's most frequent patrons: the working classes, women and children. Romantic notions of childhood were invoked and movies were denounced as violent, frightening, sexually corrupt, addictive and therefore fundamentally damaging to the naturally curious, vulnerable, naïve, imitative and emotionally susceptible mind of the child. At the same time, concepts of original sin were evident in declarations that the negative influence of cinema stimulated already degenerate young minds, leading them into even greater depths of corruption, depravity and delinquency. Concerns regarding the possible influences of cinema on children and adults quickly motivated various bodies to attempt the imposition of a regulatory framework, leading to the establishment of the BBFC in 1913.

Although debates around cinema were evident from its inception, this book focuses on the 1930s because it was a key decade – arguably *the* key decade – in the history of cinema and its regulation. Jeffrey Richards has described it as probably 'the least known and least appreciated decade in the history of the sound film'.[15] And Peter Stead considers it 'the most crucial period in the whole history of cinema in Britain and America'.[16] It is an easily identifiable period, roughly beginning with the introduction of talking pictures and ending with the start of the Second World War. Significantly, it also is the period in which the Hays Code was developed and introduced, effecting the rigorous censorship of films (see Chapter 3). Finally, it was the decade in which cinema was established as the most popular form of communal entertainment across Europe and the USA, with children of the 1930s being regarded by many as the first generation to be fundamentally influenced by so-called mass culture.

The most important facet of the decade for this book, though, is that anxiety about children and cinema rocketed with the introduction of talkies in 1927, triggering a profusion of enquiries across the world into the influence of cinema on the young. During the 1930s, literally hundreds of surveys and reports were generated worldwide, in an attempt to assess and regulate the influence of cinema on children (see Chapter 4). Most of the 'players' in the British enquiries represented groups such as church and youth organisations, which were rapidly losing their virtual monopoly on organised children's leisure. Others came from the establishments of education and government, while the remainder represented the commercial might of the cinema industry. Consequently, many of the projects began with a hidden agenda and the subject quickly became a more or less blatant battle, within and among a range of powerful bodies, for the control of children's culture and the transmission of values.

But what of children themselves in this battle? On the face of it, they apparently had little more than a symbolic role to play in what was essentially an adult debate, leading to the organisation, censorship and certification of cinema, as well as the introduction of children's cinema clubs and, eventually, the production of films for child audiences. However, this book will argue that, in fact, children took a central role as agents in the development of cinema regulation during the 1930s.

Ultimately then, this period has been chosen for two main reasons. First, it was a decade in which cinema-going had become by far the most popular commercial leisure pursuit in Britain, with children being a very important part of that trend. Second, this was the first decade of talking pictures, which prompted an escalation in anxiety over young people and film and the introduction of new, more stringent forms of censorship. The 1930s marked the zenith of all concerns regarding children and cinema; and Ellen Wartella and Byron Reeves suggest that this decade actually represented the peak of concern over children and media influence of *all* kinds in the twentieth century.[17] It is therefore clearly a key decade.

The other fundamental issue to address is the question of defining 'the child'. Historians of childhood have increasingly sought to tackle this question in recent years, interrogating established definitions of childhood, just as others have questioned definitions of class and gender. Foremost among these was Philippe Aries, whose book *Centuries of Childhood* (1960) argued that perceptions of the nature of childhood were culturally determined, giving it a flexible, rather than a universally fixed, definition. Essentially, Aries suggests, the experience of a child in any given culture is fundamentally affected by that culture's perceptions of childhood. In other words, different cultures at different times have different ideas about the nature of childhood, which inform their views on how children should behave and be treated, and this in turn directly affects children's experiences.

Following Aries, a number of historians, psychologists and sociologists have explored the ways in which definitions and experiences of childhood can vary, depending on a range of economic, social and cultural factors. Even the apparently universal biological characteristics of childhood can differ, it is argued, depending on factors such as class, culture and historical period. Thus, Michael Mitterauer has suggested that in the nineteenth century, 'unmistakable class-related differences' were apparent in the menarche (first menstruation) rates of girls, so that between 1800 and 1981 the average age of menarche decreased by several years across Europe, as standards of living rose.[18]

The majority of work by scholars in this area has focused on the history of discourses relating to childhood.[19] By 'discourses relating to childhood' I mean the shifting body of shared language and knowledge, which both creates and is created by dominant perceptions of what it means to be a child, in any given time and place. A study of such discourses necessarily draws on Aries' theory that childhood is a socially constructed category rather than a fixed reality, examining the ways in which that category – the 'child' – has been constructed through discourse. This book will follow a similar theoretical path, in that it will not be considering childhood as a fixed biological and psychological state, but rather as a socially constructed category. The main aim in this respect is to explore the role of such social construction and the discourses supporting it in the debate over children and cinema in 1930s Britain.

Nevertheless, it is necessary at this stage to consider a definition of childhood in terms of age range. This is tricky for a number of reasons. Simplistic definitions of children as 'persons aged under 16', for example, belie the fact that childhood can cover a long period of extensive mental and physical change, from infancy and pre-pubescence, through puberty and beyond. As such, childhood might be better seen as a plural rather than a singular experience. And any age at which one might choose to draw the line is inevitably problematic, not least because of the sheer variety of experiences of different children in terms of their rates of physical, mental and social development. So a fixed chronological or biological definition of the child is hard to establish. At what point does a child become an adult? And what is the difference between the two?

Justification for this basic struggle over definition is easily found, as it soon becomes clear when looking at contemporary sources that those dealing with issues relating to children and cinema in the 1930s could not reach agreement over their definitions either. One illustration of this problem comes from a meeting in 1929 of the BBFC's Mr Brooke-Wilkinson and Mr Hessey with Miss Rosamund Smith, Miss Adler and Mr Greenwood of the London County Council. In discussing the issue of children and A film regulation, conversation turned to the definition of 'children' when the meeting considered a suggested new certificate for films, which Rosamund Smith described as 'suitable for children'. Brooke-Wilkinson took issue with this phrase:

BW: Is that something different from the young person which is mentioned in the [A film] regulation?

RS: Yes, I think it is really children. Technically a child is a child up to 14, isn't that so? I don't think we discussed the age, but I think we all want really childish films...

BW: At the moment we are dealing with films for young persons, and a young person is someone up to the age of 16 years. Is your idea that this film is for some class of person younger than 16?

RS: Younger than *14*.

Miss A: I think we really thought up to 16.

BW: You are using the word children.

RS: The technical age of a child is up to the time that it leaves the elementary school, which at present is 14...

Mr G: It was understood that at present it was the school age of 14, but nothing was decided as to whether it should remain at the school age when it was 15...

RS: ...I personally thought we had 16 in our minds.

BW: In the regulation I think it is specific; it says 'no young person'.

RS: ...My view on the question is this – it might not be the view of others – that a child is a child from 1 to 14 and from 14 to 18 is a young person and then becomes an adult. That is my view. We haven't discussed it as a committee.

Mr H: I think it is perfectly clear that we deal with young persons up to 16.[20]

As this extract demonstrates, the problem of defining childhood is not solved by looking at primary source material, which is often equally undecided. This can be further illustrated by a letter to the Home Office in 1934 from a representative of the Cinematograph Exhibitors' Association (CEA), who had been asked to define *'bona fide* adult guardian'. The CEA representative writes: 'As I personally am not aware of any decision having been given as to the meaning of the word "adult" I should be very much obliged if you would kindly let me know what "adult" does in your opinion mean'.[21] The Home Office response is not known. However, when Middlesex County Council had problems with this definition, they took the plunge and stipulated that adults accompanying children had to be over 21. Unfortunately, this caused a mother of three children (who was under 21) to be refused admission to a cinema. The *News Chronicle* investigated the story in an article headed 'What is an Adult?' and suggested that the basic problem of defining childhood was simply one of variety: 'On the railway you must be over 12 and on the trams over 14; to buy cigarettes you must be 16 years old and to enter a public house you are an adult at 18'.[22]

Clearly, there were considerable problems of definition during the 1930s, but it is still important to make some firm statement about the ways in which this book will define childhood – however fluid that definition may be. So, for purposes of clarity at this stage, 'children' will nominally be taken to mean persons under 16 years of age, as this was the limit set by A film regulations. Nevertheless, there will be occasions when the primary source material suggests an upper age limit of 14, 18 or 21 years and the definition will therefore adapt accordingly.

The principal aim of this book is to explore all aspects of the debate surrounding children and cinema in 1930s Britain, with a particular focus on the mechanisms used to try to control or contain children's viewing, including an assessment of the extent to which these mechanisms were successful. Its linked themes of childhood, youth, cinema, censorship, media influence and moral panic lie at the intersection of a number of areas of academic interest, requiring a wide range of primary source material and approaches from a number of disciplines, in order to assemble a comprehensive picture of the ways in which children interacted with attempts to regulate their viewing. To this end, the debate about children and cinema is explored from various perspectives, including those of moral watchdogs and enquiry committees, the Home Office, the press, censorship boards, local authorities, cinema managers, film-makers and, perhaps most importantly, children themselves, examining not only what happened, but how and why it happened.[23]

A study of the development of official censorship is probably the best place to start. As Jeffrey Richards has effectively argued, 'it is impossible to understand the development and nature of the British cinema without a full appreciation of the work and influence of censors'.[24] Chapters 2 and 3 extend this argument to suggest that it is equally impossible to understand the development of censorship (and therefore cinema) without recognising the central importance of debates surrounding children and film in the evolution of cinema regulation. Histories of official censorship have traditionally focused on institutions and explored political themes, constructing the cinema as a cultural battlefield drawn up along class lines, with censorship being identified as a key aspect of social or cultural control. Chapters 2 and 3 offer an alternative overview of the history of censorship, arguing that the primary driving force behind the development of cinema regulation, both in Britain and beyond, was concern regarding the medium's influence on children.

The 1930s saw a proliferation of enquiries, conferences and reports generated by various interest groups, local councils and committees, who often met with the Home Office and/or the BBFC to discuss their findings. Such investigations are of particular interest inasmuch as they highlight the preoccupations and tactics of those trying to influence the regulation of children's cinema-going and they are therefore examined in detail in Chapter 4.

This chapter focuses particularly on the four main British enquiries of the early 1930s, conducted in Birmingham, Birkenhead, London and Edinburgh, looking in detail at the main 'players' and their various preoccupations and strategies. The chapter has two main objectives: first, to examine the terms of the debate as they are presented in the reports of these enquiries, including an analysis of the language used and the ways in which children are represented; second, to assess the extent to which concerns over children and cinema in the 1930s might be considered a moral panic.

It is important to discuss the term 'moral panic' here, as it is extremely problematic, having no agreed definition even among those who routinely use it. It was first coined by British sociologist Jock Young in 1971, when he described growing public concern over apparently rapid increases in drug abuse. It was then explored more thoroughly as an analytical concept by Young's colleague Stanley Cohen, in his study *Folk Devils and Moral Panics* (1972). Since then, it has been used by various sociologists, psychologists, historians and journalists, who have employed a variety of definitions and approaches to the subject, creating a range of theoretical models for the study of specific incidents. This has therefore spawned an array of isolated studies, but little in terms of a systematic approach.

The meaning of the term 'moral panic' is often considered self-evident, yet it is a highly equivocal and loaded expression. Essentially, the word 'panic' suggests an irrational and negative response – if not an overreaction – by a naïve or ignorant subject, who is often being manipulated by the media and others for a variety of reasons. Meanwhile, the word 'moral' implies that those 'panicking' consider themselves morally superior in terms of the problem. The ambiguity of the expression is also evident in its broad application, encompassing areas that may not directly involve morality, but relate, for example, to food, health and the environment, such as recent 'panics' over BSE, GM crops and foot-and-mouth disease.

Furthermore, as Peter Horsfield has argued, the term 'moral panic' can itself be used as a tool of social control, being 'invoked by those in positions of power…in order to discount and defuse legitimate challenges'.[25] This alone renders it highly questionable. I would suggest that the major underlying weakness of the term, however, is that it emphasises issues of manipulation and irrational concern, while obscuring the fact that those involved in 'panics' are usually responding in what they consider a rational way to a genuine threat. Moreover (as will be shown in the case of cinema), these players may be ambivalent rather than dogmatic in their views; they may be media-aware, rather than the blind subjects of press manipulation; and they may even be aware of the history of moral panics and their place within it. For this reason, I will use the term moral panic advisedly when discussing anxieties relating to children and cinema in the 1930s.

One good reason for retaining the term moral panic, however, is that it identifies this book with other studies of a similar nature, including John Springhall's *Youth, Popular Culture and Moral Panics* and Kenneth Thompson's *Moral Panics*, which provides a long-awaited, carefully integrated overview of moral panic studies, tracing their history and (as Springhall does) treating panics 'not simply as separate episodes but in relation to systems of representation and regulation, and as possible symptoms of wider social and cultural tensions'.[26] Following Thompson, this book will adopt a contextual constructivist approach, examining not only the construction of a moral panic, but also the socio-cultural context of that construction. That is to say, it will look carefully at the perceived threat posed by cinema to children in 1930s Britain, but will also consider the ways in which this threat was amplified by interest groups, institutions and sections of the media. Thus, the sources will be used to explore both the context of a potential moral panic and the means of its construction.

However, the problematic nature of the term moral panic should be considered implicit throughout. Use will be made of various moral panic theories, rather than adopting any one model for, as Thompson suggests, the field has generated numerous idiosyncratic approaches and it is therefore probably best to 'adopt insights from each...in an eclectic manner or to combine them where appropriate'.[27]

Notably, Chapter 4 draws on 'interest group' theories, such as that of Philip Jenkins, who argues that moral panics involve 'individuals, pressure groups and bureaucratic agencies, each with a complex and often shifting pattern of alliances between them'.[28] This chapter will demonstrate that cinema enquiries of the 1930s relied on networks of individuals, groups and organisations with overlapping interests, including religious, educational and political allegiances. In addition, analysis of the language of the debate will draw on theories of 'convergence' and 'signification spirals', which suggest that moral panics may escalate when pre-existing, apparently dangerous discursive formations are combined.[29] In this way, it will be argued, anxieties about childhood, juvenile delinquency, social class and mass culture may have combined to intensify the apparent social threat regarding children and cinema in 1930s Britain – although whether this constituted a moral panic is nevertheless debatable.

Chapter 5 represents a radical departure from most histories of censorship, which focus on the official practices of institutions and the bodies that influenced them. For, instead of examining the official mechanisms of cinema regulation, this chapter questions whether the strategies of such institutions were effective in real terms at all. As the preceding chapters will establish, attempts were certainly made to control children's viewing in the 1930s, but we should not therefore assume that these attempts were always completely successful.

In order to assess the effectiveness of adult strategies, in addition to examining the documents of official censorship bodies, it is essential to engage with the child's perspective and sense of autonomy. Chapter 5 therefore explores the role of individual viewers in the regulation of their own viewing, exploring ways in which children (and their parents) were personally involved in the censorship of cinema during the 1930s. In particular, it examines the self-regulation practised by children regarding choice of films and the methods used by children to handle screen images they considered frightening or otherwise undesirable. It also explores the interactive relationships between the BBFC certification system, cinema management, parental authority and children's own preferences, inasmuch as they all affected the autonomy children had in choosing the films they watched. In this way, several key questions are addressed: Who controlled children's cinema viewing during this period? What was the relationship between official censorship, parental authority and children's choices? To what extent did children resist adult attempts to control their viewing? And by what means did children regulate their own viewing once they were in the cinema?

In an attempt to access the child's perspective, Chapter 5 utilises a wide range of oral history interviews and correspondence. As with all kinds of primary source material, there are problems associated with such evidence, not least the whole question of memory, which has been the subject of much research in recent decades.[30] The findings of psychologists suggest that memory is largely constructed rather than simply recalled and is therefore never entirely objective or wholly reliable. Nevertheless, it has been found that anecdotal memories generally 'do not violate the meaning of the recalled episode; in fact, if anything they seem to emphasize the meaning'.[31]

In the case of this book, one of the main potential pitfalls is that of nostalgia, as the topic under consideration is one which often evokes fond memories. It is important to recognise, therefore, that memories are constructed and mediated by those who remember. And, as Annette Kuhn suggests, informants' accounts should be 'treated not only as data but also as discourse, as material for interpretation'.[32]

Despite its problematic nature, 'memory evidence' regarding cinema-going has two important strengths. First, recollections of childhood cinema-going can often be extremely vivid, reinforcing the suggestion that anecdotal memories 'emphasize the meaning' of recalled episodes. And second, many recollections are verifiable to some extent, as the films themselves provide something of a timeline. Thus, if a respondent born in 1932 recalls that at the age of 5 they went to see *Snow White and the Seven Dwarfs* on its first release, the fact that this occurred in 1937 helps to verify their statement. In addition to the release dates of films (which varied depending on location and type of cinema), other known dates help to verify information, such as the coming of sound pictures in 1927 or the introduction of the H certificate in 1937.

Original oral history research was not conducted for this book. Instead, existing sources were used from three main locations: the Cinema Culture in 1930s Britain project, housed at the Institute for Cultural Research at Lancaster University; the Oral History

Collection at the Scottish Film Archive in Glasgow; and the Going to the Pictures correspondence project, housed at the Scottish Life Archive in Edinburgh. This approach had obvious limitations, in that I could not frame questions or witness the interviews at first hand. However, the benefits were that hundreds of responses from numerous geographical locations could be accessed in a relatively short space of time and, as all three projects used an open style of questioning (rather than preset questions), there was a great deal of opportunity for respondents to mention issues directly related to this study.

As Paul Thompson has argued, 'in some contexts, oral evidence is the best; in others it is supplementary, or complementary, to that of other sources'.[33] In this case, oral and other 'memory' evidence makes an essential contribution to the overall picture, in that it provides an opportunity to assess the perspective of young cinema-goers of the period, which can then be used to test the claims of the official documents.

Chapter 6 tackles the topics of children's matinees, cinema clubs and children's cinema culture, exploring the ways in which children related to film as a cultural phenomenon and the extent to which this informed the debate in the 1930s. Importantly, this chapter considers ways in which debates surrounding children and cinema were productive, as well as prohibitive in nature. It suggests that while there were areas of overlap between adult and child viewers, children in 1930s Britain had a distinct cinema culture, involving various activities and rituals both inside and outside the cinema. It also suggests that children essentially colonised the space provided by cinema, enjoying liberating escapism and a new and somewhat subversive form of children's culture. Finally, it examines attempts to 'tame' this culture in the late 1930s, when raucous children's matinees were increasingly replaced by more formal children's cinema clubs, and it provides examples of children who initially avoided such control by managing their own cinemas.

As previously stated, the principal aim of this book is to explore all aspects of the debate surrounding children and cinema in 1930s Britain. Overall, this debate will be represented as an arena of complex power play, with the key players including children, parents, educators, clergy, cinema managers and staff, social and youth organisations, the film industry, the press, the censors and the state.

Ultimately, this debate may illustrate something of the nature of power relations between children and adults, both in the 1930s and in ongoing controversies surrounding children and popular media in the twentieth and twenty-first centuries. For this reason, although the cinema debate is often couched in terms of a desire to protect young people, it is important to bear in mind when reading the chapters that follow that, as Catherine Lumby has argued, there may well be a complex relationship at work between the avowed desire to protect children and the desire to control them.[34]

2

How Bridget Served the Salad Undressed: The Regulation of Cinema 1895–1929

The classification of films suitable for young
persons bristles with difficulties, for it is not
easy to know where to draw the line.
British Board of Film Censors Annual Report 1930

One of the first films to be banned in Britain contained neither sex
nor violence, but cheese. Shot through a microscope, it was part
of a series entitled *Unseen World*, and showed moving bacteria on a
piece of stilton. And although its producer Charles Urban would later
persuade the British High Command to allow filming at the Battle of
the Somme in 1917, in 1903 he was unable to withstand the vociferous
protests of the cheese industry. The 90-second *Cheese Mites* was
unceremoniously withdrawn from exhibition.

This incident was something of an exception, as early cinema
attracted little censure, despite some potentially offensive content.
Many early cinematic attractions at fairgrounds and amusement
arcades were saucy celluloid animations, such as *How Bridget Served
the Salad Undressed* (1897). More overtly erotic films (the most
explicit being produced in South America) were confined to private
screenings in 'smoking rooms' and brothels. In addition,
kinematographs regularly screened short, violent documentary films.
Executions were particularly popular and although such films were

not made in Britain, early 'snuff movies' were imported, including footage of six beheadings by Chinese soldiers in Manchuria and the hanging of a cattle rustler in Missouri. Other, rather gruesome, mini-documentaries at the turn of the century included films of operations (often on women), animal fights and violent attacks on animals. One French director even forced a horse over a cliff, to film it plummeting onto the rocks below.

Early films represented a new medium, initially outside the control of local authorities, but as cinema became increasingly popular and moved from fairgrounds to penny gaffs (cheap popular theatres) and music halls, and (from 1906) into purpose-built cinemas, so pressure to control this new medium became increasingly apparent. Calls for the stricter regulation of cinemas and films often drew on concerns regarding the impact of cinema-going on so-called vulnerable groups – particularly children – and such arguments would drive the development of censorship and the regulation of cinema-going, both in Britain and worldwide. This chapter will provide a brief overview of the history of British cinema regulation from 1895 to the 1920s, exploring in particular the pivotal importance of debates surrounding children's viewing on the evolution of cinema regulation, both in Britain and elsewhere.[1]

Early Entertainment Legislation and the Cinematograph Act 1909

The beginnings of film censorship legislation in Britain can be traced back to laws established in eighteenth-century London for the control of theatres and other places of public entertainment. Two types of establishment were recognised in this respect. First, the patent theatres of Drury Lane and Covent Garden, which were the only theatres permitted to stage 'legitimate' plays. These were censored by the Lord Chamberlain under the Playhouse Act of 1737 (superseded by the Theatres Act of 1843, which ended the patent theatres' monopoly and extended the Lord Chamberlain's powers of censorship to include other theatre plays). Second, London boasted many minor theatres and places of entertainment, which could only legally stage operettas, burlettas, mime, singing and dancing. These were controlled through the Disorderly Houses Act of 1751.

The 1751 Act was expressly designed to control the leisure activities of 'the lower Sort of People'. It applied to 'any house, room, garden or other place kept for public dancing, music, or other public entertainment of the like kind' and required such places to be licensed. Under this Act, unlicensed premises could be declared 'disorderly' and raided by the police, who could 'seize every person' within and arrest the keepers of the establishment. This Act also set a significant precedent for the indirect control of the *content* of public entertainment, as licensing bodies had the power to refuse licences or to withdraw them from establishments whose entertainment was considered unsuitable. Thus, by 1870, music hall proprietors often censored the material of their performers, in order to protect their own licences under the Disorderly Houses Act.

As many entertainment providers tried to practise outside the control of licensing authorities, there was some legal debate as to the scope of the 1751 Act. The Act could be enforced if music or dancing were considered an integral part of the entertainment; this was usually a discretionary matter. Thus, in 1868, one court found that music played during a religious meeting did not fall under the Act, while in 1877 it was deemed that roller-skating to music did. From the outset, there was some question as to whether film images of activities like dancing might also come under the Act, but while this was discussed in the cinema trade press, it was not really tested in court.[2]

In 1888 England's organisational and legislative structure was transformed by the creation of local county councils and related legislation. While the Disorderly Houses Act of 1751 had only initially applied to places within 20 miles of the cities of London and Westminster, the new 1890 Public Health Acts Amendment Act extended the provisions of the 1751 Act to any local council that chose to adopt it. Many did. However, fairgrounds, penny gaffs and early purpose-built cinemas still did not come under the licensing powers of the authorities (apart from a few building and safety regulations, which were seldom carefully enforced).

Calls for the control of cinema grew with the new industry's rapid expansion from the turn of the century. The issues cited by those demanding stricter controls were mainly concerned with safety – particularly fire safety – and, to a lesser extent, with the content of the films themselves.

Fire was a very serious concern in theatres across Europe and

America in the nineteenth century, as many were burned to the ground with considerable loss of life. Table 2.1 details a selection of these incidents. London's patent theatres were both destroyed by fire – Drury Lane in 1809 and Covent Garden twice, once in 1808, when 20 people died, and again in 1856. The Theatre Royal, Exeter, was razed to the ground in 1885 and although it was rebuilt and reopened in October 1886, it burned down again in September 1887, with 186 fatalities. The issue of fire safety in places of public entertainment was raised repeatedly in the House of Commons from 1865, as a result of these and other fires.

Table 2.1 Theatre Fires of the Nineteenth Century

Year of Fire	Location of Theatre	Fatalities
1808	Covent Garden	20
1809	Drury Lane	
1836	Lehmen Theatre, St. Petersburg	800
1846	Theatre Royal, Quebec	100
1856	Covent Garden	
1876	Consays Theatre, New York	283
1878	Coliseum, Liverpool	37
1881	Ring Theatre, Vienna	450
1885	Theatre Royal, Exeter	
1887	(Rebuilt) Theatre Royal Exeter	186

Created using data derived from Neville March Hunnings, *Film Censors and the Law* (London, 1967), pp. 35–6.

Probably the first serious fire involving film also involved children and occurred in 1897 at the annual *Bazar de la Charité* in Paris. One of the exhibition's attractions was a small cinema show for children, during which the projectionist accidentally started a fire. This spread rapidly, causing general panic and many fatalities, including '140 eminent people'.[3] From the very outset, therefore, anxiety regarding theatre fires was extended to include cinema shows. Indeed, cinema posed a much greater threat for three reasons. First, nearly all commercial film footage (until the late 1940s) was on highly inflammable nitrate stock. Second, the very popularity of cinema contributed to the hazard, as venues were often rapidly built, overcrowded and ill equipped to deal with fire. Third, most penny gaffs and purpose-built cinemas fell outside the existing licensing requirements (and, therefore, the safety regulations) of local councils. In 1898, for example, London County Council (LCC) issued safety regulations dealing specifically with cinematograph performances in licensed places of public entertainment, but by 1909 the city still had over 300 unlicensed music halls and picture palaces, which could simply ignore these regulations. Other local authorities, such as those in Middlesex and Newcastle, also introduced new regulations and in 1898 the major insurance companies jointly issued safety requirements for cinematograph use in buildings they had insured against fire. However, such efforts were considered piecemeal and ineffective and by 1909 local councils were demanding that the Home Office extend their powers to impose safety regulations on all cinema venues.

The other major concern associated with early cinema related to the content of the pictures themselves. From the turn of the century, showmen attracted more and more custom by increasing the size of their screens, the number of their shows and the variety of their films. They were aided in this respect by the industry as it became more organised from the mid-1900s so that films could be rented rather than bought, thus facilitating far more performances to satisfy the apparently insatiable public demand. However, highly popular films of executions, animal fights and operations were immediately attacked by the press and in the House of Commons. Fictional films also drew criticism, such as *The Black Hand* (1908), in which two intruders take a sleeping child from its bed, put a rope around its neck and string it up over the door, leaving the child's feet swinging two or three feet from the floor.

As the vast majority of early film audiences were from the working classes, it is hardly surprising that denigration of film viewing came mainly from the well-to-do. Criticism generally related to issues of class, taste and respectability, with major targets being film images of vulgarity, crime, drunkenness and licentiousness. In particular, from the early years of cinema, films were commonly blamed for causing juvenile delinquency. Thus, in 1908 an article in the *Sheffield Telegraph* argued that juvenile crime was caused by the cinema, while in 1905 the *Optical Lantern and Cinematograph Journal* reported that three boys caught breaking into a shop explained that they had learned their technique from films.[4] This issue will be explored in more detail later.

Despite the 'undesirable' content of many films, local authorities again found themselves largely powerless to intervene, although some council control was attempted. In 1904, for example, the LCC granted a music and dancing licence to the Earls Court Exhibition, on the understanding that the pictures and titles in their Mutascope machines would be carefully supervised.[5] Successful attempts were also made to place some cinema performances under the Disorderly Houses Act of 1751, as musical accompaniment was argued to be an integral part of the entertainment. However, considering the rapid escalation of the cinema industry, such individual measures were felt to be insufficient and, again, local authorities petitioned the Home Office for some kind of central control. In February 1909, the Metropolitan Police also put significant pressure on the Home Office to control film content, when they expressed grave concern over the glorification of crime in cinema shows.[6]

The culmination of repeated calls for government intervention was the passage of the Cinematograph Act of 1909 (effective from 1 January 1910). This Act required the licensing of all premises used for the 'exhibition of pictures or other optical effects by means of a cinematograph', thereby including penny gaffs, peepshow arcades and purpose-built cinemas. Although the legislation applied only to England and Wales, exhibitors in Scotland apparently complied with it voluntarily.

The detail of the Act was ostensibly concerned with imposing safety regulations on premises licensed to show films, particularly with regard to fire hazards, but it became apparent that this legislation could also be used to impose control on other aspects of cinema performances, including film content. Certainly, fire safety was a genuine concern and this forms the sum and substance of the Act. But almost a year before it came into force, Walter Reynolds of the LCC (the man primarily responsible for the Bill) revealed another agenda, announcing to the trade press that the Act would enable licensing bodies to control film content:

Will the power given to the Council [under the 1909 Act] enable it to control the nature of the entertainments given? It is the duty of the police to stop any entertainments of a doubtful character, but certainly the Council would have the power...to refuse to license places which had presented undesirable shows.

> The knowledge that they possessed that power would be another powerful factor in securing a high class of entertainment, to the general good of the trade.[7]

Thus, it was clearly intended, at least by Reynolds, that the power to license would also imply the power to censor, just as it had under the Act of 1751.

From the outset, local authorities sought to exploit the indirect powers of the Act to various ends. Indeed, before it had even come into force, the LCC announced that they would require premises licensed for cinema shows to remain closed on Sundays. Other councils followed suit and by August 1910, a 'six-day licence' was the norm across Britain. The LCC was legally challenged on this issue in December of the same year, but the court found in their favour, stressing that councils should be allowed to impose specific conditions on licensees at their own discretion, 'so long as those conditions are not unreasonable'.[8] This was a critical precedent and immediately other councils started to impose a variety of conditions on cinemas before they would grant licences. In some regions, barkers (circus-style salesmen) were banned from cinema doors and in others fixed hours of opening were required. Elsewhere children could not gain admittance to cinemas after 9 p.m., while other councils refused licences simply because they considered the district unsuitable, or felt that there were enough cinemas in that area already.[9]

In July 1910, the LCC became the first local authority to use its licensing powers officially to censor a film, as they effectively banned cinemas from showing the world heavyweight championship boxing match, in which black boxer 'Big' Jack Johnson defeated his white opponent James J. Jeffries in over 40 bloody rounds. Soon after, Fulham Borough Council made more subtle overtures regarding the indirect censorship of films when they decreed to would-be licensees in 1911 that 'the character of all picture exhibitions should be carefully supervised' because of the large number of children in attendance.[10] On nearly every occasion when conditions imposed on cinemas were challenged in court, the results went in favour of the local authority. Thus, it soon became apparent that, under the Cinematograph Act of 1909, local councils would have significant powers to control and censor cinema performances across Britain.

The British Board of Film Censors

The reaction of the British film trade to the Act of 1909 was somewhat mixed. Initially, exhibitors protested that the danger of fire had been exaggerated; that projectionists were increasingly skilful in their handling of nitrate stock and that no serious conflagration had ever occurred in a British cinema. Nevertheless, the trade finally decided to support the Bill – not least because exhibitors were seeking wider audiences and they anticipated that the 1909 Act would promote an image of picture palaces as places of 'clean' entertainment and safety as well as comfort, thus attracting the highly lucrative middle class market which had so far been elusive.

Once the 1909 Act was in force, cinema owners and film-makers were appalled by the powers given to local authorities over the exhibition of films. Yet this local, *ad hoc*, indirect system of censorship was considered insufficient by the councils, who called on the Home Office to establish a central, state-run film censorship system. In an attempt to pre-empt such a move, a deputation of 13 film manufacturers and exhibitors went to Home Secretary Reginald McKenna, on 22 February 1912, in order to propose a self-governing censorship system to be run by the film trade and industry itself. The delegation suggested that this new Board of Censors be led by a Home Office-appointed president, who would act as mediator between the board and the film industry. Three to five censors could then be employed to view films and give (or refuse) them a certificate, similar to the mark of approval used by the National Board of Censors in New York. The board would then be financed by charging a fee to producers seeking certification for their films. Although not immediately successful, the details of this proposal were thrashed out during 1912 and in November of that year it was announced that the industry-run British Board of Film Censors (BBFC) had been founded. Significantly, its first president, George Redford, had recently retired from the Lord Chamberlain's Office as Examiner of Plays.

The BBFC started work on 1 January 1913, beginning with only two rules – no nudity and no personification of Christ. It announced that all films released in Britain after 1 March would be subject to a system of certification, whereby each film would either be rejected or would receive one of two certificates – Universal (U) or Public (A).

Both U and A films were considered suitable for children as well as adults, but the former were 'especially recommended for Children's Matinees'.

This system will be discussed in more detail later; suffice it to say for now that there was initially some confusion over the precise meanings of U and A certificates, which changed over time and varied in their local interpretation. Crucially, it was a system directly motivated by concerns over children and cinema. As a BBFC document sent to the Home Office in November 1912 stated: 'The object of these two certificates is to meet, as far as possible, the complaints that have been made by licensing authorities in respect of the non-suitability of certain films for children's entertainments.'[11]

Despite its apparently thorough approach, the early years of the BBFC were dogged with problems, including the nature of films, staffing difficulties and, not least, the board's relationships with the Home Office, local authorities, the church and other moral watch-dogs. Although it had been hoped that local councils would recognise the authority of the BBFC, the board had no legal imperative and it therefore relied on the will of local authorities to demand that cinemas show only BBFC-certified films. However, most councils considered the BBFC a self-serving organ of the film industry that was far too liberal in its decisions. They therefore ignored the board's advice and continued to appoint their own local censors who would ban, re-cut or pass films that had already been passed, cut or banned by the BBFC. In fact, at the end of 1914, only 23 of the 688 licensing authorities specifically required cinemas to adhere to BBFC certification guidelines. This number rose to 35 by the end of 1915 but by 1919, just 20 counties and county boroughs stipulated that cinemas must only screen BBFC-approved films.[12]

Neither was any support forthcoming from the Home Office after December 1915, when a cabinet reshuffle instituted Sir Herbert Samuel as the new Home Secretary. Samuel considered the BBFC too lenient and he responded to calls for an official film censorship system by holding a conference to discuss the matter in April 1916. By the end of November, all but two of the licensing authorities in England and Wales had agreed to surrender their local autonomy in order to establish a unified state system of film censorship. Neither Ireland nor Scotland was properly consulted (Scotland refused on the grounds that the plan was illegal) and the cinema trade – led by the CEA's

Chairman Anthony Newbould – was adamantly opposed to the scheme. Nevertheless, it looked as though Samuel's plan would go ahead, until a number of incidents led to an abrupt turnaround in the fortunes of the BBFC from 1916.

Probably most important among these was the election of a new government at the end of 1916, and the appointment of a new Home Secretary, Sir George Cave, who chose to shelve Samuel's censorship scheme. Under Cave, Home Office support for the BBFC improved immeasurably. Although this support was unofficial and did not offer, for example, legislative backing for the board, the Home Office did take a strong advisory role, sending numerous circulars to local councils, encouraging them to support the board's decisions. By the mid-1920s, therefore, the BBFC had become independent of its trade links and, as many historians have noted, it was now, if anything, an unofficial arm of the Home Office.

The second key event was that the BBFC finally found a strong leader in 1916. The first president, George Redford, had fallen sick within weeks of his appointment in 1912 and he never really recovered. Following his death in November 1916, Redford was replaced by the dynamic Thomas Power O'Connor – a Catholic and a Liberal MP, with a background in journalism and a knowledge of the film industry (having been president of the CEA from 1913 to 1916). In place of a sick, absent leader, the BBFC gained a wily, determined and gifted negotiator, with very useful connections to boot. O'Connor's powerful friends included Ramsay MacDonald, Winston Churchill and the leader of the new coalition government, David Lloyd George. His links with the CEA were also a great strength, as the BBFC had previously been thought to favour film manufacturers rather than exhibitors. Now, under O'Connor, bodies such as the CEA and the Kinematograph Renter's Society felt sufficiently confident to add their crucial support to the BBFC.

A third important development in 1916 enabled the board to demonstrate its usefulness by defusing the potentially incendiary increase in controversial films made during and after the First World War. War films themselves were initially banned by the British government and although this ruling was soon relaxed to allow for films supporting Britain and its allies, this whole area was still very sensitive indeed. Meanwhile, a range of 'propaganda' pictures emerged, which aimed to heighten public awareness regarding delicate social issues, including the proliferation of sexually transmitted diseases, abortion, prostitution and contraception.[13] Finally, radical political issues were raised by Russian films of the 1920s, such as Sergei Eisenstein's *Battleship Potemkin* (1926), which was banned in Britain until 1954, and Pudovkin's *Mother* (1926), which was also banned. This increase in controversial films, together with a massive growth in the popularity of cinema during the war, created something of a headache for the BBFC, but it also served to underline the need for a censorship body, thereby justifying the board's existence.

Importantly, T.P. O'Connor demonstrated that the board was capable of dealing with controversial films by announcing a new set of censorship rules in 1917. While the BBFC claimed that it still had not adopted a rigid code of censorship, it did add to its criteria for exclusion as films came along. The resulting set of rules, known as O'Connor's 43, aimed to deal with all kinds of controversial film content (see Appendix 1). Although this list was only originally intended to be in force until the end of the First World War, it had expanded to number 67 rules by 1919.[14] O'Connor presented his 43 rules to the Cinema Commission of Inquiry conducted by the National Council of Public Morals in 1917 and the favourable report of this inquiry proved helpful in stabilising and enhancing the reputations of both the BBFC and cinema in general (see Chapter 4).

One final critical development was an enormous improvement in the relationship between the BBFC and local authorities at the beginning of the 1920s. The LCC had long been considered the key to the other councils and in 1923, after two years' deliberation, they issued a new set of licensing regulations, stipulating that 'no film...which has not been passed...by the British Board of Film Censors shall be exhibited without the express consent of the council'. The Home Office then circulated a new set of model conditions to local authorities in July 1923, which fully endorsed the work of the BBFC and called on councils to follow the LCC's lead in supporting the board's certification decisions. Over the next year, most local authorities agreed to do so.

By the mid-1920s, the position of the BBFC was therefore firmly established. Although its guidelines were still advisory and not legally enforceable, O'Connor's skill in public and political relations had gained the board far more support from the government, local authorities and the film trade. The BBFC finally listed its criteria for bans and cuts as a systematic code in 1926 (see Appendix 2), but O'Connor was still careful to take the middle ground regarding censorship, explaining: 'I feel I have a great duty to safeguard not merely the decency of the film, but also its liberty.'[15]

Children, Censorship and Certification

Children and Cinema Regulation in Britain

Issues relating to children were a central force in the early years of official cinema regulation in Britain and, of these issues, probably the two most significant were the perceived impact of films on juvenile delinquency and the need for age-restrictions on children's cinema viewing.

Claims that the cinema promoted youth crime emerged from the early 1900s and became increasingly vociferous as cinema grew in scope and popularity. Thus, in 1913 Accrington magistrates 'urged that licensees should take care not to select films...likely to incite young people to crime – pictures of bandits and the like'.[16] Meanwhile in Oldham, the Chief Constable warned cinema managers about films 'calculated to prove harmful to the morals of the public, especially those of young persons'.[17] Critics of the nascent BBFC also referred to this issue in their calls for stricter, official censorship. In 1916, for example, the Chief Constables' Annual Report asserted that 'the establishment of a central Government censor of cinematograph films is essential and *will conduce to the reduction of juvenile crime* in the country' (my emphasis). Similarly, new Home Secretary Herbert Samuel told representatives of local authorities in April 1916:

I have lately obtained the opinion of a number of Chief Constables, who declare with almost complete unanimity that the recent great increase in juvenile delinquency is, to a considerable extent, due to demoralizing cinematograph films.[18]

This opinion was reiterated by Samuel in a Home Office circular of May 1916, which argued for a state-run censorship system on the basis that the 'recent increase in juvenile delinquency' was directly due to the influence of 'demoralising cinematograph films'.[19]

Some local authorities disagreed with such assertions, yet they paradoxically supported the sentiments behind them. The Town Clerk of Leicester wrote to the Home Office in June 1916:

> I am requested to point out that in Leicester there has been a decrease in the number of youthful delinquents since the War, and that it is the opinion of the Chief Constable that the Cinematograph exhibitions in Leicester have not been the cause of more than one or two prosecutions since they have been licensed. At the same time, he and the Watch Committee are of the opinion that there is need of a centralized control of films ... which might induce mischief, if not crime, in the minds of the younger part of the audience.[20]

Such concerns were so pronounced that even the influential Cinema Commission of 1917 failed to draw a line under the issue, despite the fact that it took a *positive* view and recommended neither the banning of crime films nor the exclusion of children from cinemas (see Chapter 4).

By 1919 the BBFC Annual Report listed several subjects considered unsuitable for film content, with crime and juvenile delinquency high on the agenda:

> One of the most difficult subjects with which the Board has had to deal is the question of crime ... Stories of crime make a strong appeal to the imagination of the Public, especially to the less educated sections. When a story of crime is accompanied with the further elements of daring adventure, or romance, and of mystery, there are the elements of a popular success. It is also true that to young people, especially boys, with their ingrained instinct for adventure, uncorrected by experience of life, such 'crime' films make a special appeal, and it may be added, a dangerous appeal.[21]

Evident here are issues of class and gender, as well as age, with those considered most at risk being identified as 'the less educated' and 'young people, especially boys'. Moreover, this argument rests on many unquestioned assumptions, such as those regarding the 'ingrained instinct' of children and the 'dangerous appeal' of films. Such arguments will be examined in more detail in Chapters 3 and 4.

In addition to issues of age, class and gender, the BBFC displayed a cultural bias in their definition of crime. Specifically, the 1919 Annual Report carefully distinguishes between the dangerous influence of 'stories calculated to familiarize young people with theft, robberies and violence, leaving them to conclude that such are normal incidents', and innocuous content, including '"costume" crime, such as cowboy films, Mexican robberies, etc.'. The Report continues, 'it is felt that the latter incidents are regarded simply as...adventures with no connection whatever in the lives, or probable experiences, of young people in this country'. Thus, films of crime in a historical, non-British context were considered less likely to corrupt the morality of children than depictions of contemporary British crime.

The BBFC was particularly concerned about crime content in serials, since these were hugely popular with young people, and they stipulated in their 1919 Report that 'no serial in which crime is the dominant feature, and not merely an episode in the story, will be passed by the Censor'. They also required that all serials involving crime be submitted for censorship in their entirety and that *all* crime films avoid emphasising 'the methods of crime', treating crime as comedy, or making 'the detective element...subordinate to the criminal interest'.

Throughout the 1920s, the BBFC continued to express concern about the impact of crime films on children. President T.P. O'Connor was said to have made this issue a priority, as he 'considered most carefully the question of "crime" films, and the effect such films had, particularly on the child mind'.[22] In 1921 the board cut scenes from films that were thought to be 'teaching children methods of crime'.[23] In 1923 even a classic adaptation suffered the censors' scissors when the board required cuts to *Oliver Twist* (1923), involving scenes in which Fagin (Lon Chaney) teaches Oliver (Jackie Coogan) to pick pockets.[24] While all grounds for censorship listed by the BBFC in 1926 were said to be established with 'vulnerable' audience members – particularly children – in mind, specific reference was also made to the unacceptable nature of scenes depicting 'dangerous mischief easily imitated by children' (see Appendix 2).[25]

In addition to censorship, the main means by which the BBFC sought to regulate children's cinema viewing was through the certification system, instituted in 1912 to address 'the complaints that have been made by licensing authorities in respect of the non-suitability of certain films for children's entertainments'.[26] Both A and U films were initially intended to be suitable for child viewers, as it was felt that any film not suitable for them would also be unsuitable for adults. Thus, an official BBFC leaflet of 1913 stated that while U films were 'especially recommended for Children's Matinees', only films that were 'clean and wholesome and absolutely above suspicion' would receive a certificate of any kind.[27] In its first year, the board examined 7,510 films – 22 were rejected, 6,861 were passed with a U certificate and 627 with an A. Of those passed, 144 had sections that needed cutting before they were certified.[28]

Despite initial intentions for clarity, the meanings of these certificates varied widely and changed over time. Some early attempts were made to ban children from cinemas altogether or to adapt the A certificate to mean 'adults only', and in 1921 this came to a head when the Theatres and Music Halls Committee of the LCC recommended that only adults be admitted to A films. The BBFC objected and in December of that year a conference was held by the LCC with members of the cinema trade, the BBFC, the Home Office and the Lord Chamberlain's Office. At this meeting it was decided that children under 16 should only be admitted to A films in the LCC area if they were accompanied by a parent or *bona fide* adult guardian.[29] (The age limit of 16 was actually a compromise between the Home Office suggestion of 18 and the trade's preference of 14.)[30] Further important steps taken at this conference included the decision that only BBFC-certified films would be exhibited in LCC-licensed cinemas (except for newsreels or films with specific permission) and that the BBFC certificate would be prominently displayed at the beginning of each performance.

Although other local councils followed the LCC example, the Home Office still felt it necessary to call a wider conference of licensing authorities in June 1923 to discuss the lack of uniformity in licensing rules across the country. As a result the Home Office circulated a new set of model conditions to local authorities in July 1923, and in 1924 a Home Office survey reported 'fairly satisfactory progress in the direction of greater uniformity'.[31] Soon after, a test case appeared at Lambeth Police Court, where magistrates found it 'reasonable' for the LCC to require cinema licensees to exclude unaccompanied children under 16 from A films. An appeal in 1925 upheld and endorsed the first decision, giving legal support to any local authority that chose to follow the LCC example.[32]

Confusion and contention over the certification of films continued throughout the mid-1920s. For example, Dr Humbert's report to the Child Welfare Committee of the League of Nations in 1926 erroneously suggested that in Britain A certificate films were 'adjudged to be satisfactory for display to adults only and not to children'.[33] Meanwhile, in 1924 the National Council of Women called for stricter censorship of films shown to children under 16 and in 1926 several groups approached the BBFC to express concern over this issue, including representatives from the National Association of Head Teachers, the London Public Morality Council and the LCC.[34] By 1928, the issue had still not been resolved; agitation continued and some local councils argued that children under 16 should be banned from cinemas altogether.[35] This situation was only to be exacerbated by the introduction of talking pictures in the late 1920s, as will be shown in the next chapter. But before discussing the further developments of censorship in 1930s Britain, it is important to recognise the parallel experience of other nations – particularly America – in the development of cinema regulation and issues surrounding childhood and censorship, in the years before the coming of sound.

Children and Cinema Regulation in America

America was not the world's most significant film-producing nation in the early years of cinema.[36] However, it soon grew to be so and it is therefore important to consider the development of censorship in this context for three reasons. First, its evolution broadly paralleled that of Britain and it therefore offers an interesting comparison. Second, it was American films, rather than British films, that would become the favourites of many children in 1930s Britain, as Hollywood grew to dominate the market. Third, the relationship between the BBFC and the American Production Code Administration (PCA) was an important feature of censorship in both Britain and America after 1930 and it is therefore useful to provide some explanation as to the growth and development of the PCA.

The regulation and censorship of cinema in America followed a similar time frame and was often motivated by similar concerns to those already described for Britain. Foremost among these was a perceived need to protect 'the impressionable classes' from the potentially harmful influence of cinema. This particularly meant children, but also included the illiterate and immigrant peoples. Interestingly, America did not adopt an age-classification system for films until 1968 and even then this was purely voluntary, enforced at the complete discretion of cinema managers and local communities. Yet it would be inaccurate to interpret this as an indication that there was little concern regarding children and cinema in America, because the main reason behind the lack of an age-classification system was economic, with film-makers strongly resisting any narrowing of their potential audience. Therefore, as Ruth Vasey has argued, 'Hollywood movies were broadly designed to be consumed by people of both sexes, all ages, and all levels of experience...so children, their parents, and their grandparents regularly consumed the same entertainments.'[37] Consequently, it was the very *openness* of access which made calls for censorship in America particularly vociferous. In this sense, Gregory Black's argument regarding a 1915 Supreme Court decision might describe much of the early history of film censorship in America:

> Had filmmakers been willing to produce films for specialized audiences (adults only, family, children), the impact [of reformers] might have been lessened; but the movers and shakers of the movie industry wanted or needed the largest possible market.[38]

Progressive reformers expressed serious concern over the impact of film on American children from the first few years of the twentieth century. And, as in Britain, a causal relationship between the cinema and juvenile delinquency was readily assumed. In 1908, for example, one minister referred to cinemas as 'schools for degenerates and criminals', while another asserted in 1910 that movies were 'schools of vice and crime...offering trips to hell for [a] nickle'.[39] Yet many argued in favour of the cinema and against censorship, suggesting that children were robust enough to withstand its impact, including the Mayor of Topeka, Kansas, who contentiously advised: 'if you have a boy who can be corrupted by the ordinary run of moving picture films you might as well kill him now and save trouble'.[40] Nevertheless, many reformers called repeatedly for the institution of a film censorship system and their campaign, based primarily on the need to protect children, was ultimately successful.

In 1907, after a decade of the cinematograph, Chicago was the first city to attempt film censorship and they did so under the auspices of their Police Department. Two years later, this system was challenged in court over the legality of banning biographical films about outlaws. When the court found in favour of the censors, children were seen as centrally important to this case, with the court surmising that such films 'would necessarily be attended with evil effects on youthful spectators'.[41] Despite the pioneering nature of censorship in Chicago, however, this system was still criticised as inadequate. Reformer Jane Addams wrote in 1909 that she found it 'astounding' that Chicago allowed 'thousands of its youth to fill their impressionable minds with [movie] absurdities which certainly will become the foundation for their working moral codes'.[42] Meanwhile, Chicago's censor, Sergeant Charles O'Donnell, reassured his critics that films would only be passed by him for exhibition if they were 'proper for women and children'.[43]

While censors and reformers were battling in Chicago, issues relating to children and the cinema were also being hotly debated in New York – the centre of the American film industry in the years before Hollywood. This escalated in late 1908 when pro-censorship agitators virtually forced Mayor George B. McClellan to call a pivotal debate at New York City Hall. Again, the major cause for concern was the impact of films on children. Film-makers were castigated as amoral opportunists that 'profit from the corruption of the minds of children', while the city was criticised for spending millions of dollars on education, while allowing cinemas to 'contaminate and corrupt' the children of New York.[44] In a shocking climax to the debate, on Christmas Eve 1908, all 550 of the city's cinema licences were revoked and every movie theatre in New York City was closed down. Although a legal appeal enabled most to reopen within a few days, it was clear that the pressure to regulate cinema (based on arguments of child protection) had become critical.

As in Britain, key figures in the American film industry decided to act quickly, to institute their own censorship system in order to avert the imposition of external constraints. Thus, just as the BBFC was established in 1913, the New York Board of Motion Picture Censorship was created as an industry-run self-censorship system in

1909. This board made the fundamental mistake, however, of not directly addressing concerns regarding children and film. They asserted that they would pass any film that did not undermine 'fundamental morality', but refused to become a body that defined 'good taste' or protected 'children, or delicate women'.[45] Almost immediately this board was vetoed by several states and cities which established their own censorship boards instead, including Pennsylvania (1911), Ohio (1913) and Kansas (1913).[46] In each case, issues relating to children and media influence were paramount. For example, in Kansas City, Black suggests that a censorship board was created principally 'to protect children from the corrupting influence of movies'.[47]

In 1915, when a Supreme Court decision supported the right of Ohio censors to cut and ban films, the New York Board of Motion Picture Censorship sought to halt this trend of local film regulation. They tried to improve their image, changing their name to the National Board of Review (NBR), reviewing nearly all films exhibited in America and stamping those which were acceptable with a seal of approval: 'Passed by the National Board of Review'. By 1917, the NBR employed 225 volunteer workers, notably including members of child welfare organisations.[48] They reviewed films according to published standards, cutting 'vulgarity...prolonged and passionate love scenes, insufficient clothing, unnecessary and detailed showing of opium joints or dance halls, improper dancing, unnecessary brutality...and detailed exposition of crime'. They also addressed the issue of juvenile delinquency, insisting 'on the punishment of the criminal when his crime might be considered by the young and impressionable spectator as an excusable act'.[49]

The centrality of issues surrounding children to the work of censors was highlighted in 1916, when the NBR established a National Committee on Films for Young People, 'to further the discovery, production, selection, distribution and use of selected motion pictures and programmes for young people'. They referred to this committee as the 'most important department of the Board's work' and claimed to be proactive in trying 'to develop a demand for special programmes for children; to increase the manufacture of films for children; and to further the now rapid growth of special performances for them'.[50]

Despite these attempts, however, the NBR, like the BBFC, reached a crisis point in the early 1920s, when their ability to censor was slammed by critics as ineffective, self-serving and far too liberal. In 1921, over 100 anti-movie bills were introduced across America and various states and cities continued to establish independent censorship systems. Most importantly, New York State set up its own local censorship board in 1921. Meanwhile, those pushing for federal censorship claimed that movies were increasingly immoral – an argument fuelled in the 1920s by a spate of scandals in the film-making community itself (now based in Hollywood), involving extramarital sex, drugs, rape, murder, suicide and general debauchery.

In order to try to regain control over censorship and to allay public concerns, the leading Hollywood producers joined forces in January 1922 and established the Motion Picture Producers and Distributors of America (MPPDA) which became a united front for the industry in public relations. They appointed politician Will H. Hays to oversee this organisation, which then became known as the Hays Office. In 1927, Hays established a new, industry-run censorship body within the MPPDA: the Studio Relations Department (SRD). He then circulated film-makers with a document detailing all forms of unacceptable film content, called the list of 'Don'ts and Be Carefuls' (see Appendix 3).

The Hays Office was not taken seriously by film-makers until the mid-1930s however, and in the meantime local authorities continued to pass their own regulations regarding children and cinema attendance. Notably, several cities prohibited the cinema attendance of children unless accompanied by an adult, either at all times, during the school day, or in the late evening. By 1926, the Chicago censors were labelling certain films for exhibition to over-21s only, while in Maryland, New York and Virginia, boards of censors were legally required 'to prepare lists of pictures suitable for children, to be available on request' for parents.[51] Meanwhile, the Hays Office was 'advocating special performances of specially chosen programmes for children' and they prepared 'a collection of 52 such programmes, including educational and historical films, dramas and comedies of a wholesome type, chosen for their attractiveness and value to youthful audiences'.[52]

Reformers were still not convinced by such measures, which seemed to be driven by pragmatism rather than genuine principles. As Ruth Vasey has suggested, the main aim of the Hays Office was not to act as a moral watch-dog, but 'to ensure that the movies could be distributed domestically and abroad with a minimum of disruption through censorship action or consumer resistance'.[53] Calls for a federal censorship system therefore continued throughout the 1920s, becoming particularly significant in the American Catholic community. Two Catholics then put forward the idea of setting a single censorship standard for films in America by creating a formal Production Code. Martin Quigley (publisher of the trade paper *Motion Picture Herald*) and public relations officer Joseph 'Joe' Breen presented their idea to the Catholic hierarchy and corporate film executives in 1929 and both welcomed it. The code was then drafted by Father Daniel Lord, a priest, professor of dramatics and editor of a popular Catholic youth publication, who also worked as technical adviser on Cecil B. DeMille's *The King of Kings* (1927). When Lord's code was presented to Will Hays at the MPPDA, he declared it exactly what he had been looking for. By February 1930, it had been approved and adopted by all the major film studios as an advisory standard and, to the annoyance of the others involved, it was immediately dubbed The Hays Code.

Interestingly, in writing the code, Lord was particularly influenced by issues relating to children and cinema. In 1929 he had attended a matinee performance of *The Very Idea* – a film that addresses the thorny subject of surrogate parenthood. Although he found the film basically responsible, Lord was shocked to note that children responded in an apparently inappropriate and 'less sophisticated' way to the material.[54] He therefore considered children to be in particular need of the protection afforded by a code of censorship, especially with new sound films which he felt 'would be irresistible to the impressionable minds of children, the uneducated, the immature, and the unsophisticated'.[55]

Ruth Vasey agrees that the adoption of the Hays Code was directly related to concerns surrounding children and cinema:

> The industry's main public relations problem in the 1920s and 1930s was the widespread conviction that children would learn 'sophisticated', violent, or antisocial behaviour from watching motion pictures. The Production Code was largely designed to assuage these anxieties, which had been exacerbated by the introduction of sound.[56]

As in Britain, therefore, issues regarding children and the cinema were one of the main driving forces behind the development of censorship in America.

Children and Cinema Regulation: An International Perspective

Although this book focuses on Britain, cinema was and is a global medium. It is therefore useful to investigate the impact of concerns regarding children and cinema on regulatory practices worldwide, in order to establish how widespread this phenomenon might have been. It should be noted that this only represents a brief exploration based on two contemporary sources: an appendix to the Report of the Cinema Commission of Inquiry of 1917, entitled 'Cinematograph Censorship Regulations in Other Countries', and a report on children and international cinema legislation given by Dr Humbert to the Child Welfare Committee of the League of Nations in 1926.[57]

By 1914, all countries with cinema as a form of popular entertainment had adopted some system of censorship, be it locally organised or state-run and, as in Britain and America, issues surrounding children were nearly always absolutely central to this process. By 1930, special regulations regarding the exhibition of films to children had been passed all over the world.

By the 1920s, for example, many countries had passed regulations regarding minimum ages and times of cinema-going for children. Those under 6 years old were legally prohibited from cinema attendance in Germany, Latvia and Danzig, while children under 5 years old were excluded in Hungary and children under 3 years old were excluded in Salvador.[58] Some countries had far stricter legislation, including Romania where all children under 18 years were banned from cinemas unless films were 'of an instructive and educative nature'.[59] Many countries also either forbade the attendance of children at evening performances or required that they be accompanied by adults. Thus, children under 8 years old were not legally admitted to cinemas in Salvador in the evening, while in Spain children under 10 years old were 'absolutely forbidden' at evening shows and could not attend unaccompanied at *any* time unless it was a performance intended solely for children.[60] Meanwhile in Sweden, children under 15 years old had to be accompanied by an adult to performances ending after 8 p.m. and in several Canadian provinces unaccompanied children were banned from cinemas both during school hours and after 6 p.m.[61]

In some Japanese provinces, children under 14 were only admitted to cinemas if accompanied by an adult and even then they were prohibited from admission after 9 p.m. Moreover, any child already in the cinema at this time would receive a ten-minute warning before being asked to leave.[62] Italian legislation passed in 1925 went further by providing a means of enforcement for cinema regulations. The 1925 law stipulated that on occasions when children had to be 15 to attend the cinema they must pass a height test, with those under 150 cm tall being 'presumed to be under 15 ... unless proof to the contrary [was] furnished'.[63]

The majority of legislation, however, concerned film *content*, including both broad standards of censorship and the age-related classification of films. In some countries, the content of children's matinees was heavily restricted. For example, in Romania children's films all had to be 'educative or instructive'; in Salvador 'only instructive and moral films' could be shown at matinees; and in Spain matinee films were required to be 'of an instructive and educative character'.[64] Elsewhere, children were given a wider range of films, albeit a limited one. In Uruguay, a 1921 decree specified the genres acceptable for exhibition to children: 'popular scientific films', 'panoramic films', newsreels, comedies, and generally 'films providing simple and harmless amusement'. Those considered unsuitable included anything 'likely to injure the child's development ... detective films, intensely dramatic films, films which have a painful effect on the child's imagination [and] films which encourage feelings of hostility towards other countries'.[65]

Such themes recurred worldwide in interwar legislation pertaining to children and the cinema and in nearly every case regulations stressed the need to protect the mind, morality and imagination of the child from the powerful influence of films. In Latvia, children were prohibited from viewing 'films likely to produce a harmful effect on the *moral development of youth* or capable of *over-stimulating youthful fancies*'.[66] In Germany, no films could be shown to children that were 'liable to have a detrimental effect on their *moral, mental or physical development* or unduly to *excite their imagination*'.[67] Such themes were also evident in the official cinema regulations of Czechoslovakia, Danzig, Norway, Austria, Sweden and the Orange Free State of the Union of South Africa, to name but a few.[68]

In a number of cases, legislation drew on moral rhetoric by referring to the potentially 'evil' influence of cinema over children. For example, in Saskatchewan, Canada, any film 'which may offer evil suggestions to the minds of young people or children' was prohibited, while on the Island of Formosa local authorities censored films prior to public exhibition and banned any that might 'exercise an evil influence on the minds and morals of children'.[69] Similarly, in Salvador, no film was permitted which was considered 'liable to implant evil sentiments in the minds of the young or encourage vicious propensities'.[70]

As in Britain and America, a particular concern frequently mentioned in foreign legislation was the potential impact of crime films on the behaviour of young people. In Italy a 1926 decree reinforced regulations from 1923 that 'children and young persons' should be 'excluded from all cinematograph performances with a love or crime interest' that might 'corrupt their morals by force of suggestion'.[71] Similarly in New South Wales, Australia, censors specified four types of scene that would not be passed for exhibition in cinemas, including 'successful crime, such as bushranging, robberies, or other acts of lawlessness which might reasonably be considered as having an injurious influence on youthful minds'.[72]

In Imperial Germany an apparently rapid increase in juvenile crime was attributed directly to the influence of the cinema; an attribution expressed through a range of censorship and cinema regulations.[73] In 1911 the leading authority on German cinema law, Albert Hellwig, conducted an extensive investigation and concluded that 'popular crime films have a decided effect on juvenile criminality'. He continued, with unashamed presumption, 'although it is not possible to demonstrate this link with any certainty in even a single specific case, the correctness of this view can undoubtedly be deduced from general psychological principles'.[74] Such views were endorsed by police chiefs, judges and state legislatures, as in 1913 when the state government of Württemberg restricted children's viewing on the grounds that 'the cinema can push a child into actually imitating the crimes and misdeeds that he sees portrayed'.[75]

Hunnings suggests that in interwar France, too, the main concern regarding film content was 'criminality and the effect of the cinema on juvenile crime', generating prolonged litigation and municipal bans on certain types of film.[76] In 1921, the Prefect of the Var issued a ban on realistic crime films, reasoning that as 'cinemas are much frequented by young people...public order and tranquillity cannot be maintained, any more than can morality, with this continual instigation of young people to unhealthy exploits'.[77] Meanwhile, the Procureur de la République at Roanne wrote to the Prefect of the Loire regarding a number of incidents in which young people arrested for theft had named themselves after gangs and criminals in films. He concluded, 'it is unquestionable that most young delinquents...have their moral sense obliterated by the sight of crime films'.[78] Similarly, in 1926 a French delegate reported to the League of Nations that 'the magistrates who sat on the children's courts in Paris had always realized the pernicious influence of certain films on a large number of crimes'. He then cited a 'band of young thieves who called themselves "*La Main qui etreint*"'(The Grabbing Hand), explaining that this was 'a name taken from a film'.[79] Such concerns were also expressed in local cinema regulations across France, such as the ban at Sablé-sur-Sarthe on 'all police [gangster] films, all films based on cheap/serial stories and, in a general sense, any films likely to warp/mislead the imagination of children'.[80]

In several countries, one proposed solution to the problem of media influence on children was the classification of films as either suitable or unsuitable for child viewers. In Denmark, as in Britain, early cinema legislation was adapted from existing theatre laws and by 1914 a Board of Censors was established, which passed films in two categories: suitable for all audiences, and for over-16s only. Children were banned from the latter, although this only involved around 5 per cent of all films passed.[81] While BBFC certification was merely advisory, the Danish film classification system was established under law in 1913 and was legally reinforced in 1933. They then introduced a second age limit and a classification band for films especially suitable for children, which were also exempt from taxation.[82]

Certification was popular in other countries, including India, where A certificates were used; in Bombay, films considered unsuitable for children were 'certified on the condition that their exhibition is restricted to adults'.[83] A similar certification system was adopted by Hungary, and in Poland children under 17 were only permitted to see films passed by the Board of Censors and an advisory committee 'of experts composed of school teachers'.[84]

Although this evidence is brief, it demonstrates that both concerns over children and cinema and the consequent regulation/legislation of the medium were essentially global phenomena. Indeed, several international committees were established to discuss these issues and their interaction continued well into the 1930s (see Chapter 4).

In many countries it can be argued that the issue of children and cinema was not merely one factor, but was the *main force* behind the development of censorship and cinema regulation. A key example is Japan, which had the world's second largest film industry by 1939. Here the entire censorship system revolved around children, as a decree of 1925 stipulated that (except under special conditions) *no* films would be passed for exhibition in Japan that were 'likely to be harmful to the mental and moral development of the young and to their good education', or that might 'suggest unhealthy ideas to children or weaken the authority of teachers'.[85] Consequently, *all* films were passed with a view to the apparent vulnerability of child audiences and there was therefore no need to restrict the access of children to films in Japanese cinemas.

The centrality of children to the development of cinema regulation can also be seen in Denmark, where Hunnings suggests 'a major consideration in the development of film censorship...has always been a concern for the protection of young people'.[86] He notes that such concern motivated the vast majority of Danish censorship legislation from 1907, while from 1933 '*all* the changes in the [Danish] censorship system...have been concerned with children'.[87] Meanwhile, the key importance of issues surrounding children was also evident in post-revolutionary Russia, where all film censorship came under the People's Commissariat of Education from its foundation in 1917 and initially, within that Commissariat, under the School Extension Department.[88]

Perhaps the most telling example, however, is Belgium. In this liberal nation there has never been any official censorship of films for adults, yet it was considered necessary to institute severe restrictions on the cinema attendance of children. Thus, in 1920, a new Belgian law stipulated that 'minors of either sex who have not reached the age of sixteen shall not be allowed to be present at any public cinema performance', except in cinemas that *only* showed films licensed for exhibition to children by a special commission.[89] An almost identical law was passed in Luxembourg in 1922, with an age limit of 17 years.[90]

Two important conclusions can be drawn from this early history of censorship and regulation. First, that the regulation of children's film viewing in Britain should be viewed not in isolation, but within the wider context of regulatory practices across the world. A range of countries considered the impact of film on children's morality, education, imagination and health to be potentially dangerous, if not 'evil'. Also, although most of the international examples given involved legislation, many other nations adopted similarly robust systems of regulation regarding children's cinema-going without a legislative mandate, as occurred in Britain under the BBFC.

The second conclusion is that evidence from Britain, America and many other countries strongly suggests that the principal driving force behind the early regulation of cinema was concern regarding the influence of the medium on children. As the next chapter shows, such concern would continue to drive the development of cinema regulation in Britain and America in the 1930s, as anxieties escalated with the arrival of talking pictures.

3

It Ain't No Sin: The Regulation of
Cinema 1929–1939

Will Hays is my shepherd, I shall not want,
He maketh me to lie down in clean postures.
                    Gene Fowler, 1930s/40s screenwriter

In the late 1920s, controversy surrounding children and cinema
intensified owing to a number of factors, the significant catalyst
being the coincidence of two major events: the introduction of talking
pictures and the Great Depression. 'Talkies', first produced in 1927,
proved immediately successful – so much so, that as early as 1928 the
BBFC could report that 'synchronised films' had 'taken deep root'.[1]
Indeed, by 1930, the major Hollywood studios had all decided to stop
making silent films.

With talkies the industry standard, studios and cinemas rapidly
poured money into sound conversion, but just two years after the
introduction of sound, with mass conversion well under way, the
industry was rocked by the Wall Street Crash and the Great
Depression, which crippled the strongest studios and exhibitors and
ruined many others. Debts due to sound conversion and loss of
financial holdings were compounded by competition from radio (an
increasingly popular source of entertainment) and a slump in box
office revenue (particularly in America) as audiences felt the bite of the
Depression and stayed home. The *Film Daily Year Book* of 1934

estimated that weekly cinema attendance in America had fallen from
'a boom high' of over 100 million in the 1920s to 'a Depression low'
of under 40 million. Meanwhile in Britain, in 1930 alone, at least 50
corporations related to the film industry were liquidated.[2]

By 1930 the industry was committed to, and utterly dependent
upon, the continued popularity of sound films. Struggling to weather
the financial storm of the Depression, studios started producing
reliable, crowd-pulling talkies of various kinds, aiming to fill cinemas
with patrons regardless of the feelings of censors, reformers, or moral
watch-dogs. These crowd-pullers were often sensational in nature and
several hugely popular genres emerged, provoking heightened levels
of protest about the potential impact of films on children. By the mid-
1930s, this protest would culminate in extensive changes in cinema
regulation, an irrevocable shift in (power) relationships between film-
makers, reformers, censors, licensing authorities, exhibitors and
audiences, and ultimately a massive sea change in film content itself.

The Problem of Talkies

Overall, sound pictures posed two main problems for censors. First
was the sheer technical difficulty of editing films where sound and
picture had to be synchronised. In silent films, offensive intertitles or
suspect visual sequences could be removed cleanly and with relative
ease, but this was extremely difficult to accomplish with sound-on-
film and virtually impossible with sound-on-disc.[3] Therefore, censors
had to use a blanket approach with early talkies, passing or banning
them *in toto* (although sometimes a silent film was passed and its
sound version banned, or sound and silent versions of a film could be
given different certificates).[4] A solution to technical censorship
difficulties was soon found, however, as censors asked producers of
'synchronised pictures' to submit scenarios and/or scripts *before*
production commenced, rather than simply presenting finished films
for censorship. This then became increasingly common practice for
most British producers and the handful of American studios
submitting films to the BBFC during the 1930s.[5]

Above and beyond technical problems, sound films posed a serious
challenge to censors in terms of their content. As novelist Compton
MacKenzie remarked in 1931: 'it was bad enough before Talkies

became the rule, and when only the *eyes* of children were offended. It is worse now.'[6] Swearing and lewdness were already censored in silent film intertitles. For example, in 1919, 1921, 1923 and 1925 the BBFC reported cuts to 'suggestive sub-titles' and 'sub-titles in the nature of swearing'.[7] Slang was also considered a problem, as in 1925 when the board objected to American film-makers 'constantly producing alien idiomatic phrases'.[8] But such transgressions in silent pictures made up relatively little of the finished film. Talkies, on the other hand, could deliver far more offensive language and innuendo per reel and could be both subtle and racy, using combinations of quick-fire dialogue, meaningful pauses, colourful language, slang, wisecracks, *double entendres* and sexual innuendo. When sound effects were added to hot dialogue, screen sex suddenly became more sexy and screen violence more violent. As early as 1929, the BBFC declared:

> The introduction of sound films has unquestionably raised new problems from the point of view of censorship. Generally speaking, it is found that the dialogue far more emphasises the situation than is the case with titling.[9]

Meanwhile, one newspaper wittily suggested in 1932 that 'the increase in innuendo in talkies' was owing to the fact that British censors were 'too old and innocent to understand the meaning of many of the lines they pass', having an average age of about 60 years.[10]

Although the Hays Code was introduced in 1930, it was relatively ineffective for its first few years due to film industry intransigence and popular public demand. Until 1934, Hollywood film-makers took advantage of this position, deliberately spicing productions with the most popular aspects of film content in order to fill seats. Consequently, over the five years from 1930 to 1934 (usually dubbed the 'pre-code period') they produced a steady stream of arguably the most subversive and salacious films that had ever been seen, or that would be seen for another quarter of a century, and cinema-goers witnessed a rush of fast-talking, hard-hitting films, crammed with thrills, sex and violence, which flouted the social order and defied Hays and his largely impotent colleagues.[11]

Unsurprisingly, the sudden rash of sensational pre-code talkies caused great concern to reformers, not least because such films tended to occur in groups or 'cycles', as studios sought to repeat their most successful film formulae. Thus, one offensive film might be followed by several more of the same kind, each seeking to out-do their predecessor. Among the most popular, prolific and controversial were the pre-code gangster, sex and horror cycles. These were not only numerous and subversive, but attracted large numbers of children and were thought by many to be the biggest threat to child viewers to date. Consequently, important trends can be explored by examining these films in terms of their silent predecessors, controversial content, popularity with young people and responses they elicited from reformers and censors in America and Britain.

The Gangster Cycle

As previously mentioned, crime films were denounced from the early days of cinema because of their perceived impact on juvenile delinquency, but they nevertheless continued to be popular with both adults and children, especially after the coming of sound. The BBFC noted with regret at the end of 1928 'a marked revival in the production of films dealing with crime in a way which is considered detrimental to the public interest'.[12] Such concern escalated in the early 1930s as film-makers expanded the already popular genre to include gangster films. Drawing on sensational contemporary reports of organised crime and underworld vice in Prohibition America, gangster films rapidly capitalised on the huge public fascination in Britain and the USA with shocking events such as the St Valentine's Day Massacre of 1929 and the notorious exploits of figures such as Al Capone, Baby Face Nelson and bank robber John Dillinger.

Importantly, the protagonists of early gangster movies were usually hoodlums rather than law enforcement officers (a trend that was reversed after 1934). Key examples were Edward G. Robinson as Caesar Enrico Bandello in *Little Caesar* (1930), James Cagney as Tom Powers (based on Capone's Irish rival, Dion O'Bannion) in *The Public Enemy* (1931) and Paul Muni as Tony Camonte (based on Capone himself) in *Scarface* (1932). Other early examples, released within a few months of each other, were *Doorway to Hell* (1930) and in 1931, *The Finger Points*, *City Streets*, *The Secret Six*, *The Vice Squad*, *Quick Millions* and *Star Witness*. In all, Hollywood produced nine gangster movies in 1930, 26 in 1931, 28 in 1932 and 15 in 1933, when Prohibition ended and the cycle's popularity began to wane.[13] The success of gangster films also spawned related pre-code cycles, including prison and chain-gang movies, which questioned the justice system and encouraged audiences to sympathise with criminals rather than with the brutal establishment.

Pre-code gangster movies were fast and furious, full of sharp, slangy dialogue, dark humour, sexual impropriety, flashy cars and violent gun battles. They were not just talkies; they were aggressively noisy extravaganzas. The main characters were antisocial, insubordinate, selfish and immoral, yet they often enjoyed glamorous, successful lifestyles, in stark contrast to the harsh Depression experiences of most cinema-goers. As a small concession to the censors, the protagonist generally died in the last reel, giving lip service to the view that crime ultimately does not pay.

American gangster films were immediately popular with British youngsters, particularly boys, many of whom copied the speech and mannerisms of their swaggering, smart-mouthed heroes.[14] Jim Godbold recalls that when he was around 14 years old, he and his friend went regularly to see gangster films in Stowmarket, including *Little Caesar*, *Public Enemy* and *Scarface*:

> When we went to gangsters [my friend] would really come out, you know, he was aping the gangsters. He'd strike a match on the wall, and that... You see, gangster films were glorifying the gangster... And that was having an effect on people... My friend and me, we bought a black shirt and a white tie because one of the gangsters had this.[15]

The popularity of American gangster films with British children was also reported in cinema enquiries of the early 1930s (see Chapter 4). The Birmingham enquiry asked 38 boys aged 11 which kind of films they preferred and 19 chose 'murder, war and Chicago gangster' films, owing to their 'thrilling' content.[16] Birmingham children said that such films had taught them about 'life in Chicago and the underworlds of London and Paris', 'a lot about American gangsters and raketeers' and, one child claimed, 'how to shoot people through my pocket'.[17] Similarly, children in the Birkenhead enquiry claimed to have learned 'the history of the gangster wars' and 'how the gangsters rob the big banks of America'.[18] In the 1932 Edinburgh enquiry 12.5 per cent of boys chose 'Underworld or Gangster' films as their favourites, ranking gangster films the third most popular out of 15 genres (after War and Westerns). Interestingly, it was ranked as the top genre by subgroup Senior B (working class boys aged 13–14), 24 per cent of whom chose it as their favourite film type.[19] But gangster films were less popular with girls in this study. Only 2.6 per cent rated it as a favourite film type and 11.5 per cent said it was the category they disliked the most.[20] However, as this questionnaire asked children to select just one favourite film type, excluding all others, gangster films were probably more popular with both boys and girls than the results suggest. More importantly, as the Edinburgh figures show, gangster films were highly popular in that demographic 'danger zone' – working class male youth.

As with other genres, reformers complained about various aspects of the gangster cycle, but the fact that *children* enjoyed these films and were imitating their speech and mannerisms was usually the main cause for concern. Thus, the *Kansas City Times* argued in 1931 that although gangster films were not harmful to adults, they were 'misleading, contaminating and often demoralizing to children and youth'.[21] Similarly, at the opening of *Little Caesar* on New York's Broadway in January 1931 (when 3,000 people smashed two glass doors, raiding the box offices for tickets) young people were immediately considered at risk from the film's moral tone.[22] James Wingate (head of the New York censorship board and later of the PCA) told Will Hays that he had been inundated with complaints from people who were horrified to see the children at *Little Caesar* 'applaud the gang leader as a hero'. Wingate also prioritised children when complaining to Hays that the gangster's eventual death in this film was an ineffective lesson, as 'the child unconsciously forms the idea that he will be smarter and will get away with it'.[23] Even Al Capone claimed to be concerned about the impact of gangster films on children. In an interview with *Motion Picture Herald* in 1931, he allegedly said:

> These gang pictures – that's terrible kid stuff... They're doing nothing but harm to the younger element of the country. I don't blame the censors for trying to bar them. Now you take all these youngsters who go to the movies. Well, those gang movies are making a lot of kids want to be tough guys.[24]

In April 1931, Will Hays responded to critics by appointing former police chief August Vollmer to investigate the impact of gangster films on children. But in his report (used by the Hays Office to defend the gangster cycle) Vollmer argued that such films were essentially harmless and realistic. If anything, he suggested, they were rather too favourable in their depiction of police efficiency.[25] Reformers were not easily pacified, though, particularly when two young boys were involved in a tragic accident in New Jersey, playing cops and robbers after watching the gangster film *The Secret Six* (1931). One killed the other, shooting him with a gun he thought was empty. There was an immediate outcry blaming the film for this incident, and as Black notes, 'only a few pointed the blame toward the parents who kept a loaded gun in the house'.[26]

Although much questionable material got through, censors were by no means silent regarding early gangster films. New York State alone cut over 2,200 crime scenes in films between 1930 and 1932, and by mid-1931 gangster films were banned in a number of American cities because of the actions of pressure groups, many of which argued that such films posed a threat to children. There were particularly energetic battles over the last major film in the cycle, Howard Hughes' *Scarface* (1932). The Hays Office demanded extensive cuts and required Hughes to give the film the subtitle *Shame of the Nation*. Even then, local American censors initially refused the cut version, allowing it only when Jason Joy of the Hays Office visited them personally and assured them that the cycle was coming to an end.[27]

In Britain, the BBFC took their lead from the Hays Office and were relatively relaxed about gangster films, so long as they were set in America. In 1932, for example, BBFC senior script examiner Colonel J.C. Hanna rejected the proposed film *When the Gangs Came to London*, explaining that the board had 'had a good deal of trouble with "gangster films" in recent years and it was only because they were obviously American that they finally passed'. He added, 'wholesale machine gun murders in the streets of Chicago possibly are deemed to come under the head of "topicals", but in London would be quite prohibitive'.[28] Meanwhile, most Hollywood gangster films were passed as A films in Britain with minor cuts or delays, including *Little Caesar. Public Enemy* was initially refused a certificate, but was eventually passed in June 1932, a month after the heavily cut *Scarface* was given BBFC approval.[29]

In general terms, therefore, despite the complaints of moral watch-dogs and censors in America and elsewhere, the pre-code gangster cycle ran a fairly natural course, with popular demand and the drive of film-makers to meet that demand prevailing over the wishes of reformers. Over 78 Hollywood gangster films were made between 1930 and 1933 and while many were censored, most still contained scenes of violence, sexual impropriety and glamorous immorality.

The Sex Cycle

As the gangster cycle waned, it made way for another controversial series of films, this time involving the popular theme of sexual relationships. In December 1931, Jason Joy wrote a frustrated letter to the Hays Office, noting that while the MPPDA was discouraging the production of gangster pictures, many film-makers had simply turned to pictures about sex instead:

> With crime practically denied them, with box-office figures down, with high pressure methods being employed...it was almost inevitable that sex, as the nearest thing at hand and pretty generally sure-fire, would be seized upon. It was.[30]

Although these films were not popular with young children, the impact on youth was again perceived to be of primary concern among cinema watch-dogs and censors.

In the same way as crime, sexual content had already been heavily censored before talkies came along. Together with saucy intertitles, the BBFC cut 'suggestive amorous advances', 'suggestive... shadowgraphs' and inadequate clothing.[31] They had also dealt with a procession of seductive, predatory, sexually aware silent female characters, from Helen Gardner's *Cleopatra* (1912) and the 'vamp' roles of Theda Bara, to the sultry heroines of the 1920s played by Clara Bow, Gloria Swanson, Pola Negri and Greta Garbo. These films were generally passed by the BBFC, albeit with some changes. Of this list, only Garbo was really successful in transferring her sexy image to talking pictures, but she was soon joined by a fresh batch of hot *femmes* in the early 1930s, including Hedy Lamarr, Marlene Dietrich, Jean Harlow and Mae West.

If silent sex pictures had been inflammatory, the talkie cycle was positively incendiary, as dialogue and sound effects were fully employed in a proliferation of films exploring themes of adultery, divorce, promiscuity and prostitution. Many tackled the thorny subject of the Depression and the ways in which financial hardship forced people into morally dubious decisions. Women were sympathetically portrayed using sexual favours or prostitution to save themselves or their families from penury, including Marlene Dietrich in *Blonde Venus* (1932), Tallulah Bankhead in *Faithless* (1932) and Clara Bow in *Call Her Savage* (1932). By the end of 1932, Joy was also complaining about a sub-cycle of 'kept woman' films, which portrayed adultery as a viable alternative for the unhappily married.[32]

Other troublesome sub-cycles were backstage dramas (with plenty of costume-change sequences) and raunchy sex comedies, notably the hits written by and starring Mae West. Homosexuality also featured in a number of pre-code films, including *Sailor's Luck* (1932), *Our Betters* (1932) and *Cavalcade* (1933), with taboo content colloquially described in the trade press as 'queer flashes', 'pansy comedy', 'mauve characters' and 'male magnolia'. This represented a serious challenge to the censors; by 1932 *Variety* predicted that, while producers were 'going heavy on the panz stuff in current pix', the Hays Office would probably not tolerate 'more than a dash of lavender', as they were 'attempting to keep the dual-sex boys and lesbos out of films'.[33]

As with gangster films, censors objected less to individual sex films than they did to the constant barrage of an entire sex cycle. By 1929, the BBFC reported that it was handling a 'large number [of] Back Stage Drama' films, which were considered 'sordid' and 'unmoral in practice and principle'. While 'one such film by itself may not be prohibitive', the board argued, 'a continuous succession of them is subversive, tending to inculcate a lower outlook, and to invest a life of irregularity with a spurious glamour'.[34] Within two years the board claimed to be inundated with films based on 'lust or the development of erotic passions', many of which seemed, 'on every conceivable occasion, to drag in scenes of undressing, bathroom scenes and the exhibition of feminine underclothing...solely...for the purpose of giving the film what is termed in the trade "a spicy flavour"'.[35] And by late 1931, they reported (with an amusing lack of irony) that the sex cycle had 'increased [the board's] work...enormously', for such films 'had to be viewed over and over again' by censors, to ensure compliance with BBFC standards.[36]

Still, film-makers were more disposed to hearing the sound of cash in tills than the complaints of censors and watch-dogs and so the sex cycle continued. By September 1932, the Hays Office deemed 24 of the 111 American films in production to contain illicit sexual content.[37] And *Variety* estimated that in 1932–3 'over 80 per cent of the world's chief picture output was...flavored with the bedroom essence', with 352 of the 440 films released that year containing 'some sex slant', 145 having 'questionable sequences' and 44 being 'critically sexual'.[38]

Although young children generally poured scorn on 'sloppy stuff' (see Chapter 5), sex films were popular with older children in Britain. Denis Houlston remembers that from the age of about 13 he and his friends considered Jean Harlow 'a favourite'.[39] Harlow plagued censors as a sultry man-eater in gangster and sex films including *Hell's Angels* (1930), *The Public Enemy* (1931), *The Secret Six* (1931), *Red Dust* (1932) and *Red-Headed Woman* (1932). They also enjoyed Marlene Dietrich's *Blue Angel* (1930). In one memorable scene, Dietrich strips to her underwear and the camera follows her stockinged legs as she ascends an open spiral staircase. When only her legs are visible at the top of the stairs, she carefully removes her french knickers and drops them onto a man waiting below. Denis recalls:

> *Blue Angel*! *Blue Angel*! Oh those frilly knickers in *Blue Angel*! They sent us, you know! As you can *imagine*. Well, of course, we liked the legs of course. Legs Dietrich.[40]

The erotic charge of sex pictures for adolescent boys is also evident in Denis's enthusiastic recollection of the entire pre-code era:

> In the *early* thirties, anything went...they showed you virtually anything...As a schoolboy [with my friends]...we loved it because you got plenty of leg shots and the *décolletage* was quite generous, more generous than later on. Eh, so we would see bits of those female bodies which, you know, we'd only dreamed about [laughs]. And...shots of stocking tops was a favourite thing and *always* in pictures the leading lady would *have* to adjust her stockings some time. So up would come her skirt and we'd all be *goggle-eyed*.

Concern regarding the impact of sex pictures on the young was two-fold and heavily gendered. Essentially, reformers worried that such films would prematurely inflame the unhealthy passions of boys with unsuitable erotic images of women, but more seriously, they feared that sex pictures would corrupt innocent girls and lead them into inappropriate sexual behaviour. Consequently, whereas gangster films were primarily considered a danger to boys, sex pictures were mainly believed to threaten the virtue of girls.

One of the principal targets for reformers in this regard was Mae West, who was dogged by 'child-protecting' censors from the outset of her writing career. In 1926 her first Broadway play *Sex* was closed down by New York authorities who argued that it was 'corrupting the morals of youths'.[41] She was fined $500 and sentenced to ten days in prison for indecency, but proved unrepentant, writing and staging two more controversial plays: *The Drag*, about homosexuality, and the vice-laden *Diamond Lil*. She then adapted the latter to create her first starring role in a movie, the instant box-office hit *She Done Him Wrong* (1933).

West's wisecracking, sexually rampant screen persona – highly popular with women – was immediately perceived as being a threat to girls. Beatrice Cooper recalls that she was forbidden to see Mae West films during her teenage years:

Mae West. My mother would never allow me to see Mae West... She was a SEX SYMBOL, you see. So they thought I might be spoiled if I saw her.[42]

The apparent double vulnerability of young women (not to mention the double-double standards of adult men) was demonstrated in a MPPDA memo to Will Hays in 1933, which argued:

The very man who will guffaw at Mae West's performance as a reminder of the ribald days of his past will resent her effect upon the young, when his daughter imitates the Mae West wiggle before her boyfriends and mouths 'come up and see me sometime'.[43]

'Serious' sex films were also considered dangerous viewing for girls. For example, one local American censor reviewed the romantic drama *Possessed* (1931), in which bored factory worker Joan Crawford becomes the kept mistress of Park Avenue lawyer Clark Gable. The censor complained to Hays that there were many young people in the audience and she was particularly appalled to hear a girl whisper to her friend: 'I would live with him too, under any conditions'.[44]

In addition to age and gender, concerns regarding sex pictures were informed by perceptions of class. Just as working class adolescent boys were considered at most risk from gangster films, so working class adolescent girls were seen as especially susceptible to the temptations provoked by sex pictures. In 'Children and the Cinema' (written around 1930), author Marianne Hoffmann describes several reformatory school girls led astray by films. She argues that working class girls are particularly unable to withstand the lure of the cinema, citing the story of a 'country girl of 15', left to mind her employer's baby one evening, whose 'desire [for films] was so strong that...she ended up by strangling the child and rushing off to the cinema'.[45] In the specific case of sex pictures, Hoffmann is convinced that working class girls are a particularly vulnerable group:

> The danger to poor girls is immense...The love of luxury which is gaining a hold on our towns starts at the pictures. The sensual film, even if not pornographic, poisons the moral sense of young girls. By awakening their sensual instincts it is...a training ground for the streets.[46]

The sex cycle created a headache for the censors to equal, if not exceed, that caused by gangster films. This was exacerbated by the practice of 'pinking': labelling certain sex pictures as suitable for 'adults only' to increase their box office appeal. While such a 'warning' might be seen to mollify critics, it was also widely recognised as a cynical way of emphasising the sexual content of a film, so as to attract large numbers of both adults and young people. Pinking was credited with helping make a smash hit of Mae West's *She Done Him Wrong*. It was also used to great effect on *Baby Face* (1933), in which Barbara Stanwyck played a speakeasy bartender who sleeps her way to the top. *Variety* declared 'anything hotter than this for public showing would call for an asbestos audience blanket'.[47] Yet they also reported that the film utilised pinking, with 'an ad campaign that's bringing in the kids by warning them to stay away; also the grown ups in paying numbers. It's the same old gag and it's working again'.[48]

The Horror Cycle

Despite the fact that hundreds were made, including *Frankenstein* (1910), *Dr Jekyll and Mr Hyde* (1920) and *Nosferatu* (1922), unlike silent crime and sex films, silent horror films aroused surprisingly little concern.[49] Nevertheless, when the new cycle of popular talkie horror films hit the cinema in the early 1930s, they were almost immediately controversial. This probably related in part to a general increase in concern regarding the cinema. But it was also due to the enhanced quality of talkie horror, since atmospheric music and sound effects, creepy-voiced macabre dialogue and a liberal dose of blood-curdling screams combined to make these films far more thrilling than their silent counterparts.

The pre-code horror cycle was the result of yet another studio seeking to avoid insolvency through box office success. Mae West kept Paramount afloat, gangsters put a fortune in the bank for Warner Brothers, RKO was rescued by King Kong and it was Universal that first hit pay-dirt through the horror cycle, with instant hits *Dracula* (1931) and *Frankenstein* (1931). They immediately built on this success in 1932, producing *Murders in the Rue Morgue*, *The Mummy* and *The Old Dark House*. Other studios followed suit with films including the Oscar-winning *Dr Jekyll and Mr Hyde* (1931) and in 1932, *Freaks*, *Doctor X*, *White Zombie* and *The Hounds of Zaroff*. The horror cycle continued to peak well into the mid-1930s. Key films of 1933 included *The Invisible Man*, *Island of Lost Souls*, *Mystery of the Wax Museum*, *King Kong*, *Murders in the Zoo* and *The Ghoul*. By 1935, Universal were still successfully harnessing the pulling power of Boris Karloff and Bela Lugosi, with *Mark of the Vampire*, *The Raven* and the critically acclaimed *Bride of Frankenstein*, along with another horror film, *Werewolf of London*. The cycle became less prolific by the late 1930s, but continued to be popular until at least the end of the decade.

The innate threat of horror films was their combination of sex, violence and the supernatural, which broke taboos, challenged Christian values and subverted the social order. For example, in Universal's *Murders in the Rue Morgue* (1932) Bela Lugosi plays the evil Dr Mirakle, a mad scientist trying to prove his own theory of evolution. He abducts prostitutes and injects them with gorilla blood in search of a match and when the women die, he throws their bodies in the Seine. The film's content includes a monster, sexual/scientific experimentation, prostitution and murder, along with sexual innuendo, the implied rape of a woman by a gorilla and strongly sacrilegious imagery. In one scene, Mirakle takes his latest subject and lashes her to a wooden crucifix. He checks her blood, declares it to be 'rotten – black as your sins' and, being disappointed yet again, he falls to his knees before her, apparently praying to the crucified whore.

The pre-code horror cycle was extremely popular with children (see Chapter 5). Tom Walsh enjoyed watching a number of horror films in 1931-2, when he was 9 or 10 years old, including *Frankenstein*, *Dracula* and *Dr Jekyll and Mr Hyde*. When asked whether he went to see all kinds of films as a child, he recalls exercising discretion and notes the mixed feelings of fear and fun that seem to have made horror films attractive to many young people:

> No, I chose as carefully as I could, because, eh, gangster films I loved as a boy. James Cagney, Humphrey Bogart, that sort of thing. Eh, horror films. Children have a strange fascination for horror films. They're afraid of them but they like them.[50]

Neither was this mixed attraction gender-specific, as horror films were extremely popular with girls as well as boys. Joan Donaghue recalls a similar mixture of fear and enjoyment when watching pre-code horror films with her female friends, aged between 7 and 9 years old, in the early 1930s:

> We went especially to be frightened by Boris Karloff in *The Old Dark House* or *Frankenstein* and we would cling to each other and squeal or shut our eyes. It didn't take much to set us off in those days![51]

It is perhaps to be expected, given the highly questionable content of pre-code horror films and their popularity with children, that this cycle provoked most anxiety among reformers in Britain, leading to the introduction of a special H certificate, which ostensibly prevented children from seeing horror films at all. This important development will be examined in more detail below.

Responses to the Pre-code Threat

America and the Hays Code

As Chapter 2 shows, the regulation of silent cinema was essentially a global phenomenon. With the coming of talkies, this trend continued and concern intensified and increasingly focused on the output of the world's leading film producer: Hollywood. Initially, although studio heads in America agreed in principle to abide by the Hays Code, film-makers, motivated by financial pressures and popular demand, largely ignored it, generously lacing their films with subversion and 'spice', not only in the three cycles just described, but in many other genres, including comedies and musicals.[52]

With the growth of talking pictures, American critics and reformers, already up in arms about silent films, were incensed by what they perceived to be an uncontrolled upsurge in the power and immorality of screen images. Once more, local censorship was deemed inadequate and there were renewed demands for a federal censorship system, fuelled by the findings of the Payne Fund Studies into the impact of cinema on children (see Chapter 4). This groundswell culminated in the formation of a dedicated movement known as the Legion of Decency – a campaign by the Catholic Church of America to boycott both offensive films and the cinemas that screened them.[53]

The Legion campaign posed a serious threat to both the film industry and the Hays Office, for Catholics represented 20 per cent of the American population (largely in urban areas, where cinema was most lucrative). Moreover, the Legion was backed by American Jewish and Protestant groups and by Catholics in key foreign markets such as Italy and Spain. Issues surrounding children were central to the campaign. The Legion Pledge (taken by over seven million Americans by mid-1934) denounced 'vile and unwholesome moving pictures' as 'a grave menace to youth'.[54] Meanwhile, Dr A.H. Giannini (the Catholic president of the Bank of America in Los Angeles) warned Hollywood producers that he was prepared to withdraw finance from the kind of offensive films that were 'prostituting the youth of America'.[55] Finally, films were classified by age for the first time in America, as the Legion adopted a four-category rating system, identifying movies as either suitable or unsuitable for children.[56]

By 1933, the major studios and the Hays Office were buckling under pressure from reformers in general and the Legion in particular, and steps had to be taken. In December 1933 the head of Hays' Studio Relations (censorship) office, James Wingate, was replaced by a new, Catholic director, Joe Breen. In June 1934 Breen's department was renamed the Production Code Administration (PCA) and given the remit to oversee the strict application of a new, binding Production Code to replace the previous advisory one. All Hollywood studios were then required to appoint representatives to work with Breen at the PCA. The MPPDA agreed that their members would not begin production on a film until the PCA had approved the script. Completed films would also be resubmitted for a PCA 'purity seal', without which they could not be distributed or exhibited. Studios that failed to comply would be fined $25,000. For the first time, the Hays Code had the genuine backing of film-makers who agreed, under severe pressure from the Legion of Decency and others, to clean up their act.

Breen was by all accounts stricter and more stubborn than his predecessors. He soon became known as the 'supreme pontiff of motion picture morals'; indeed, Doherty suggests Breen's impact was such that it would be more accurate to call the pre-code period the 'pre-Breen' period and the Hays Office, the 'Breen Office'.[57] Almost immediately, Breen was able to test-drive the now-enforceable Hays Code, proving his own mettle as chief censor and PCA director with his first test case: Mae West's new production, *It Ain't No Sin*.

Whereas Wingate compromised in censoring West's previous films (to help keep Paramount from bankruptcy), Breen allowed no such concessions. He rejected the entire first script for *It Ain't No Sin* as 'a glorification of prostitution and violent crime without any compensating moral values of any kind'.[58] He rejected two further drafts and, when Paramount defied him and made the film anyway, he refused it a certificate. Paramount then tested the Legion of Decency and advertised the film on Broadway with massive billboards announcing '*It Ain't No Sin*'. They were picketed by Catholic priests with placards declaring 'IT IS'.[59] Eventually the studio realised that defiance was futile; the climate of film production and exhibition was changing to such an extent that they would have to comply. To West's dismay, Paramount implemented the dialogue changes and cuts demanded by Breen and changed the movie's title from *It Ain't No Sin*, to *Belle of the Nineties* (1934). This saucy but sanitised film was then approved for public exhibition by the PCA.

Throughout, children remained central to the passionate debate around censorship. As late as July 1934, the *New York Herald Tribune* argued that the Legion should 'find some more serious matter to fight against than Mae West's terrible influence over the ten-year-old mind'.[60] Meanwhile, others opposed to the censorship crackdown argued that it would all be averted if children's viewing was restricted, for this was the main bone of contention.[61]

However, such opposition was in vain. By the midsummer of 1934, the Hays Code was firmly in place, Breen was established as the ultimate arbiter of Hollywood film content and a watershed had been reached. Finally, as box office figures started to rise from 1934 (alongside initial financial recovery from the Depression) the PCA chose to interpret this as confirmation that there was indeed public demand for morally clean films, suitable for both children and adults to see.

Britain and the A Certificate Problem

It was predictable that the debate surrounding children and cinema in pre-code America should focus primarily on the content of films, since Hollywood was, by and large, the source of the 'problem'. In Britain, however, the BBFC had already established fairly effective control over domestic film production by the early 1930s, so the threat posed to British children by the cinema was often seen as essentially alien – namely, the multitude of popular yet 'unsuitable' films imported from America. Cinemas wanted to screen these lucrative films and audiences wanted to see them; nevertheless, British reformers launched a bi-frontal attack on the transatlantic invasion of monsters, gangsters and harlots. There were renewed calls – first for stricter censorship and second for more effective restrictions on the access of children to cinemas. In particular, the debate continued to revolve around one issue: the admission of children to A films.

By the early 1930s, the BBFC had seen a number of significant changes, particularly in personnel: in 1929 president T.P. O'Connor was replaced by former Home Secretary the Rt. Hon. Edward Shortt; and in 1930 chief censor Husey was replaced by retired artillery officer Colonel J.C. Hanna. Hanna became the BBFC's vice-president and senior script examiner, assisted from 1934 by Shortt's daughter, Miss N. Shortt. This pair, described by Jeffrey Richards as 'a rather tetchy retired army officer and a sheltered upper-class spinster', were primarily responsible for vetting film scenarios submitted in advance by producers (about one-third of British film projects were processed in this way during the 1930s), passing judgements that often seemed rather fastidious, prudish and naïve.[62]

As already explained, from the outset in 1913, the board had given approved films one of two certificates – Universal (U) or Public (A). Both were said to be suitable for children, but the former were 'especially recommended for Children's Matinees'.[63] Importantly, the BBFC argued that parents were primarily responsible for decisions regarding children's viewing and they recommended that only children accompanied by parents or *bona fide* guardians should be admitted to A films.

This stance was maintained by the BBFC into the 1930s, despite the fact that A film regulations were ignored in Scotland, while in England and Wales unaccompanied children habitually circumvented

1. 'A' or 'U'? *Punch* cartoon. (Reproduced in Richard Ford, *Children in the Cinema*, London: Allen & Unwin, 1939.)

them, either by sneaking into the cinema without paying or, more commonly, by asking adult strangers to accompany them past the box office. Herein lay the key problem of children and A film attendance: the ineffectual nature of current regulations. When under fire on the issue, the BBFC invariably reiterated their position and placed the onus back on parental responsibility, but this did nothing to placate reformers concerned that children were achieving more or less unrestricted access to films of all kinds.

There were two other controversial issues related to the A film category. First, some argued that there was no need for two certificates; films were either suitable for all audiences, or they were unsuitable. Second, some critics argued that A film regulations did nothing to protect working class children who were often taken to the cinema by their parents, regardless of the nature of the films, because there was no alternative childcare. But although this led to calls for an outright ban on under-16s from A films, they were opposed by the CEA, who argued that such restrictions would fatally impact cinemas in working class areas.[64]

Throughout the 1930s, the attendance of children at A films continued to be the subject of much debate, exacerbated by the coming of talkies and controversial pre-code film cycles. Notably, access to gangster and horror films was increasingly problematic, because they were hugely popular with children and were generally given (ineffective) A certificates.

In 1931, Sir Herbert Samuel returned to the Home Office as Home Secretary, still maintaining a great interest in the influence of cinema, but apparently more kindly disposed towards the medium than he had been in 1916. By now there was considerable demand for action on issues surrounding children and A films. The BBFC and the Home Office both received frequent deputations on the matter from interest groups and licensing authorities and there was growing pressure from local boards of enquiry in places like Birmingham and Birkenhead (see Chapter 4).

In an attempt to examine the extent of the A film problem, the Home Office sent out a questionnaire in February 1931 to all 764 licensing authorities in England and Wales.[65] The questionnaire enquired about the extent to which local authorities were complying with the 1923 model conditions regarding cinema licensing – in particular, conditions concerning the admission of children to A films.

While many historians refer to this questionnaire, few if any recognise that debates surrounding children and cinema were undoubtedly its driving force, for government records confirm that the entire investigation was being conducted for a report on the Home Office Children's Branch.[66]

Of the 764 authorities contacted, 723 replied, including every County and Municipal Borough in England and Wales. Most of the 41 that did not reply had no cinema within their jurisdiction, while of those that did respond, 120 had no cinema and 97 had just one. Table 3.1 shows the extent to which the 603 responding authorities with cinemas claimed to comply with the seven model conditions of 1923 regarding cinema licensing and management.

Table 3.1 Responses to Home Office Questionnaire on Model Conditions, 1931

Model condition	Authorities complying	
	No.	%*
1) That no films injurious to morality or inciting crime should be shown	511	84.7
2) That no film which the BBFC had not passed should be shown	445	73.8
3) That children should not be admitted to A films unless accompanied by a *bona fide* parent or guardian	**396**	**65.7**
4) That the BBFC certificate should be shown on the screen for at least 10 seconds before the beginning of the film	267	44.3
5) That the certificate as indicated by A or U should be shown at least 1¼ inches high in advertising outside cinemas	246	40.8
6) That there should be no immoral advertising outside cinemas	479	79.4
7) That there should be complete lighting in cinemas at all times when open to the public	484	80.3

* Percentages relate to the 603 responding licensing authorities with cinemas in their jurisdiction.
Source: PRO–HO45/14731: Children and the cinema 1929–1932.

As this table suggests, 65.7 per cent of responding licensing authorities with cinemas in their jurisdiction in 1931 claimed to comply with Model Condition 3 (MC3) – that is, 'that children should not be admitted to A films unless accompanied by a *bona fide* parent or guardian'. There was a rural/urban variation in these figures: 83.3 per cent of authorities reported compliance in rural areas, compared to just 60 per cent in urban areas. Thus, children in towns and cities were apparently more likely to gain unaccompanied access to A film performances. A few authorities noted that they had introduced tougher conditions (Liverpool and Newbury had both banned under-16s from A films altogether) or more lenient ones (two had cut the age of unaccompanied attendance from 16 to 14).

However, although 65.7 per cent of authorities claimed to adhere to MC3, further questioning revealed a range of practical problems regarding the effectiveness and enforcement of this condition. When asked about the *application* of MC3, 84 licensing bodies claimed, rather cagily, to have 'no evidence that the condition has not been effective'. Meanwhile, 28 authorities admitted that MC3 was 'difficult to enforce', 13 confessed that 'children ask strangers to act as their guardian', eight explained that programmes including a mixture of U and A films caused problems of enforcement and six protested that it was 'difficult to determine a child's age'. One authority complained that parents took their children into the cinema and left them there and a remarkable 15 authorities suggested that all under-16s should be banned from A films.

Thus, of the 396 authorities claiming to have adopted MC3, only 244 reported that they actively enforced it. Most of these used inspections (commonly, police inspectors or visits by the authority), while others sent reminders to cinema managers regarding children and A films. But 57 authorities reported that their compliance relied solely upon the co-operation of licensees, 152 said that they took no special action to enforce conditions regarding the admission of children and, despite the common practice of sneaking in with strangers, only two authorities had successfully pursued prosecutions in this regard.

In 1931, therefore, while the BBFC argued that unaccompanied children should not be admitted to A films, only two-thirds of local authorities in England and Wales even claimed to comply with this regulation and just 40 per cent actively enforced it (probably less in urban areas). Furthermore, as will be shown, even if MC3 *was* adopted and enforced, many children still efficiently evaded this attempt to control their viewing. The Home Office therefore concluded that the current regulations were ineffective, and in November 1931 Samuel established a new Film Censorship Consultative Committee (FCCC) to tackle the problem of 'the admission of children to exhibitions of A films'.[67]

At its first meeting on 26 November 1931, the FCCC comprised Samuel himself, Shortt and Brooke Wilkinson from the BBFC, two representatives from the LCC, four from other county councils and four from municipal corporations (including two chief constables).[68] This soon expanded to include representatives from other licensing authorities and, on the committee's insistence, at least one woman. They met frequently over the next two years, aiming to get a firm grip on the problem of children and A films – primarily because a lack of central control was spawning wild variations in licensing across Britain, which threatened the fragile position of the BBFC.

While most local authorities claimed to comply with BBFC/Home Office advice in the early 1930s, the 1931 questionnaire had clearly demonstrated that this was by no means unanimous. Neither did the nominal assent of authorities necessarily signify their genuine compliance or unquestioning loyalty. Local bodies still had power of veto over all BBFC decisions and they often used it. Many still considered the BBFC too liberal, including Beckenham Council, who created their own board of censors in 1933.[69] Conversely, other authorities found the BBFC too conservative and they allowed banned films to be shown. As Tom Johnson notes, 'it was not unusual to see film posters in the early thirties screaming, "Banned by the Censors – Passed by _____ County Council!"'[70]

Unsurprisingly, British local authorities also displayed a variety of responses to the problem of children and A film attendance in the 1930s. Policies ranged from the aforementioned total ban on children at A films in Liverpool and Newbury, to a complete disregard for A certificate regulations in Scotland, where unaccompanied children could attend freely and A films were frequently shown at children's matinees.[71] Authorities prohibiting under-16s from attending A films did so on the grounds that such films were unsuitable for all children, whether accompanied or not. However, they usually added the concession that exhibitors could apply to the licensing board for a 'suitable' A film to be reclassified as U, so that it could be shown to children. This strategy invariably backfired, as in Portsmouth, where exhibitors deliberately overloaded the system in order to render it unworkable.[72]

Probably the best-known ban on under-16s from A films occurred in Liverpool in 1930. It was sparked off when a boy asked a stranger to take him into the cinema, unaware that the stranger in question was magistrate Mrs Steuart Brown. The outraged magistrate consequently persuaded Liverpool justices to impose a ban on under-16s from A films, whether accompanied or not.[73] Explaining their decision, in defiance of the BBFC, the justices argued that A films were potentially harmful to children and that parents were 'not always the best judges of what a child should see'.[74] As in Portsmouth, a provision was made that 'suitable' A films could be reclassified as U films on appeal.

Other areas adopting a similar approach included Newcastle, Leicester, Hove, Sheffield and Birmingham. The FCCC managed to dissuade some authorities bent on banning children; for example, Dorset County Council postponed their decision to ban under-16s from A films in March 1932 pending FCCC deliberations.[75] In May the same year, however, nearby Bridgewater informed the CEA that they were banning under-16s from A films, asserting that they would not be placated in the same way that Dorset had been.[76]

Just as the compensatory reclassification system backfired in Portsmouth, so it was found to be unworkable elsewhere.[77] In Beckenham, examiners 'found themselves forced to allow almost 90 per cent of the A films to be shown as U films, with no restriction whatever upon the admission of children'. Similarly, Liverpool examiners left it to the 'honour' of exhibitors which A films to exclude children from, only to find that around 130 A films were then shown with no restrictions on child admissions in the licensing year 1931–2.[78] Meanwhile, dissenting authorities were assailed by the persuasive arguments of the CEA and FCCC, who reiterated that A films were not necessarily 'Adult' films; they were simply those for which the BBFC *advised adult guidance*, and the system had been devised to allow parents to make individual decisions, based on the nature of a given film and the age and personality of their own children. The BBFC Annual Report of 1930 made their reasoning clear:

The classification of films suitable for young persons bristles with difficulties, for it is not easy to know where to draw the line...Such well-known pantomime stories as Red Riding Hood have had a terrifying effect upon some few neurotic children. A few mothers have also complained that their children have wakened up with fright ... after seeing a beautiful and educative natural history film.[79]

As children varied considerably, the BBFC, FCCC and CEA argued, the solution was not to ban them, but to inform parents more clearly as to the suitability of A films. By December 1932, all the dissenting authorities had conceded defeat, reinstating the proviso in their regulations that children should not be admitted to A films, 'unless accompanied by a *bona fide* parent or guardian'.[80]

After meeting for one year, the FCCC made a number of recommendations regarding children and A films to the Home Office. These were then embodied in a Home Office circular and sent to all licensing authorities in England and Wales on 6 March 1933, together with a new set of model conditions.[81] The emphasis was on improving parental awareness, not least because the February questionnaire had revealed that film certification categories were displayed outside cinemas and before performances in only a minority of jurisdictions (see Table 3.1). Moreover, many cinemas only displayed this information briefly, in tiny lettering, or in obscure places. Therefore, the 1933 circular recommended that authorities require cinemas to display 'easily legible' category notices, 'in a prominent position at each entrance to the premises' and 'over every pay box', in addition to projecting the film's certificate clearly on the screen before each performance. The BBFC also arranged that film posters and other publicity would now display certification details of all films.

Lastly, the circular recognised that 'children are able to persuade adults whom they meet outside the cinema to take them ... in'. Yet it did not really propose a viable solution, merely suggesting that cinemas should post notices outlining the regulation regarding *bona fide* guardians and 'expressing the wish of the management that patrons will not encourage children to evade this regulation'.[82] The Home Office also recommended that cinema staff and managers condoning such practices 'should be reminded that any such action ... imperils [their] licence'. There were additional suggestions regarding 'horrific' films, which will be outlined shortly.

Interestingly, a copy of this circular was requested by a Stormont official, because the issue of children and A film attendance was also being hotly debated in Northern Ireland.[83] This official betrayed a rather cynical attitude to the problem, however: 'I do not think we have the least intention of doing anything about the matter here', he wrote, 'but we are constantly being badgered about it, and would like to seem bright and enthusiastic when receiving deputations of old ladies on the subject'.[84]

Finally, the FCCC advised the Home Office that the meanings of BBFC certificates should be more widely publicised, so that people would understand them. This had previously been raised at a BBFC/LCC meeting in 1929, where frustration with the system was very apparent. The board's Mr Hessey complained that nearly all the letters they received involved 'a misunderstanding about the [A] certificate'; his colleague Brooke Wilkinson mused 'whether it might not be wise to exclude children altogether from the cinema'; and Rosamund Smith of the LCC (later of the FCCC) exclaimed: 'We want to drum it into them; the public are so stupid...I know that thousands of them don't want to know. They haven't got the brains.'[85]

One method of publicising the meanings of certificates quickly presented itself in 1933, when the Joint Committee of the Mother's Union, the National Council of Women, the National Federation of Women's Institutes and the Public Morality Council decided to support the Home Office circular on Children and A Films. They publicised the circular widely and arranged 'The Influence of the Cinema', an event at Caxton Hall on 29 May 1933, to promote the new model conditions and 'to press upon all Licensing Authorities the vital necessity of adopting [them] *in toto*'.[86] This represented the first real consensus between the Home Office, the BBFC, local licensing authorities, the CEA and moral watch-dogs in dealing with the issue of children and A film attendance. However it was, of course, neither the end of the problem, nor of the debate.

Throughout the early 1930s, arguments concerning children and A film attendance had repeatedly come to a head over one pre-code cycle in particular: horror. Reformers were exercised by this genre which was not only highly offensive, but massively popular with children. The resultant dispute would lead to key changes in British cinema regulation.

A flash-point was reached early in the pre-code horror cycle, when *Dracula* (1931) was rapidly followed by the release of *Frankenstein* (1931). Both films received only minor cuts before being passed with A certificates, feeding existing anxieties regarding the access of children to A films. These were spectacular thrillers, highly popular with audiences of all ages and, as one quickly followed another, it became apparent that a new cycle was being born. Reformers sought to nip this in the bud.

The launch of *Frankenstein* in Britain was a great cinematic affair. Lobbies boasted massive cut-outs of the monster with flashing eyes and teaser slogans including 'The monster is loose!' and 'Beware the hand of the monster!' Publicity stunts were also arranged. Cinemas stationed ambulances outside their buildings or nursing staff within and at least one administered joke 'nerve tonic' medication (sugar capsules) to potential patrons.[87] The film was a smash hit and adults queued for hours to see it. Of course, many children were also fascinated by its appeal and attended in droves.[88]

Almost immediately, complaints came from the National Society for Prevention of Cruelty to Children (NSPCC), the LCC and Surrey County Council and children were banned from *Frankenstein* in Manchester, London and elsewhere.[89] Probably the most concerted campaign was by the Order of the Child, who opposed the admission of children to previews of *Frankenstein* at the Tivoli Theatre in London, in January 1932. The Order then campaigned for the exclusion of all children from this film on its general release in May. They argued that it was 'too thrilling for children to see' and sent letters to the Home Office, the BBFC, CEA, LCC, the Tivoli Theatre and Gaumont British (the renters for the film). Gaumont British consequently agreed to include in their advertising the statement: 'in our opinion, this film is unsuitable for children'.[90]

Frankenstein was a pivotal film in the children and cinema debate in Britain. It was by far the most frequently mentioned film in correspondence to the FCCC and was repeatedly discussed at length in their meetings.[91] After consultation with the FCCC, the CEA set a precedent by contacting its members just before the film's general release to recommend 'in very strong terms that all exhibitors showing this film should make an announcement [that] *Frankenstein* is... not suitable for children'.[92] This recommendation was repeated on the release of *Dr Jekyll and Mr Hyde* (1931) and *Murders in the Rue Morgue* (1932), thus setting a pattern; the CEA would now inform exhibitors whenever a horror film was released.[93]

The new approach to horror was formalised in May 1933 with the introduction of a special BBFC category. If appropriate, particularly strong horror films could now be passed with both an A certificate and the label 'Horrific', signifying that they were unsuitable for children. The procedure was supported by the 1933 Home Office circular mentioned above, which announced that a list of horror films would be kept at the Home Office for the information of licensing authorities. The first Horrific label was applied to *Vampyr* (1931), which had been delayed pending the new category and was passed uncut for release as a Horrific A film in May 1933. At the Caxton Hall meeting that same month, FCCC chair Sir Cecil Levita declared: 'We have for the first time definitely nailed to the counter that the Censor – and...the Local Authority... – can define at any time a film to be horrific or terrifying, and order notices to be put up that it is unsuitable for children.'[94]

The Horrific label was seen as a step in the right direction by those who had long sought the introduction of a 'third BBFC certificate' for the protection of children. In 1921, for example, an NC or Not for Children certificate had been proposed, while in 1929 the LCC had argued that A should mean Adults only, with a C certificate being introduced for films 'especially suitable for children'.[95] A similar suggestion had been made to the BBFC by the Public Morality Council in 1930 and to the FCCC by Middlesex County Council in 1932.[96] Such ideas were invariably blocked by the BBFC who argued that the existing system, if adhered to, provided adequate protection and that a C certificate might ruin a film's potential for adult audiences.[97] Finally, with the release of *Frankenstein* in 1932, the Order of the Child called on the BBFC to introduce a third certificate for films that 'cannot in any circumstances be shown to children'.[98] Thus, the Horrific label was a compromise; it signified that some films were unsuitable for children, but it did not prohibit their attendance. Crucially, however, the Horrific label was not a *certificate* and it therefore did nothing to stop unaccompanied A film attendance by young people. Indeed, it may have been a variation on 'pinking', simply attracting children to the forbidden fruit of 'unsuitable' films. So reformers persisted in campaigns for tighter restrictions on children's viewing and local authorities continued to take independent action. In June 1933 the LCC backed the new label, stipulating that Horrific films should be advertised outside cinemas with the phrase 'This Film is Unsuitable for Children'.[99] However, St Helens and Birmingham banned children outright from the Horrific *King Kong* in September 1933 and, in December 1935, Middlesex banned children from all films *they* deemed horrific, regardless of their BBFC category.[100] By January 1937, Middlesex was joined by Surrey and Essex, the LCC were considering a similar move and Finchley and Hendon Education Committees had resolved that 'under no circumstances should children under 16 years of age be permitted to attend performances of A films'.[101] The ideal of central BBFC control was starting to slide once again.

The situation was aggravated in 1936 when newly-appointed BBFC President Lord Tyrrell declared that the horror cycle was over and that the Horrific label could therefore be scrapped.[102] While well informed (the cycle was indeed starting to wane), Tyrrell's comments did nothing to appease those who were concerned that existing regulations were already woefully ineffective in excluding children from unsuitable films. When protests were lodged by the Joint London, Middlesex and Surrey County Councils Viewing Committee, Tyrrell was forced to retract his comment.[103] Rather than defusing the situation, his assertions had simply strengthened the resolve of those seeking an effective third certificate.

Increasingly, calls for this third certificate came to focus on horror. In July 1935 the LCC proposed to the FCCC and the Home Office that the only solution was officially to exclude all children from Horrific films.[104] Between October 1936 and March 1937, the LCC then tried to convince the BBFC that 'in addition to the two existing categories of films...there should be a third category 'H' (passed as 'horrific', i.e., for public presentations when no children under 16 are present)'.[105] Further pressure was applied in February 1937, when Odeon boss Oscar Deutsch announced that, because of persistent problems with child attendance, he would no longer show Horrific films in his cinemas.[106]

Finally, in April 1937 the LCC requested once again that the advisory H label be made a formal certificate in its own right, to exclude children from horror films. This time the BBFC complied and in June 1937 the first H certificate was given to MGM thriller *The Thirteenth Chair* (although this film was not particularly horrific and, as *Today's Cinema* suggested, 'the usual adult certificate would have suited it equally as well').[107] The decision as to whether a film was passed A or H continued to be rather arbitrary and inconsistent for the rest of the decade, but children were now officially banned from some horror films and could only gain access to them by illicit means.

It should be recognised, though, that the Horrific label and the H certificate were applied to only a handful of films. Just 18 were labelled Horrific between 1932 and 1936 and from 1937 to 1950 only 37 were given an H certificate (less than three per year), 21 of which were certified in just two of these years, 1946 and 1939 (see Appendix 4). Nevertheless, the H certificate was a significant development, being the first official ruling to exclude all children in England and Wales from certain films, regardless of their own wishes or those of their parents.

Conclusions

With the introduction of sound films in the late 1920s and the growth of controversial pre-code film cycles in the early 1930s, concern surrounding children and the cinema escalated. This culminated in the increased regulation of film content and, in Britain, new limitations on children's cinema attendance. A watershed was reached in the summer of 1934 when the campaigns of the Legion of Decency and others spawned a new, enforceable Hays Code, which effectively sanitised Hollywood and went a long way towards solving the problems associated with children and film. In both Britain and America, these fundamental changes in film content and cinema regulations were principally driven not by political factors or issues of social class, but by ongoing concerns regarding children.

After many years of protest, the sanitisation of Hollywood took place almost overnight and from July 1934 (as Black argues), 'making a film "as Breen as possible" became good business policy'.[108] The alternative was a lengthy and expensive process of re-writing, re-shooting and re-editing to gain PCA approval. Thus, from 1934, Hollywood movies eschewed nudity and suggestive humour; divorce and extramarital sex were portrayed as unacceptable; and crime no longer paid, with law enforcers rather than gangsters being the heroes of films such as *G-Men* (1935) and *Special Agent* (1935). Also from mid-1934, in stark contrast to previous film cycles, a new, respectable cycle emerged of literary adaptations, eminently suitable for both children and adults, including *Treasure Island* (1934) and, in 1935, *Alice Adams*, *Becky Sharp*, *David Copperfield*, *A Midsummer Night's Dream* and *A Tale of Two Cities*.

The watershed of 1934 can be seen in the contrasting fortunes of two stars: one considered a highly inappropriate role model for children; the other, a paragon of wholesome childhood. As already shown, 1934 marked the beginning of the end for Mae West, who only made six more films before returning to the stage. Stripped of their sexy edge, these films lacked the sparkle and therefore the box-office appeal of West's earlier work. Meanwhile, Shirley Temple became a star in 1934 at the age of 6, appearing in no less than seven films that year and earning a Special Oscar, 'in grateful recognition of her outstanding contribution to screen entertainment'. While there were clearly other factors at play, the divergent career paths of West and Temple really epitomised the pivotal changes that occurred in Hollywood in 1934.

Once the Hays Code became established and film content came under far stricter controls, reformers and critics were appeased. In July 1936, Pope Pius XI issued an encyclical on films, blessing Breen, praising the work of the PCA and the Legion of Decency, and noting the changes wrought by just two years of the new Hays Code: 'crime and vice are portrayed less frequently; sin no longer is so openly approved or acclaimed; false ideals of life no longer are presented in so flagrant a manner to the impressionable minds of youth'.[109]

In Britain, an additional calming factor was the growing alliance between the Hays Office and the BBFC from the mid-1930s. This collaboration aimed to smooth the path of exhibition for both British and American films, setting uniformly high moral standards and discussing particular national sensibilities, such as the British aversion to animal cruelty. As in America, therefore, concern over film content rapidly declined in Britain from 1934 and by the end of 1935 the BBFC could report 'a marked diminution of hostile criticism'.[110] Meanwhile, the FCCC became largely redundant, meeting only once between 1934 and 1938 and again in 1946 when they disbanded.[111]

It is important, however, to note that censorship control was by no means absolute after 1934, for there were still significant areas of compromise in the regulation of cinema, as film-makers sought to create within and beyond limits set by censors. Consequently, although Doherty suggests that from July 1934 'cinematic space was a patrolled landscape with secure perimeters and well-defined borders', I would argue that these borders were in fact negotiable and unstable.[112] A notable example of such negotiation is the making of

Dead End (1937), a film that portrays a street gang of sharp-talking delinquents, who spend their time in perpetual truancy, swimming in a filthy downtown river, playing cards, fighting and stealing.

Several changes were made to the original *Dead End* stage play, including the removal of references to syphilis and the replacement of the outspoken, crippled protagonist, Gimpty, with a clean-cut, democratic, social pioneer played by Joel McCrea. However, the final film still overstepped censors' boundaries. Socio-economic inequality was highlighted and heavily criticised. There were references to prostitution, police brutality against women strikers and criticisms of the reform school system. Not least, juvenile delinquents were sympathetically portrayed as victims of circumstance; some riddled with tuberculosis, some carrying knives, all living by the law of the concrete jungle. Yet despite these irregularities, both the PCA and the BBFC passed *Dead End* for exhibition, owing to careful negotiation (before, during and after production) between the censors and producer Samuel Goldwyn.[113] This then illustrates the flexible nature of film regulation, even after 1934; the success of this film led to a popular series of five more 'Dead End Kids' films in 1938 and 1939, including *Angels With Dirty Faces* (1938), followed by other spin-offs (starring the East Side Kids, the Little Tough Guys and the Bowery Boys), going right through to 1958.[114]

After 1934, the sanitisation of Hollywood allowed British reformers and censors gradually to shift their focus away from concerns relating to the corrupting moral influence of cinema on young people and onto another, related issue: the ability of films to cause fear or psychological trauma in children.[115] Interestingly, this change represents a privileging of the romantic view of the vulnerable child in need of protection over the original sin model of the dangerous child with a natural tendency to moral corruption, reflecting more widespread changes of the 1930s in approaches to education and child welfare.[116] In 1937 a former member of the LCC Education Committee described the difference in approach: 'the interest has altogether changed. We are concerned not with the morals of the children but with their fear, of wolves foaming at the mouth and that sort of thing.'[117]

This shift in emphasis towards a concern regarding fear led directly to the creation of the H label in 1933 and the H certificate in 1937. However, neither strategy was genuinely successful. As Chapter 5 will show, children continued to circumvent attempts to control their viewing and persisted in using adult strangers to gain entrance to A films throughout the 1930s and 1940s.[118] The H certificate, while more restrictive, applied to only a handful of films in one genre – a limitation not lost on some reformers, who continued to campaign for the complete exclusion of children from all unsuitable films (not only horror films). In November 1938, the Order of the Child complained to the Home Office that children were still regularly gaining entrance to see A films with strangers, and they called for 'a Third and more restrictive certificate for certain types of films, as in the case of horrific films', which could be applied to other genres.[119] But it would not be until 1951, and the introduction of the X certificate, that most children would be effectively excluded from apparently unsuitable films of all kinds.

Overall, despite an emphasis in existing literature on issues relating to social class and politics, it would appear that the key developments in the regulation of cinema and censorship in Britain and America before and during the 1930s were directly related to specific concerns regarding the impact of film on young people. In fact, since the birth of the BBFC in 1913, film certification categories in Britain have *always* related to the protection of children. From the initial A and U certificates to the H label and H certificate in the 1930s, and on to the X (16) certificate in 1951, the AA and X (18) certificates in 1970, and the PG, 15, 18 and R18 certificates in 1982, British cinema regulation has consistently been driven by issues relating to the child.

Moral Panic or Flapdoodle?

There is probably more 'flapdoodle' in regard to the
type of film which should or should not be exhibited
to children than almost anything else.
Daily Film Renter, 15 July 1936

As the previous chapters suggest, cinema regulation in the first four
decades of moving pictures was largely driven by concerns
regarding child viewing. Such concerns were manifest in a variety of
ways, including numerous official investigations carried out into the
impact of film on the young. This chapter will focus on some of these
enquiries in detail, assessing their motivations and their findings, and
considering whether they, along with other manifestations of concern,
represented a 'moral panic' over children and cinema in the 1930s.

Overview

The first major British investigation into the social impact of cinema
took place in 1917 when the Cinema Trade Council asked the National
Council of Public Morals to undertake 'an independent inquiry into
the physical, social, moral and educational influence of the cinema,
with special reference to young people'.[1] The resulting Commission of
Inquiry had 25 members representing a broad range of interests,
including the National Union of Teachers, the Cinematograph

Exhibitors Association, religious organisations, youth organisations and local councils, plus writers and composers (notably, controversial author and birth-control campaigner Dr Marie Stopes) and BBFC president T.P. O'Connor. Their enquiry was wide-ranging, taking evidence over six months from film-makers, exhibitors, censors, educationalists, chief constables, ministers of religion, doctors and, importantly, children. Sub-committees were also appointed to visit cinemas, and sub-enquiries were conducted to canvass the opinions of chief constables, clerks to the justices of the peace and school and youth workers. There was also a specially commissioned sub-enquiry into the impact of film on juvenile delinquency in America.[2]

In 1917 the Cinema Commission of Inquiry published its extensive report of almost 400 pages. The findings were comprehensive, detailed and balanced, finally concluding that the social impact of cinema in Britain was largely positive, despite the allegations being levelled against it. Thus, the report declared, although they had been 'compelled…to give special attention to the alleged *defects* in the picture house', the commission had been 'convinced by the amount of testimony offered in [cinema's] favour of its value as a cheap amusement for the masses, for parents as well as children, especially as regards its influence in decreasing hooliganism and as a counter-attraction to the public-house'.[3]

A key focus of the enquiry was the question of whether films effected high levels of juvenile delinquency, and in this respect too the conclusions were carefully considered and generally commendatory:

> The problem [of juvenile crime] is far too complex to be solved by laying stress on only one factor and that probably a subordinate one, among all the contributing conditions… While a connection between the cinema and crime has to a limited extent in special cases been shown, yet it certainly has not been proved that the increase in juvenile crime generally has been consequent on the cinema, or has been independent of other factors more conducive to wrongdoing.[4]

Despite the thorough, authoritative conclusions of the 1917 enquiry however, concern continued to surround cinema, particularly as it related to young people.[5] This was only exacerbated with the introduction of talkies from 1927, and the 1930s saw a massive rise in enquiries regarding the social impact of cinema on children, both in Britain and overseas.

Many international projects were initiated, including League of Nations conferences in 1926, 1936 and 1938.[6] But probably the most extensive research into the issue of children and cinema took place in America between 1929 and 1933, when leading psychologists, sociologists and educationalists conducted a large collection of enquiries known as the Payne Fund Studies (PFS).[7] The findings of this broad investigation into the impact of cinema on children were published in 12 detailed volumes, but public awareness of the PFS came primarily from the controversial summary volume by Henry James Forman, *Our Movie Made Children* (1933), which selected the studies' more sensational findings (including those not yet published) in order to denounce cinema as a scapegoat for a variety of social ills.[8] Even the PFS directors (who were by no means enamoured of the cinema) considered the tone of this anti-movie polemic to be extreme, yet the media cited it extensively and it rapidly became a best-seller.

While the PFS were underway in America, several local enquiries into the impact of cinema on children were launched in Britain. Many were small-scale projects or dealt with particular issues, such as the educational use of film or the impact of war films on children.[9] Others looked specifically at the subject of children's matinees (see Chapter 6).[10] But the four key British cinema enquiries of the early 1930s were those conducted in Birmingham, Birkenhead, London and Edinburgh. These are of great interest and will now be examined in some depth, including details of their backgrounds, main players and methodologies.

Background to the Four Main British Cinema Enquiries

In 1930, the National Council of Women held a conference in Birmingham to discuss the problem of film content. Overall, they found many films morally suspect if not dangerous, and they therefore requested that the Home Office hold a public enquiry into the need for stricter censorship and cinema regulation.[11] When this request was denied, the Birmingham Cinema Enquiry Committee (BCEC) was formed to investigate the impact of cinema-going on Birmingham children.[12] Their enquiry (conducted between April 1930 and May

1931) was based on a clear prejudice against the cinema and was specifically designed to uncover sufficient evidence of the medium's shortcomings to persuade the Home Secretary to change his mind. This bias is openly acknowledged in the foreword to their published report:

> Amongst ourselves there was widespread 'dissatisfaction' (to use a mild expression) with the prevalent type of film, and particularly the baneful effect of that type on children and adolescents...Our object was to endeavour to persuade the Home Secretary to institute an impartial inquiry...the results of which we were confident would lead to drastic and beneficial changes in the regulations at present governing the exercise of the 'Censorship'.[13]

The BCEC enquiry was therefore principally concerned with the negative effect of cinema on 'children and adolescents'. The main thrust of its investigation involved the distribution of questionnaires to around 2,300 children from 24 schools and youth groups in and around Birmingham, asking about their frequency of cinema attendance, film preferences and the effects of cinema-going. A few youths and adults were also questioned. In addition, BCEC representatives visited cinemas (including children's matinees), producing 430 visitors' reports. The enquiry's findings were published in 1931, and throughout the first half of the 1930s the BCEC continued to hold public meetings and conferences, assemble petitions and send deputations to the Home Office, in an attempt to improve the moral climate of the cinema, particularly for young people.[14]

Following the Birmingham enquiry, the Birkenhead Vigilance Committee (BVC) was inspired to conduct a cinema enquiry of its own between June and October of 1931, based closely on the BCEC model. The link to Birmingham is clear from their report, in which the BVC 'strongly endorse the appeal of the Birmingham Cinema Inquiry Committee...for "an impartial and comprehensive public inquiry into the production, classification and exhibition of films"'.[15] They go on to applaud

> with fullest sympathy the determination of the Birmingham Inquiry Committee to persist...'until...the abuses and dangers

– intellectual, physical and moral – particularly for children and adolescents, which at present make what might be an instrument of untold good into an instrument of incalculable harm, have been extirpated'.[16]

In addition to shared motivation, the Birkenhead enquiry employed a very similar methodology to that of the BCEC, including an almost identical questionnaire, completed by around 1,845 local children. BVC representatives also submitted 46 cinema visitors' reports (20 of which involved Saturday matinees). The findings of the Birkenhead Committee were published in December 1931 and the BVC continued to campaign by writing to the Birkenhead Justices, requesting amendments to cinema licensing regulations. Notably they called for the banning of all children aged under 16 from A film performances. This correspondence was published in Birkenhead newspapers, but licensing regulations were not changed at that time.[17]

Cinema enquiries then followed in London and Edinburgh, but these were fundamentally different from the Birmingham and Birkenhead studies in many respects. The London Enquiry was carried out by the LCC Education Committee, who published their report in March 1932.[18] The LCC had been active in cinema regulation from the turn of the century and was instrumental in the shaping of regulations regarding children's cinema attendance throughout the 1920s and 1930s. During this time it held numerous meetings on the subject with (amongst others) the BBFC, the London Public Morality Council, the Juvenile Organisations Association, the London Head Teachers' Association and the National Union of Women Teachers.[19] However, in meetings during the summer of 1929, the LCC admitted with some concern and frustration that, despite their efforts, there was still 'no effective method…for preventing unaccompanied children from attaching themselves to adults for the purpose of gaining admission to exhibitions of A films'.[20]

After a year of wrestling with the subject yet again, the Theatres and Music Halls Committee chairman Miss Rosamund Smith finally declared: 'we are almost sick of it'.[21] The baton was then passed to the LCC Education Committee, which was commissioned to produce a comprehensive report regarding children and cinema attendance. They would obtain the information for this report from an enquiry that became by far the largest of the four under consideration, involving

Figure 4.1 Relative Sample Sizes of British Cinema Enquiries 1930–33*

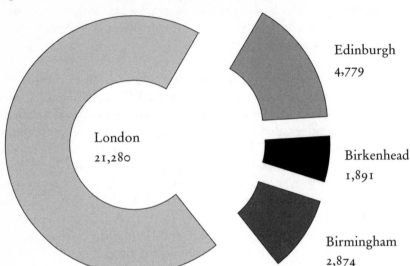

Edinburgh
4,779

London
21,280

Birkenhead
1,891

Birmingham
2,874

* Calculated from estimated number of persons consulted and cinema visitors' reports.
Sources: Published enquiry reports (see Ch. 4, n13, p.202, n15, n18, n23, p.203).

21,280 children aged between 4 and 14, from 29 London schools (see Figure 4.1).

Unlike the Birmingham and Birkenhead enquiries, the LCC enquiry apparently was not calculated to promote any particular action, neither was its agenda derived from negative assumptions regarding the impact of cinema. Instead, it seems to have been a genuine attempt to understand a complex social issue: 'the effect of the attendance at cinema performances on the minds of children'.[22] To this end, using interviews and questionnaires, the London enquiry sought information regarding the frequency of cinema attendance and viewing preferences of children, while also aiming to pin down the ambiguous 'intellectual and moral consequences' of cinema-going among young people.

The last of the four main British enquiries of the early 1930s was conducted in Edinburgh between June 1931 and February 1933. The city's Juvenile Organisations Committee had been debating issues surrounding children and cinema regulation for over a decade and, as in London, they finally concluded that 'no real progress could be made until an enquiry had been carried out', since 'until full information...had been obtained there was and could be no sufficient answer' to the problems associated with children's cinema-going.[23] An enquiry was therefore instituted to investigate the matter further, with representatives from 22 organisations being invited to form the Edinburgh Cinema Enquiry Committee (ECEC).[24]

In the same way as the LCC (and unlike Birmingham and Birkenhead), the ECEC claimed to be genuinely seeking useful, reliable information regarding children's cinema-going, with no particular axe to grind other than their desire to establish a thought-through basis for future decisions regarding cinema regulation. Thus, the preface to their report recommends an impartial approach rather than a witch-hunt, describing film as 'a vehicle of instruction and entertainment the potentialities of which for good or for evil are almost incalculable'. It continues:

> The 'pictures' have come to stay...Trepidation accordingly is of no avail. Nor need the outlook on the film and its influence be wholly suffused with foreboding. To have begun any enquiry with prepossessions against the cinema would have been merely futile.[25]

The central form of investigation used by the ECEC, as in the other cities, was a questionnaire for children. Children from 21 Edinburgh schools were involved, with 2,580 questionnaires being completed by pupils aged between 9 and 18.[26] Similar questionnaires were distributed to 350 working young people aged between 14 and 21 (mainly via youth organisations) and of these 250 were completed and returned.[27] Questionnaires were also distributed to parents (1,030 replies) and school teachers (649 replies).[28] Finally, ECEC representatives visited a selection of cinemas regularly over an eight-week period, completing a total of 270 visitors' reports.[29] This therefore constituted the second largest enquiry of the four (see Figure 4.1).

The Main Players

While they differed in many ways, the committees of all four enquiries contained a similar demographic mix of well-to-do people, including large numbers of women, with the majority representing religious groups, youth organisations, educational establishments, women's groups and social/moral campaign organisations. This confirms Jeffrey Richards' assertion that 'the cinema's influence on children greatly preoccupied society's traditional cultural elites and groups concerned with child training and welfare'.[30] Edinburgh was the only enquiry to publish a full list of committee members (see Appendix 5), but records from the other three enquiries suggest that their committees were very similar in composition and therefore the Edinburgh list can be seen as broadly representative.

The main ECEC had 57 members, including 35 women and 22 men (over 61 per cent women). This included 22 representatives from youth organisations, 11 from women's groups, nine from churches and religious organisations and seven each from educational organisations and social/moral campaigns such as the Scottish Temperance Alliance and the National Vigilance Association. Of the 57 main committee members, 25 formed an executive committee consisting of ten women and 15 men (40 per cent women). Graduates, educationalists and clergymen were most likely to serve on the executive, while single women and members of campaign groups were far less likely to do so.

It is particularly interesting to examine the involvement of women in these committees, for while women had key roles in the early stages of enquiries and at general committee level, it was men who held nearly all the executive positions. Thus, although the Birmingham enquiry arose from a conference held by the National Council of Women, five of the committee's seven office holders were men.

A second point of interest is the higher status of *married* women and, in particular, the way in which these women stressed their maternal role as a mark of authority when speaking about children and the cinema. In a meeting between the Public Morality Council and the BBFC in 1930, for example, Mrs H.W. Boustead of the Mothers' Union explained: '*as mothers* we are so largely concerned with the...daily effect of [films] upon young people we know very well indeed the allurement of the "spurious glamour" [depicted in them]'.[31]

Meanwhile, at an open meeting convened by the BCEC in 1930, Alderman Mrs Sands J.P. cited her maternal authority over and above her status as an alderman or a magistrate, asserting: 'That is what I am speaking about, the influence of the cinema on the children, and *I speak as a mother*'.[32]

Although symbols of female morality and motherhood were employed to support arguments for increased cinema regulation, they could also be used to undermine them. Birmingham magistrate W.A. Dalley, for example, dismissed the BCEC as 'an interfering lot of old women of both sexes'.[33] Meanwhile, positive and negative connotations of motherhood were both apparent in the argument of Captain G.D. Griffith (President of the London Head Teachers' Association), who called for an improvement in the quality of films in 1936. He explained: 'We don't want Mother Grundy's dictating what children shall see, but we do want to supply programmes to which the most careful parents can send their children'.[34] Here, Griffith evokes the eighteenth-century dramatic character Mrs Grundy – the personification of prudish disapproval and social propriety – and, interestingly, he renames her *Mother* Grundy. Yet although he seeks to undermine cinema's detractors by depicting them as meddling mothers, he goes on to cite 'careful parents' as the ultimate arbiters of film content – perhaps the important distinction here being that 'careful parents' might be men or women.

Finally, the key issue regarding the composition of cinema enquiry committees is that their members were nearly all from religious, educational, youth and women's organisations. In the ECEC, for example, 89 per cent of those members with specific affiliations represented such organisations, and this figure rose to 100 per cent in the executive (see Appendix 5). Although this may not be surprising in itself, the reasons for this composition deserve consideration, as they may help explain some of the motivations and methodologies underpinning cinema enquiries. Why did the majority of committee members come from such organisations? And what did they seek to gain?

Of course, individuals and individual organisations each had their own anxieties relating to the cinema. Churches were challenged by Sunday film shows and the physical conversion of church buildings into film theatres.[35] Youth organisations struggled to compete with the entertainment value of the cinema (see Chapter 6). And, as will be shown, teachers complained that schoolwork suffered because of truancy and evening cinema-going. Above all, however, cinema enquiries claimed to have one common motivation: the protection of children; and it was apparently this motivation that lay behind the composition of committees, for the church, the family, schools and youth groups were all associated with the protection of the young.

There is a fundamental flaw in this reasoning though; if their primary concern was the protection of children, this should surely have been assuaged to some extent by the reassuring, authoritative findings of the 1917 Commission of Inquiry which was in many ways still relevant. While this investigation did not render later enquiries redundant, it certainly could have formed a useful basis for them, as it provided a sophisticated appraisal of issues relating to the protection of children. Yet not one of the four main enquiries of the 1930s even refers to the Commission of Inquiry that had been conducted in 1917. This suggests that although protection may have been an issue, there was apparently an additional motivation – something that had been unresolved in 1917. I would argue that this additional driving force related to unspoken issues of social control.

Essentially, cinema was considered a massive potential influence on the behaviour and development of the young and as such it represented a direct threat to those structures traditionally considered responsible for socialisation: families, schools, churches and youth movements. Arguably, therefore, the bodies involved in enquiries had a vested interest in the regulation of cinema, because the medium challenged their apparent monopoly on the socialisation and control of young people.

There are two caveats to this argument. First, motivations of protection and control need not be mutually exclusive and both may well have been important factors in these enquiries. However, it is important to highlight the issue of social control before looking at the rhetoric of the enquiries, as they do tend to privilege aspects of protection and generally leave issues of authority and control unstated. Second, these organisations were by no means united in their opinions regarding the cinema. As will be seen, there was often great disparity of opinion between educationalists, church ministers and others concerning the relative merits and dangers of the cinema. Nevertheless, it remains the case that the main players in these and other cinema enquiries were nearly all from organisations traditionally associated with the socialisation of the young – organisations that stood to lose out significantly if cinema were as powerful a force as they feared.

Content of the Four Main Enquiries

Having given some background to the four main cinema enquiries and the players involved, the following sections will examine the content of the reports in more detail, paying particular attention to the approaches and rhetorical strategies used. While these four enquiries ostensibly had a common purpose (the protection of children), it will be shown that they adopted very different methodologies, came to very different conclusions and presented their findings in very different ways.

The London Enquiry

The LCC took great pains to be 'scientific' in their attempt to 'obtain the facts' about children's cinema-going, as is evident from their report's repeated references to issues of objectivity, reliability and validity.[36] The 21,280 children involved came from 29 London schools, 'chosen as representative of each of the inspectorial areas', creating a sample that the committee felt was 'probably large enough, and...sufficiently varied, to ensure the validity of the results'. The report suggested that this sample was 'representative not only of London conditions, but also of those obtaining in most very large English towns', but it was careful to acknowledge that conditions might vary in rural areas or cities elsewhere in Britain.[37]

The report, written by LCC Chief Examiner Dr F.H. Spencer, also refers at length to problems of reliability. The introduction notes that although answers were obtained 'by the careful (and so far as possible objective) questioning of the children', there were inevitably various levels of accuracy. Older children, frequent cinema-goers and those that did not attend at all were thought to have provided more reliable information than had younger respondents or those that attended the cinema sporadically. Statistical information was considered generally reliable, 'for in statement of fact the tendency of children to give the answer they believe to be expected is not very great, and can, with fair certainty, be discounted or checked'. However, answers relating to subjective opinion were considered less reliable, especially when given orally and particularly if inexperienced investigators were involved. It is perhaps worth quoting one section at length, to illustrate the amount of scrutiny given to this subject in the report:

> Where children are asked oral questions, and matters of opinion are involved, their answers are not to be taken at face value. The experienced questioner knows this, and in most cases he is not deceived. But this makes it no easier to get to the truth. Children are very quick to see that the questioner is going to form a judgement. They will frequently do two things: (1) give the answer they think is expected, (2) give the answer which they think will cause the questioner to think well of the individual and the class ... Consequently, different people will get different answers to a given set of questions; or the same person will get different answers on different occasions from the same set of pupils. The fashion set by the first answer may affect the whole series of answers, and answers will sometimes be given 'without thinking'. For these reasons the oral answers of a single class or a single school may be misleading. Consequently it was arranged that a good many answers should be given in writing ... Moreover the oral information was obtained by teachers and inspectors who are able to eliminate fairly well the element of suggestion.[38]

Spencer does not present his report as an unproblematic statement of fact; he goes into some detail regarding the limited reliability and validity of the enquiry's findings. Moreover, he acknowledges that the findings may not necessarily be applicable throughout Britain and he also stresses on several occasions that the report refers only to elementary school children, with potentially very different conditions applying to 'young people over 14'.[39]

After providing statistics of children's frequency of cinema attendance and film preferences (categorised by age and gender), the report addresses its main theme: the 'effects of attendance' on children, including physical effects, impact on speech (Americanisms), moral influence and potentially harmful effects. Nearly all of the findings are qualified but positive, in a style reminiscent of the 1917 enquiry.

The physical effects of cinema-going on children are found to include tiredness and 'aching eyes', but the report's conclusion in this respect is that 'the present evidence on the point of health is not sufficient to justify…a commonsense lay conclusion, still less a "scientific" one'.[40] Concerning Americanisation, Spencer concludes that 'the speech of the children is not much affected', with only a few phrases having entered the vernacular, 'such as "Yeah" or "Yep" for "Yes", or "O.K. Chief", signifying "Yes, sir", to a superior'. He even notes that 'one head master prefers this American slang to his local variety'.[41]

Regarding the sexual content of films, Spencer is unequivocal. 'All the inspectors who mention it…are convinced that the morally questionable element in films (i.e., that reserved for adults) is ignored by children of school age…[It] does, in fact, bore them.'[42] Five years later, a committee member wittily recalled that when they were asked to investigate the 'sex evil that was supposed to be rife in the films', investigators often 'came back disappointed', with one lady inspector asking: 'when are we really going to see something indecent?'.[43]

The report also tackles concerns about children imitating behaviour in films, particularly regarding the controversial issue of juvenile delinquency. It concludes:

> The younger children for a time imitate in their play what they have seen on the films. For example, children under seven who have seen a fighting adventure film come to school with rulers or pencils stuck in their belts, after the manner of weapons. But these external evidences of film influence are usually fugitive, and at least are confined to play…Film influence seems not to affect conduct outside play, and the worst delinquent in a school is sometimes a child who never goes to the pictures…Instances of children having stolen in order to get money to go to the films are negligible in number. Nor is there any evidence of imitative misconduct on the part of these school children.[44]

The report therefore concludes that cinema-going does not generally compromise the morality of children in terms of imitative behaviour. Moreover, it welcomes evidence that many children are 'running errands and doing odd jobs for parents' to earn cinema money. It also notes the unforeseen educational benefit of cinema-going for some children who, when asked about films, revealed an aptitude for learning that had not previously been apparent in the classroom. Examples include a 'backward girl of nine, who had never before been known to volunteer a remark in class'; during the investigation it transpired that she went to the cinema twice a week and when questioned in class about the pictures, she apparently 'became voluble on the subject'.[45]

Overall, therefore, the LCC report had very little to say against the cinema. The exception to this was 'one distinct evil ... that children are often frightened at the films, and that the fear remains with them and causes dreams'.[46] Spencer singled out war films and 'mysteries' (horror/thrillers) in this regard, arguing that 'terrifying incidents have undesirable, and possibly permanent, effects upon children'. Using the rhetorical tool of assumed consensus, he concludes that 'most sensible people would agree that children ought not to be shown such pictures' and later recommends that 'if it is practicable, war films should be prohibited for children'.[47]

Apart from the issue of frightening film content, Spencer reported that 'the enquiry brought out no other point upon which there was definite evidence of harm'. He therefore concluded that, 'in spite of the strong opinions of some able and devoted head teachers to the contrary, the preponderance of evidence is that the actual effect of the pictures on the children is not substantially harmful'.[48] In closing, Spencer refers with relaxed humour to similarities between film and popular literature, which he considers equally harmless to young people:

> The film is no worse that [sic] the old time 'blood', universally read by the boys only a few years ago. It is no more falsely sentimental than many of the feminine equivalents of the 'blood'. What man of fifty has not been a pirate in his youth?[49]

According to the LCC enquiry, therefore, the cinema posed no real threat to children. Interestingly, this report did not express any concern whatsoever regarding the behaviour or control of children – perhaps owing to the fact that the majority of the investigators represented the council rather than organisations associated with the socialisation of the young. Importantly, this enquiry was by far the largest and arguably the most authoritative of the four. Overall, its findings are encapsulated in the first sentence of Spencer's closing remarks: 'My general impression after reading a fairly large mass of evidence carefully, is that there is no need for serious alarm.'[50] Hardly evidence, therefore, of a moral panic.

The Edinburgh Enquiry

A sense of panic is equally hard to find in the report of the ECEC. As in London, this enquiry had an avowed aim to carry out an open-minded, scientific, objective study of children and the cinema, rather than simply searching for ammunition against the medium, as was the case in Birmingham and Birkenhead. Thus, the report asserts that the primary objective of the enquiry was to elicit 'full information; scientifically compiled and presented without prejudice'.[51] Specifically, it cites the need to approach the subject positively and to glean honest opinions from children themselves, thereby producing a report with 'value of a constructive nature...giving in considerable detail the opinions of the children on the pictures as they are'.[52]

In the same way as the London report, problems of methodology and reliability were addressed from the outset. The report explains:

When...the questionnaires came to be composed, every effort was taken to ensure that, as far as possible, the answers to the questions would reveal what those who filled up the papers actually thought and felt and not what they considered they ought to think and feel.[53]

Interestingly, the Edinburgh report does not utilise the words of children in order to present a particular argument. Rather, the results are simply tabulated and then briefly discussed in a measured way. Findings, for example, about the frequency of children's cinema attendance indicate that 'the average attendance at the cinema per child is almost exactly once a week'.[54] If anything, the report endows this information with positive connotations, noting that 'a weekly visit to the cinema has become a stable feature in the lives of the children' and suggesting that 'cinema-going is looked on as a legitimate amusement, which is nevertheless kept in its place', as homework and household chores are also accomplished.[55]

Where responses to questionnaires are inconclusive, the report acknowledges this without much further comment. For example, adolescents' responses to a question regarding the 'influence of the pictures on speech or actions' were found to be 'disappointing'. The report notes that while some adolescents believed that films affected their speech, 'as for their actions, they do not seem to know what causes them'. But rather than going on to speculate, the report simply concludes: 'this question seemed too difficult and has elicited no definite information'.[56]

The report's analysis of teachers' questionnaire responses is also interesting inasmuch as it recognises the importance of factors influencing children *other than* cinema. In response to questions regarding the potential impact of cinema-going on children's concentration and eyesight, for example, the report notes 'a considerable number of Non-committal answers' and a tendency among teachers to refer to a range of factors causing poor concentration. Thus, one respondent suggests that 'general city conditions, noise, traffic, and lack of sleep, may cause it'.[57] Similarly, when asked whether frequent cinema-going tends to 'destroy the Child's originality and creative impulse', one teacher frankly replies: 'Yes, to a limited extent, but the school as we know it seems to do that too'.[58] Finally, regarding any direct impact on schoolwork, the report notes that teachers in infant and junior school departments 'are in fairly general agreement that in their case the pictures are without effect'.[59]

Although many of the findings of this report are positive or inconclusive, there are areas where the impact of cinema is portrayed in a more negative light. One example involves the response of parents to the question of whether there are 'kinds of pictures which quite definitely…children ought not to see'. Here, key problem genres are singled out for criticism, namely: 'those dealing with Sex, Gangsters, War, Murder and Crime', plus 'weird and mysterious [horror] pictures'.[60] These genres were reportedly criticised by the majority of parents from all social backgrounds.

Nevertheless, where the report discusses apparently negative aspects of cinema-going for children, it still does so in a balanced and thoughtful way. Notably, it is careful to indicate where negative views have only been expressed by a minority of respondents. For example, the report states that some parents wanted children to be excluded from adult or evening performances, but notes: 'it is to be observed that [such] replies...were comparatively few, and must not be taken as coming from the majority of the parents'.[61] This approach stands in direct contrast to the rhetorical manipulation evident in the Birmingham and Birkenhead reports, as will be seen.

Overall, the findings of the Edinburgh enquiry are generally positive, but somewhat mixed, providing an overview of cinema 'alike in its cheerful aspects and those that are menacing'.[62] Its recommendations are largely constructive in nature; for example, it calls for 'special pictures for children as there are special books'.[63] It also asserts that the BBFC has 'done remarkable work in maintaining screen standards', but suggests that the apparently 'immense and dominating importance of the film in the lives of children' justifies the appointment of a 'Commission in Film Censorship' by the government, to look into the issue more fully (as would occur with the FCCC).[64] Above all, the ECEC argues that cinema represents 'an influence of first importance' among children.[65] However, far from using its findings to foment a moral panic, the Edinburgh enquiry's report takes care to paint a detailed and balanced picture of the issues under consideration.

The Birmingham and Birkenhead Enquiries

The remaining two enquiries of Birmingham and Birkenhead can most usefully be addressed together, as they shared the same aims and methodology and reached very similar conclusions. As already outlined, these were the first two of the four key enquiries to be conducted and they were also the smallest in terms of sample size. More importantly, they differed significantly from the enquiries conducted in London and Edinburgh, in that they adopted an overtly negative stance towards cinema's impact on children from the outset. Both the Birmingham and Birkenhead enquiries were strongly based on the premise that while cinema had potential for good, it was currently damaging and dangerous for children. This negative premise would inform both the methodology of the investigations and the rhetorical strategies used in their reports. In this sense, as will be demonstrated, the BCEC and BVC might be considered to have promoted a potential moral panic.

The enquiries in Birmingham and Birkenhead purported to be 'scientific', just as the London and Edinburgh enquiries had.[66]

However, where the former reports were cautious in their conclusions and made clear the limited reliability and validity of their data, the reports of the BCEC and BVC asserted that their findings were beyond question. They also employed the rhetorical tool of claiming to represent a consensus of 'public opinion'. As the Birmingham report states:

> We instituted a scientific and comprehensive enquiry...and public opinion is steadily consolidating itself behind our movement...We have, therefore, decided to print our report and present our evidence – which is both comprehensive and conclusive. Comment is unnecessary. But confirmation of our results from magistrates, the clergy, parents of every class, business men, working lads and girls, and teachers of every grade is daily reaching us.[67]

The tone of the Birmingham report in particular is that of a call to arms, confident in its fundamentalist assertions regarding the dangers of cinema and the need for action. BCEC president Sir Charles Grant Robertson's foreword declares: 'The...public enquiry for which we ask will come, because an organized public opinion will insist upon it; and when it does it will confirm up to the hilt what the reader will find set out in these pages.'[68]

Another interesting feature in the presentation of both the BCEC and BVC reports is the use of quotes from young questionnaire respondents. Where the London and Edinburgh enquiries use quotes sparingly and stress the difficulties of obtaining information in this way, the two earlier enquiries utilise many quotes, carefully selecting and editing the words of children, while asserting that the 'simple candour' of such evidence is almost guaranteed to be reliable.[69] One way in which the reports cleverly imply the essential reliability and truthfulness of the children's responses is by leaving the spelling and grammar uncorrected, thereby suggesting adult influence to have been minimal if not non-existent. 'Where quoted their words and spellings are reproduced as written', the BVC report explains; 'the answers are the unaided work of the children'.[70] Similarly, the BCEC report reassures its readers: 'It is to be understood clearly that these answers are the free work of the child. No assistance was given...So far as is possible the precise words of the children are used in this report.

Spelling has not been corrected.'[71] This strategy therefore suggests that the quotes are unmediated – drawing attention away from the fact that they have been carefully selected for specific rhetorical purposes, as will now be shown.

The first three items on the BCEC/BVC questionnaire ask about frequency of cinema attendance, motivation for attendance and preferences for different types of films. Only a few responses are quoted, and these are often those of young, female (and therefore supposedly 'most vulnerable') children, who claim to enjoy the dangers of violent films. The BCEC report notes:

A girl of 11¾ who goes 'once or twice a week' writes: 'I like murder pictures best'...The Commissioner adds: 'One child said she would show me how to strangle people'.[72]

There are then three leading questions about the negative physical effects of cinema:

Do you think the show is too long?
Do the pictures tire your eyes?
Do the pictures keep you, or children you know, from sleeping afterwards?[73]

In both studies, most children replied 'No' to all three questions. However, this was clearly not the response best suited to the argument of the reports and therefore the evidence is presented in a very selective manner. The Birmingham report grudgingly admits that the response to the first question was 'an almost unanimous "No"' and then it quickly moves on to the other two questions, where the number of 'No' responses is not even stated. Instead we are told that of 1,439 children, 353 reported tired eyes and 349 agreed that either they *or children they knew* claimed to have disturbed sleep.[74] Nothing is said of the vast majority who did not report problems. By reporting the minority view and ignoring the majority, this therefore diverts the reader's attention towards the less significant figure, serving the rhetorical purpose of the report. Such an approach might be contrasted directly with a similar question in the ECEC enquiry, in which parents were asked: 'After a visit to the Cinema are the children (a) nervous, (b) sleepless, (c) more difficult to control?' This report stated that,

All over, more than 90 per cent replied No to all three questions; less than 2 per cent replied Yes to all three. Quite clearly, the parents do not think that attending the cinema has an adverse effect in these respects.[75]

The Birmingham enquiry goes on to reinforce its argument that cinema is physically damaging to children by giving a selection of 12 quotes, all from the minority of children who agreed that viewing had an adverse effect on them (or someone they knew), including the following evocative examples:

'I was so afraid after it I thought burglars would be in the room.'

'The pictures have often kept my sister and myself from sleeping after by causing us to go hysterical.'

'We only dream after murders.'[76]

The penultimate question on the BCEC/BVC questionnaire is: 'What have you learned from the pictures?' This is rooted in the idea that children are blank slates, susceptible to learning from film images – a concept which is underlined in the BCEC report:

Only psychologists could satisfactorily determine the full implication [of responses to this question] and yet everyday common sense, even without much imagination, can see in these children's remarks the far-reaching usefulness or injury of the film...All will agree with the crisp and clear-sighted reply of one lad: 'I have learnt many things. If I see anything I have not seen before I am bound to learn, whether it is good or bad.'[77]

This passage therefore reinforces the blank slate theories of socialisation and assumes that cinema has the power to influence and teach children, for better or worse. It also utilises a number of rhetorical tools: presuming consensus (in the phrase 'all will agree'); appealing to the 'common sense' of readers; referring to psychologists to give an air of scientific credibility; and encouraging the assumption that a child's 'clear-sighted' remarks are inherently accurate and reliable.

In presenting the enquiry's detailed findings on the question of learning, the Birmingham report attempts to polarise films into two main categories, first by imposing headings and second by quoting responses which demonstrate either the positive value of educational films, or the negative influence of other types of film. Positive educational value is cited under the heading 'General Knowledge', with quotes which include:

'I have learnt ways and customs of other lands.'

'I have learnt that insects are industrious.'

'I have learnt to keep my teeth clean.'[78]

Meanwhile, apparently harmful lessons are displayed under the headings 'Impressions with Regard to Sex' and 'Crime and Violence'. Here, children's comments are unproblematically employed as evidence of deviant socialisation, although they could equally be read as deliberately provocative or subversive statements. They include:

'I have learnt how to love and to murder people at the same time.'

'I have learnt nothing but murder.'

'I have learnt how to shoot through my pocket.'[79]

Other statements on this theme refer to children imitating behaviour seen in films. The Birmingham report is generous with sensational quotes on this topic, including: '"I have learnt how to but someone on the head"' and '"I have learnt how to choke wild animals."' Similarly, one child declared: '"Some boys call themselves the Rusty Dagger Gang and they throw rusty knives about."' The BCEC report also cites imitation of suicidal behaviour among children, including 'two references to boys imitating hanging themselves after being at the Pictures' and a child who explains that their sister has been so influenced by cinema-going that '"when she's angry because she can't have her own way she goes to kill herself with a knife"'.[80]

One final point of interest regarding the language of the BCEC and BVC enquiries relates to the use of 'adult' and 'child' voices in the responses of children. This concept has been explored by sociologists Robert Hodge and David Tripp in their study of children and television.[81] Hodge and Tripp suggest that decoding interview responses of children includes distinguishing between responses made in a 'child' voice (used normally for speaking to other children) and those made in a 'parent' voice (used for speaking to adult authority figures). 'Child' voice responses tend to be rapid, confident and grammatically informal, with high energy and subversive content. 'Parent' voice responses, meanwhile, tend to be well-considered replies in a formal grammatical style, with conventional content and often ending with a rising intonation, like a question. The implication of this, in basic terms, is that responses in a 'child' voice might be considered to be a more reliable representation of the child's opinions, whereas responses in a 'parent' voice could be seen as the child's attempt to give the response they feel the adult investigator desires.

Interestingly, this phenomenon is very apparent in the BCEC and BVC enquiries, where children tend to offer neutral or positive comments about the cinema in the first person, with a 'child' voice, such as: 'I have learnt what life is like when we grow up' or 'I have learnt that a good laugh makes me more cheerful'.[82] However, when children make negative comments about the cinema, in support of the enquiries' hypotheses, they often do so in an 'adult' voice, referring to childhood in the third person. Thus, in the BVC enquiry, one child asserts, '"murder pictures are unsuitable for children"', while another explains, '"pictures are not good for children, because it teaches them American slang"'.[83] Likewise in the BCEC enquiry, some children confirm the investigators' expectations regarding imitative behaviour using an 'adult' voice, with one child declaring, '"children do all they see on the pictures"' and another explaining, '"when children see war pictures many of them want to be soldiers"'.[84] Interestingly, this response was also apparent in evidence from an earlier Birmingham enquiry in 1926, when a child explained that cinema '"learns children how to break into shops"'.[85]

Unlike the Edinburgh and London enquiries, therefore, which recognised and attempted to deal with problems of reliability, the BCEC and BVC enquiries set out to prove a hypothesis – that cinema was a threat to children – and they selected the most inflammatory evidence available in support of that hypothesis, regardless of whether it was representative or reliable.

In considering the four enquiries together, it is clear that although they sprang from similar concerns regarding the impact of film on children, their differences in methodology, rhetorical strategy and, most importantly, their different findings, suggest that this was not a simple matter of moral panic. The enquiries of the LCC and the ECEC were the result of long-standing concerns. They were conducted with care for reliability and balance and had largely positive findings regarding the impact of cinema. It should also be remembered that they were much larger enquiries in terms of sample size and were far more thorough in their approach than the BCEC and BVC enquiries. The latter pair might, however, represent aspects of a moral panic. They were a relatively sudden development, fuelled by an antagonistic attitude towards the cinema (mainly on moral grounds) and they were reported – especially in the case of Birmingham – in such a way as to provoke the strongest possible reaction among the public, although, as will be shown, this reaction was not necessarily forthcoming.

Moral panic or 'flapdoodle'?

Given the diversity of evidence from these four studies, it can be argued that the situation in 1930s Britain regarding cinema and children involved wide-ranging debate rather than outright demonisation, with expressions of extreme anxiety representing, to use a 1930s phrase, more of a 'flapdoodle' (commotion) than a moral panic. Undoubtedly, there was a strong reaction against the cinema in certain quarters during the decade, particularly with regard to its potential impact on the young. Moreover, this reaction drew on existing fears regarding juvenile delinquency, mass culture and the mob, creating what some moral panic theorists call a 'spiral effect' or 'convergence of discourses', which may have acted as a catalyst, intensifying fears about the threat posed by cinema to children.[86] However, it is important to remember that wholly negative or alarmist reactions to the medium were relatively rare. What is more, within key institutions, including the church, education and the media, there was a large range of opinion and a significant amount of qualified support for children's cinema-going.

A very mixed reaction was apparent, for example, in the responses of churches and other religious groups to the popularity of cinema. Some opposed film outright, some screened religious films and others set up secular matinees, showing carefully selected material. The LCC enquiry found that 'in some areas the fact that the Salvation Army throws its influence against cinema attendance seems to be effective in diminishing attendance. On the other hand, the penny performances organised by a religious mission possibly increase the attendance.'[87] Certainly, between 1930 and at least 1937, churches ran regular children's matinees in at least six cities across England and Scotland, each with average audiences of around 1,200 children.[88]

A wide range of opinion was also evident among Christians at a conference entitled 'Children and Films', conducted in February 1937 by the Cinema Christian Council and the Public Morality Council. Here the main cause for concern was not children's cinema attendance *per se*, but the nature of the films that they watched. Conference Chairman, the Bishop of London, claimed to be 'most anxious' about the impact of films on young people, having taken two children to see *King Kong* and finding to his surprise that 'the little girl was quite unmoved but...the little boy was whimpering with terror'.[89] Meanwhile, a complex examination of the problems of selecting films was provided by a conference delegate, Islington Methodist minister Rev. D.O. Soper, who had run children's film shows twice weekly since 1930. Soper explained that while even 'some of the earlier Mickey Mouse films were, frankly, indecent' and Westerns were perhaps 'not...entirely suitable for children', there was actually no 'need to trouble very much' about the impact of sex films on children. 'The double entendre goes over their heads', he explained, 'the "close-up" makes them snigger...they are generally bored stiff.'[90] Finally, William Farr of the BFI (another delegate) suggested that, quite apart from immoral or violent films, many U films were unsuitable for children simply because they were 'dull and uninteresting'.[91]

Evidence from this conference and elsewhere therefore indicates that churches in Britain were discussing children's cinema-going in a complex and measured way. Moreover, they were increasingly using film themselves for matinee shows and other events. By the end of 1937, film equipment had been installed in churches of all denominations and Roman Catholic churches had their own religious film organisation.[92] By January 1938 over 200 churches had equipment for showing talking pictures, Gaumont–British Instructional were making films for the Religious Film Society and Arthur Rank was subsidising churches that could not afford the equipment.[93] The first film screening in a cathedral was at Chichester on 9 January 1938. Three films with religious themes were shown and hymns and prayers were also projected onto a screen to a congregation of around 2,000 people.[94] During Easter 1937, one newspaper article highlighted the use of film by churches, with the headline: 'Let's take the "Sin" out of the Cinema.'[95]

Similar trends were also evident in education. By 1935 there were around 650 film projectors being used in Britain's schools.[96] In Glasgow alone, 25 schools were reportedly using cinema apparatus 'for everyday work' in 1935, and membership of the Scottish Educational Cinema Society rocketed between 1934 and 1935 from 140 to 670 members.[97] Growth continued, and between 1935 and 1936 the Edinburgh branch of this society grew from 80 members to 530.[98] By the end of 1937, 916 of Britain's 32,000 schools and colleges had film projectors (136 with sound).[99] This trend extended across Europe and, if anything, Britain lagged behind. In 1935, Germany made provision for 60,000 school film projectors (10,000 of which were to be installed that year) and, as early as 1932, France had between 16,000 and 18,000 school film projectors.[100] Even in Hungary, by the end of 1937, 400 of the total of 600 schools were reportedly equipped with projectors.[101]

Nevertheless, educationalists were concerned about the impact of mainstream cinema on children and on the last day of 1936 the Annual Conference of the National Union of Teachers discussed, among other things, the need to exclude children from A film performances.[102] In the same way as religious organisations, educational establishments therefore had mixed feelings about the medium of film and about children's cinema-going in general. Certainly, some of those expressing most concern about the impact of film on children came from these two institutions. But this is not to say that there was a unified response to the situation from either camp.

Finally, it is interesting to consider the variety of opinions expressed regarding children and film in Britain's newspapers, for again there was no unified response. Newspaper reports of the various enquiries and conferences, for example, displayed a wide range of reactions. In November 1936, a BFI two-day conference on 'Films for Elementary School Children' was covered in a variety of ways by the press.[103] The *Grimsby Daily Telegraph* took exception to the conference's claim that juvenile delinquency was not linked to cinema-going, suggesting that it was ridiculous to ignore the connection between film and petty crime, just because 'bootlegging, gunrunning, and putting citizens on the spot are not yet noticeably popular juvenile activities'.[104] The same article suggested that showing horror films to those aged under 18 was 'little less than criminal'. Meanwhile, the *Sheffield Independent* report on this conference declared that there was little cause for concern, as 'a lot of nonsense is talked about children and the films, especially about the harm that certain films are said to be doing to the child mind'.[105] However, this article goes on to denounce 'the presentation of films in which speech is vulgarised by Americanisms and the language is spoken in a hideous drawling way that is an offence to the ear and to the mind', concluding that 'there is more cause to worry about the inartistic film than about the so-called morally obnoxious'.

There is certainly a great deal of evidence that newspapers and individual journalists took a wide range of stances on the subject of children and film. In looking at the issue of moral panic, it is essential to note that many journalists recognised the place of the cinema debate in recurring arguments about children and leisure, spotting the potential for a panic and deliberately opting not to encourage it. A good example of this comes from the *Birmingham Mail*'s report on the 1931 BCEC enquiry, which saw through the rhetoric and came down firmly in favour of the cinema:

> Personally we think [the BCEC] are exciting themselves unduly. It is the old story of the child and literature over again. It used to be the 'penny dreadful' which was corrupting our young innocents, now it is the pictures...the cinema is the most wonderful and most potent educational force yet evolved, and children probably get a great deal more good than harm from it.[106]

Unsurprisingly, the harshest critics of conferences were to be found in the cinema trade press and these provide the strongest examples of newspaper reports refusing to encourage the development of a moral panic. This final example from the *Daily Film Renter* makes its opposition very plain indeed:

LEAVE THEM ALONE!

How far, we are tempted to ask, are the majority of children... really interested in their elders and betters providing them with special picture programs? We feel constrained to put this query in the view of the announcement that another conference in this connection is to be held in the autumn, under the joint auspices of the BFI and the Cinema Christian Council. There is probably more 'flapdoodle' in regard to the type of film which should or should not be exhibited to children than almost anything else. We do not doubt the good intentions of those responsible for these conferences but, quite frankly, are they likely to achieve any real or lasting purpose?... Children, like grown-ups, demand first and foremost, entertainment. Secondly, most of them desire to be left alone so far as the provision of their amusement is concerned, and we doubt very much whether any of them are likely to be particularly thrilled at the prospect of bodies of well-meaning folk indulging in weighty pronouncements as to what the citizens of tomorrow shall see when they visit the Kinema. There is nothing whatever wrong with the influence of films, as we have pointed out over and over again.[107]

Conclusion

Despite their idiosyncratic nature, most moral panic studies consider certain common elements to be important. Initially, moral panics are characterised by a sudden, high level of concern regarding a certain issue or event. This creates a volatile and hostile response, which may exaggerate the level of perceived danger. The threat and those who perpetrate it may be branded as 'folk devils' and, finally, the panic may result in a diminution in the threat itself and/or increased regulation.[108] Is this pattern apparent in concerns and responses relating to children and cinema in 1930s Britain? I would argue that, overall, it is not and that this did not therefore constitute a moral panic in the classic sense.

First, although there was a great deal of concern about the cinema's impact on children, this was not a sudden reaction. As Chapters 2 and 3 have demonstrated, by 1930 the issue of children and cinema had already been debated for over three decades. Second, it was not generally speaking a wholly hostile, volatile, groundless, or irrational reaction. Issues were often discussed in a complex, thoughtful and positive manner, reaching largely productive conclusions. Furthermore, as Chapter 6 will show, cinema did indeed pose a potential challenge to the influences of home, school, church and youth group; it spawned a distinct children's cinema culture involving alternative role models, an ambiguous moral code, a new learning environment and a largely unregulated arena of play. Therefore it is hardly surprising that parental, religious, educational and youth organisations should have considered it a potentially dangerous phenomenon. Third, there is no easily identifiable 'folk devil' (although Hollywood might qualify for such a label). Nevertheless, it must be conceded that increased regulation did result from this debate during the course of the decade and, after changes to censorship in 1934, there was a marked diminution in the overall level of concern.

Perhaps most importantly, in considering the nature of this debate it is crucial to recognise the wide range of perspectives that were represented. If it was a panic, then who was panicking? Although this period saw a proliferation of enquiries, conferences and reports, representing a high level of interest in the subject, these displayed a variety of agenda, they used different methodologies and rhetorical strategies and they reached very different conclusions about the issue. Meanwhile, the key establishments of church, education and the print media were by no means uniformly opposed to the idea of cinema for children. There was a great deal of ambivalence and division within these groups as to the potential of the medium and a large range of opinions regarding any possible threat that it might pose. Therefore, while debates surrounding children and cinema were vibrant and widespread during the 1930s, and while these debates had a central influence on the development of cinema regulation and censorship in Britain and elsewhere, this did not ultimately constitute a moral panic in the classic sense.

5

Children as Censors

The time is past. We no longer see headlines in the
paper, 'Should children go to the cinema?' If children
want to go to the cinema they will go.[1]
                        Miss E.M. Fox, Headmistresses Association
                                                  12 January 1931

Most histories of film censorship are based on a common
assumption: that censorship solely or principally involves the
impact of certain institutions, and the bodies that influence them, on
the content of films. Indeed, this assumption is so pronounced that
most historians in the field do not even seek to define censorship.
Instead, the 'censorship system' is taken to mean those official
practices of regulation that endeavour to control material in the public
domain (ostensibly to protect public order and morality). Thus the
agents of film censorship in Britain are taken to be the local
authorities, the BBFC, the Home Office and sometimes film
exhibitors and production companies.[2]

Annette Kuhn has provided an important critique of this approach,
characterising it as a 'prohibition/institutions' model, which assumes
that censorship is something 'done' to films by certain bodies in order
to cut or ban undesirable content. She argues that this approach is
unnecessarily limited, and ultimately even misleading, in its setting of
boundaries:

If this model provides a certain purchase on the historical study of film censorship, this is only because it constructs, *a priori*, an object of inquiry which is relatively amenable to empirical investigation. By the same token, though, the definition of censorship which both emerges from and sustains the prohibition/institutions model is a constricting one, for it allows only one story – and not necessarily the most interesting or important one – to be told about film censorship.[3]

Kuhn suggests that censorship was a far more complex, interactive process than is often acknowledged, involving 'an array of constantly shifting discourses, practices and apparatuses' and being productive, as well as prohibitive, in nature.[4] Similarly, I would argue that while a grasp of the history of official censorship is essential in gaining an understanding of the regulation of cinema-going, this represents 'only one story' – or one part of the story – about children and censorship in Britain and it certainly does not fully explain the ways in which children's viewing was censored during the 1930s.

Specifically, what is fundamentally lacking in existing histories of censorship is an appreciation of the cinema audience as regulators of their *own* viewing. Kuhn has considered the relationship between official censors and the audience as a collective body.[5] But it is also essential to recognise that audiences contain *individuals*, centrally active in the practices of censorship, who each have some ability to regulate their own viewing. Put simply, film-goers can effectively 'ban' a film for themselves by refusing to watch it, or make 'cuts' in a film's content by hiding their eyes, leaving the room, or engaging in some other activity. Consequently, in order to explore the processes of regulation fully, we must investigate the ways in which children (and their parents) were personally involved in the censorship of cinema during the 1930s, noting in particular the ways in which such autonomous self-regulation subverted, over-ruled or simply ignored the mandates of official censorship bodies.

In examining processes of self-regulation used by child cinema-goers in the 1930s, useful parallels can be drawn from the fields of cultural and media studies and education, particularly theories regarding the ways in which children interact with television.[6] Clearly, this involves a different medium and a later period, but important similarities do exist.

Theories of children and the media essentially fall into four main groups. 'Effects' research broadly sees the relationship between screen images and child behaviour as one of cause and effect. This is often labelled the 'hypodermic' or 'magic bullet' theory of media influence by its detractors, and it informed most of the 1930s studies into children and the cinema described in Chapter 4. 'Critical' mass communications research, meanwhile, does not focus on the impact of media on behaviour as such, but is concerned with the role of media as a force of socialisation, drawing on dominant ideologies in order to influence beliefs and values. The third theoretical stance, derived from cognitive psychology, differs from the first two in that it emphasises the active role taken by audiences in the construction of meaning, rather than suggesting that the audience is a passive recipient of a fixed meaning, delivered by the text. But it is the fourth approach, known as the 'uses and gratifications' model, and the theoretical approaches it has helped engender, that I wish to explore in more detail.

Uses and gratifications research reverses the media–audience relationship described in the first two theories since it does not examine ways in which media impact audiences, but ways in which people actively choose and use media in line with their own needs and preferences. Furthermore, it does not treat audiences as homogeneous groups, but highlights the importance of individual differences, such as personality, gender, class, race and, of course, age, as variables in the relationship between individuals and media. While audience research in media studies has moved on from the uses and gratifications model, its emphasis on individual agency has surely benefited subsequent approaches.[7] Thus, for example, Barie Gunter and Jill McAleer argue that 'children do not simply sit passively and watch the images displayed before them on the screen...instead, they often actively select what to watch to satisfy particular needs or moods'.[8]

Privileging the agency of viewers, this chapter will consider children's choices and preferences and examine ways in which these related to official attempts to regulate their viewing. This does not mean to imply that children in 1930s Britain were necessarily self-aware, autonomous, or successful enough for their viewing behaviour always to reflect their personal preferences. But neither was the regulation of children's viewing conducted solely, or even primarily, by institutional and other authorities. As will be shown, children exercised a great deal of choice in regulating their own viewing; choice which clearly varied from child to child depending on their preferences and situations; choice which often involved subtle negotiation, blatant subversion, or complete disregard of official and parental censorship.

Academic consideration of the role children play in regulating their own television viewing, often focusing on the agency of the viewer, is, itself, a relatively recent development. A key study in this field is David Buckingham's *Moving Images: Understanding Children's Emotional Responses to Television* (1996), in which the author examines not only how children and their parents control their viewing, but also the ways in which children respond to a range of television material, including melodrama, documentary and horror films. Having interviewed a number of children from a variety of backgrounds, Buckingham suggests:

> Children are not merely passive objects of adults' attempts at regulation – nor indeed do they uniformly resist them. On the contrary, children actively learn to regulate their own emotional responses to television. They develop very definite ideas about what they can and cannot 'handle', and hence what they will or will not choose to watch.[9]

As will be shown, evidence suggests that this may also have applied to the regulation of film viewing by children in the 1930s; three of Buckingham's conclusions, summarised below, are particularly pertinent in this respect:

1. Official regulation of children's television viewing (including video ratings and the television watershed) is often used for guidance, but is otherwise largely ignored by parents and children, who claim the right to make autonomous decisions about their viewing.

2. While parents often attempt to restrict their children's viewing, these attempts become increasingly ineffective as children grow older and use a range of strategies to evade or challenge parental regulation.

3. Most children deliberately avoid material they find frightening or otherwise undesirable, but many others enjoy and actively seek out

such material, using a variety of coping mechanisms to deal with their own responses.[10]

Given that histories of official regulation are only part of the story, the remainder of this chapter will explore self-regulation practised by children in the 1930s regarding film choice and strategies used to avoid undesirable screen images. The interactive relationships between official censors, cinema staff, parents and children will also be examined, inasmuch as they affected the autonomy of young viewers, and the prohibition/institutions model will be re-evaluated in the light of this evidence.

Regulation of Film Choice

This section will look at the theme of children's film choice from three different perspectives: the impact of BBFC certification regulations; the role of parental authority; and the ways in which children exercised autonomous control over their cinema attendance.

BBFC Certification

As detailed in Chapters 2 and 3, the principal means by which the BBFC sought to control children's viewing choices in the 1930s was through certification: while U and A films were open to all ages, A films could only officially be seen by children under 16 if they were accompanied by a parent or *bona fide* adult guardian. From 1932, A films labelled 'horrific' were said to be completely unsuitable for children and, while initially this was only advisory, in 1937 the institution of an H certificate formalised the exclusion of children under 16 from all such films, whether accompanied or not. Cinemas not adhering to these regulations, established by the BBFC and supported by local authorities and the Home Office, might be fined or could lose their licence to exhibit films. However, this alone does not give a full picture of children's cinema-going for, as previous chapters have indicated, young people habitually ignored and circumvented all such regulations.

For children who liked musicals, comedies or westerns, getting into see these pictures seldom proved a problem, as most of these had

U certificates. But many also liked genres that tended to attract A certificates – notably, gangster and horror films – and in order to see these, if parents or guardians were not present, the use of strangers as 'accompanying adults' was widely practised. Interestingly, this activity is not remembered by oral history respondents as an overtly subversive act: they were not sneaking in under age to assert their right to see 'inappropriate' films; they simply preferred certain films and negotiated their way around official regulation in order to see them.

The common nature of this activity is reflected in the number of respondents who mention it. Betty Verdant notes that 'you had to be 14 [*sic*] to get in unaccompanied, but if you were alone you could wait outside and ask a grownup if you could go in with them'.[11] Brigadier J.B. Ryall also recalls that when going to A films as a boy, he 'would wait for a man or couple to come along and say "Please Mister, here's my money would you please buy me a ticket". This way', he explains, 'you dodged the censor.'[12] The widespread use of this technique is also described by Bernard Goodsall, who remembers, 'like others of my generation, asking people to take you in when an A certificate film was on the menu'.[13] Similarly, Olive Johnson suggests that this was a common practice:

> As ['chillers'] were restricted to adults, we had to implore older folk in the queue to 'take us in' with them! Very naughty, but all children did it if they were unaccompanied by their own parents.[14]

Conversely, some children who looked old enough to attend A films alone also used this device when seeking to pass as a child and gain admission at a cheaper rate. Bill Grant lived in Scotland, where A certificates were not enforced, but he also recalls sneaking in with strangers:

> I can remember wanting to go to the Picture House in Springburn and I would watch maybe a couple going down the street. 'Hey, mister! Will you take me in with you?' I would give him my money, but being accompanied with him I'd get in for four pence. If I'd been on my own it would have cost me six pence.[15]

Some managers, however, did adhere to the rule that under-16s must be accompanied to A films. Denis Houlston found this something of an obstacle as a rather diminutive 16 year-old in 1933, although he still managed to assert some autonomy: 'I used to go with my friends... and they wouldn't let us in on one occasion 'cos I was always small, so I probably looked younger than I was... so I took the huff and I *boycotted* them, and I never went there again'.[16] However, the practice of children gaining entry with strangers was often accomplished with the collusion not only of the strangers, but also of the cinema staff. While many cinemas required children to be accompanied, they often ignored the stipulation that this companion must be 'a parent or *bona fide* adult guardian', turning a blind eye to unaccompanied children who routinely procured adults from the cinema queue, just to get past the box office. Thus, many cinema staff outwardly upheld certification regulations, while unofficially condoning the techniques used by children to circumvent them. Olga Scowen remembers going to the Harrow Coliseum during the school holidays:

> And if it was an A film, you see, I couldn't go in on my own. So you used to wait for somebody to come and say, 'Please, will you get me a ticket?' [Laughs] And the people behind the cash desk knew very well what was going on, but they never stopped you. [Laughs] So I saw quite a lot of A films when I shouldn't have done.[17]

A notable example of adult collusion occurred in Bristol where, on 5 March 1932, a Mrs Saviour went to the Saturday matinee at the Metropole Cinema and found 45 children outside, unable to gain entry. The film being shown was *Never the Twain Shall Meet* (1931), a romantic comedy about a man who 'goes native' after falling in love with an uninhibited, sexy, young Polynesian woman. As the film had an A certificate, the unaccompanied youngsters could not enter alone, so Mrs Saviour gamely agreed to buy their tickets and accompanied all 45 into the cinema. Following a timely visit from a police inspector, the case went to Bristol Police Court. The defence argued in vain that the regulation was ridiculous, as it prevented under-16s from seeing a 'sex film' which would probably bore them, while allowing 16–21 year-olds to see it, even though 'the age of puberty rendered them more susceptible'. Eventually, the cinema owners were fined £10 on the grounds that a stranger was not a *bona fide* guardian, thus setting a legal precedent.[18]

Nevertheless, many cinema managers and staff continued to collude in the practice of children gaining entry with strangers and, when cases came to court, the legal authorities also often colluded to some extent by setting minimal fines. In 1931, legal action was taken against the Manor Picture House, Sheffield, for admitting 200 unaccompanied children to see Hitchcock's *Murder!* (1930), an A film that touches not only on murder, but also on suicide and transvestitism.[19] In March 1933, Victor Harrison and Charles Crotch, the owners of the Plaza Cinema, Norwich, were fined for allowing 400 unaccompanied children to see the A film *Death Ray*. Although their defence was weak (they claimed that they thought the film had a U certificate) they were only fined £1.[20] Similarly, in February 1937, when a cinema manager was found guilty of exhibiting an A film to children, Salford magistrate Mr Percy Macbeth fined him just £1 and undermined the regulations further by commenting: 'I can never understand why children's morals are more likely to be corrupted if they see a film alone than if they are accompanied by an adult.'[21] Meanwhile, in Southampton, the council was troubled by numerous cinema managers admitting children to see 'horrifics', and when Alderman Mouland naively suggested: 'I do not think any cinema manager would run the risk of breaking the [BBFC] regulation', his colleague Alderman Lewis simply retorted: 'Oh, don't be silly!'[22]

Although, as has been shown, cinema staff generally disregarded children's use of strangers as accompanying adults, some did frown upon the practice and these individuals had to be carefully avoided. James Barton recalls that from 1933–4, when he was aged 10 and 11, he would 'haunt the cinema queues, asking "Will you take me in mister" when an A film was showing'. But he also remarks that 'at these times one did of course need to keep an eye out for Mr Race – a tall, stern doorman, in a glorious fading red uniform'.[23] Similarly, film critic Leslie Halliwell recalls that as a boy, when he tried to see *King Kong*, he found that 'the Odeon had acquired a brisk and hawk-eyed new commissionaire, who shooed me off at every attempt'.[24]

The generally relaxed attitude of cinemas towards unaccompanied children attending A films is indicated by the fact that the only policing of this activity took place on the door. For while usherettes often tried to regulate other kinds of children's behaviour in the

auditorium (see Chapter 6), children without adults at A films were
not apparently in danger of being challenged once inside the cinema,
where they could leave the 'accompanying adult' and sit elsewhere to
enjoy the picture. Ellen Casey recalls:

> If it was an X film [*sic*] you had to go in with adults. Well we
> used to stand outside and ask people, would they take us in? So
> they used to do that. Soon as we went in, like, we just left them.
> It was just that you had to be with an adult to go in.[25]

The introduction of the 'horrific' label apparently posed little problem
either, since only 18 films received this label between 1932 and 1936
(see Appendix 4) and several respondents remember seeing these as
unaccompanied children anyway, including *The Invisible Man* (1933)
and *The Werewolf of London* (1935).[26] A more serious obstacle,
however, was posed by the H certificate, which banned children from
some films whether they were accompanied or not. As a boy in North
London, Mr A.M. Peary would check the local newspapers with his
friend before deciding which film to see, but at 12 years old, they
found the newly introduced H certificate to be a tougher obstacle:

> If there were A (ADULT) films, this would necessitate asking
> some kindly adult to 'take us in' if our parents could not take
> us. It was bad news if H (HORROR) certificate films were on
> as no person under 16 was admitted.[27]

A similar problem is recalled by film producer Richard Gordon,
who went to the cinema with his brother when they were boys in the
1930s. They used a variety of methods to circumvent BBFC and LCC
regulations, including trying to pass for 16 at the box office and using
strangers to accompany them. 'Once in a while', he relates, 'a cinema
manager would allow us in alone to an A program on condition that
we sat next to an adult in case an inspector came round to check the
audience.'[28] However, Gordon notes that 'films rated "Adults Only"
or with an "H" certificate were an insurmountable problem', recalling
'the ignominy of being turned away from . . . *The Ghoul*, despite being
accompanied by our grandmother who valiantly tried to convince the
manager that we were over 16'.[29]

Essentially, unless cinemas were prepared openly to flout licensing regulations, the only children who could see H films would be those that could pass for 16 years of age. H film rules were certainly more closely adhered to by cinemas; in fact, only one oral history respondent of those studied recalls attending an H film as a child. Anthony Venis gained admission to see *The Cat and the Canary* (1939), when 14 or 15 years old. He was alone and remembers that the cinema had a back projection system, which rendered the auditorium very dark indeed, making the experience 'a bit eerie' and more frightening for him:

> Of course...the cinema was very dark, and I was quite young, obviously, then. Eh, it begs the question as to how I got in! [Laughs] I can't remember really. Because 'H'...I'd have thought I'd have been banned from that.[30]

There were some other exceptions. Although Richard Gordon was initially unable to gain admission to Universal's 1939 re-release double bill of *Frankenstein* and *Dracula* in its early smash-hit run in the West End of London, when he was aged 13, a certain amount of persistence eventually paid off:

> When the double bill went on general re-release shortly thereafter, a schoolmate and I were able to see it in a suburban cinema where an usherette, who was a friend of my mate's mother, sneaked us in through the fire exit. *Son of Frankenstein* [certified H] arrived in London but by that time, I was taking no chances. I forged a school document to show that I was sixteen and got in to see it on my own.[31]

Despite the more stringent regulations, it is important to reiterate that the impact of the H certificate on children's choices was slight, as it affected only a handful of films. Meanwhile, for the majority of children, A film regulations were apparently no obstacle to their cinema attendance. Eileen Barnett's recollection is typical of the matter-of-fact ease commonly associated with the activity of unaccompanied attendance. She explains that she and her friends constantly asked strangers to take them into the pictures:

> They never refused. So *you could get into any film you wanted*

to. You just had to ask somebody and they'd take you in as if you belonged to them.[32]

Thus it can be seen that children easily negotiated their way around BBFC certification rules (and, occasionally, zealous cinema staff) in order to see their films of choice. As Eileen Barnett puts it, 'you could get into any film you wanted to'. This system did rely, however, on the collusion of adults: those who 'accompanied' children, cinema staff who turned a blind eye and magistrates who imposed tiny penalties on cinema managers. In this sense, while children's choice of films was barely restricted by BBFC regulations, it was still dependent to some extent on adult sanction.

Parental Authority

The other adults with a potentially strong direct bearing on the cinema attendance and film choices of children were, of course, parents. Parents did exert control over children's choices, particularly over the choice of cinema venue and the time of attendance, and, less frequently, over the choice of film itself.

Winnie Lees lived in Glasgow's West End during the 1930s and one of her nearby cinemas as a child was the Seamore, Maryhill, which, she explains, 'I wasn't really allowed to go to. I don't really know why. But my mother didn't think that it was very suitable.'[33] Her mother therefore regulated Winnie's viewing in terms of venue. This may have been because the Seamore was rebuilt by eccentric showman A.E. Pickard in 1926, with a Moulin Rouge-like, illuminated, revolving windmill on the roof and an auditorium ceiling decorated with paintings of female nudes. Hence Pickard's slogan, 'You'll see more at the Seamore!'[34]

The main form of parental regulation over children's viewing involved the time of performance attended and the amount of supervision required. In these respects, many parents appear to have imposed a series of age-restrictions on their children's cinema-going. Most did not allow small children to attend the cinema unsupervised, unless it was a children's matinee and, for the many whose parents were not cinema-goers, this generally meant being taken by an older sibling or other relative. A fairly typical example is Vera Entwistle, from Bolton, who started going to the cinema in about 1935, when she was 8 years old. She went three times a week: on Tuesday and Thursday evenings with her older sister and to Saturday matinees with a group of friends.[35] The age at which children were allowed to go to the cinema alone varied, but for many it appears to have started when they were aged about 10. Ellen Casey was 10 when she reached this milestone in 1931, while James Barton remembers that it was 'around the age of ten (1933) I would have "gone solo" to early evening "First House"...performances'.[36]

This example mentions the other age-restriction often imposed by parents, regarding time of attendance. Most cinemas offered two identical performances per evening, known as the first and second houses, starting at around 5.30 p.m. and 8 p.m. respectively. (This was particularly true of the early 1930s, before continuous shows were more widely introduced.) A number of respondents recall that their parents did not allow them to attend the second house, as this was considered too late for bedtime. Moreover, cinema owners preferred to sell tickets for the second house to adults paying full price. As Bob Surtees explains, 'children were not allowed evening cinema or at least not encouraged'.[37] Consequently, going to the second house was often perceived as a sign of maturity. Mr Murray recalls with some pride how reaching this landmark made him feel like an adult:

> One thing I wasn't allowed to do was go into the second house of the pictures, which started at eight o'clock at night and finished at ten. Not until I was 14. And when I was 14, Father said, eh, 'You can go in the, eh, second house.' WE-ELL! You were about 25 year old then, like!...Just started work then he said, eh, 'Oh, you can go to second house now.' You know, 'You're working and you're 14', like, you know. Cos you worked till half past five.[38]

It is interesting to see a parallel here with Buckingham's study, as he has noted that most children seem to subscribe to developmental models of childhood and look to shifts in parental regulation of their viewing as indications of their maturity. Thus, when Mr Murray was allowed to attend the second house, although he had already passed the milestone of gaining paid employment, it was this change in *viewing practice* that he recalls made him feel 'about 25 year old'. This upholds Buckingham's suggestion regarding children, that the definition of what it means to be an 'adult' or a 'child', or a child of a certain age, is established partly in response to their parents' regulation of their viewing. The discourse and the knowledge that it claims to embody are thus intimately connected with the operation of power.[39]

In the same way it appears that in the 1930s parental regulation of the time at which children attended the cinema became an integral part of the process by which they were defined in terms of their age.

While children largely ignored age restrictions imposed by the BBFC and local councils, parental age restrictions on child attendance were more closely adhered to. Most restriction was on younger children, who often could only attend the cinema when genuinely supervised. Meanwhile, children that could attend alone were not normally allowed to go to second house performances. (That being said, as the two evening performances were usually identical, the latter restriction made no difference regarding children's choice of films.) So although BBFC certification apparently provided no real barrier to the attendance of children, the choices younger children could make regarding which films they saw were often limited by the preferences of those that supervised them.

This generally meant that younger children saw whatever their parents or guardians chose to see. But it should certainly not be assumed that younger children were always taken to tame or otherwise 'suitable' pictures. Sheila McWhinnie remembers being taken to her first talking picture, *Madame X* (1929), which she reasonably describes as 'not all that suitable for a 10 year old'.[40] And 6 or 7 year old Margaret Walsh was taken to see *Les Miserables* (1935); a rather harrowing version of the film, which includes repeated, lengthy flashbacks of the main character being strung up by a gang of guards and beaten senseless with solid wooden sticks. She remembers 'crying terribly' and explains, 'I was *horrified*'.[41] Molly Stevenson's first memory of films is from the age of 8 or 9, when her parents took her with them to see the brutal social issue film *I Am A Fugitive From A Chain Gang* (1932). She cried throughout, but justifies her parents' selection, speculating that it was probably a double feature programme, with the other picture being 'a *funny* film, cos I can't imagine them taking us to *The Chain Gang*'.[42] Meanwhile, Joan Howarth remembers 'being taken by my mother to watch a film about

2.   Full house at a children's matinee. (Reproduced in Richard Ford, *Children in the Cinema*, London: Allen & Unwin, 1939.)

a werewolf and I was terrified'.[43] A respondent in Mayer's study of British cinema-going, a woman born in 1928, also recalled: 'To begin with I did not go to the pictures because I was *interested* – but because my parents wanted to go, and I could not be left at home.' She continues, 'I was hardly introduced to films in the best way; for, at the age of 8 my grandmother took me to see a Boris Karloff Horror Film!' (an experience which she said gave her nightmares for two years).[44]

A second assumption to be avoided is that younger children could never opt to see films unless their parents wanted to see them – for on some occasions, it was the child rather than the parent who selected the film. Les Sutton remembers a 'moderately startling' trip with his father to the cinema in 1932 when he was 10 years old:

I persuaded my father to take me to see Karloff as *The Mummy*. He hadn't much time for fantasy, but took me, as youngsters were not admitted without parents or guardians. What there was of horror in the film – the burying alive scene – annoyed him (to think that I should want to go to such films).[45]

Similarly, Jessie Boyd was desperate to see *Dracula* (1931), when she was just 8 years old, although her local cinema was reluctant to admit her, and her mother had some misgivings:

I begged Mum to take me along, and she pleaded with the doorman... 'My little girl has been *so* looking FORWARD to this'. He was moved by her appeal. Consequence, the 'little girl' took her FASCINATED terror home, and was haunted by vampire dreams for years![46]

So some young children chose the films they saw, *despite* their parent's preferences. Other families reached a consensus regarding their choice of films, whereby no one's preferences were necessarily undermined. Mrs Schneiderman recalls:

I was born in 1931 and remember going to see 'suitable' films from a very early age...My mother used to take me to see all the Shirley Temple films, and the Hollywood musicals...Any other kind did not interest me anyway.[47]

It would therefore seem that young children had a range of experiences regarding their exercise of choice at the cinema. For many, interaction with parental authority in this respect involved a subtle process of negotiation – a process which is clearly demonstrated in the case of Ralph Hart. Ralph was born in 1921 and lived with his Jewish family in Golders Green. He and his mother both enjoyed going to the cinema and shared a love of musicals, which they saw together. Ralph's memory of his interaction with his mother over film choice is detailed and complex. His mother forbade some films and Ralph appears to have accepted this parental ban, which included gangster films:

> Well. *My mother did not like me to see those.* [Deliberate voice] *They were not for children*...she said they were for *older* people...A good straightforward murder mystery – Charlie Chan – yes. But not *gangster.*[48]

Meanwhile, although Ralph's mother did not like horror films, she allowed Ralph to go and see them on his own (presumably gaining entrance with a stranger). The two films he especially recalls, *King Kong* and *The Invisible Man*, were released in 1933 when Ralph was 11 or 12 years old. The latter was one of only five films labelled 'horrific' by the BBFC that year. But neither film scared him and, presumably, this contributed to the fact that Ralph's mother did not consider horror films harmful for him and that she therefore allowed him to go:

> One of the *great* films, and again my mother wouldn't see it, was, em, *Invisible Man*...I saw that on my *own*. She let me go and see it, because she said it would be too *horrific*. It had no effect on me whatsoever.

> My mother wouldn't go and see *King Kong* so I went down and saw it by myself...I went down to the Grand to see it myself. I enjoyed it to the nth degree! I was not in any way frightened whatsoever! *King Kong* did not frighten *me*![49]

Ironically, Ralph's abiding memory of a traumatic cinema experience relates to a film his mother chose and which they saw together. *Outward Bound* (1930) involves a young couple, played by Douglas

Fairbanks Jr and Helen Chandler, who attempt suicide by turning on the gas tap in their dingy London flat. They fall unconscious and the man starts to dream. The couple then find themselves travelling through thick fog on an eerie ship with no lights, and they soon discover that they and the other passengers are dead and bound for purgatory. Finally, in the dream, a young clergyman on board redeems the couple and they are physically saved by their dog, who breaks a window in the flat and then dies. This film was successful in New York, but was banned by the BBFC who objected to its depiction of attempted suicide and its questionable religious theme. However, three local authorities – Middlesex County Council, Sussex County Council and the LCC – chose to overrule the BBFC ban and showed the film in February 1931 on the strict grounds that it was not to be shown to children under 16.[50] Consequently, Ralph Hart was one of the few people in Britain to see this film, even though he was only 9 or 10 years old. It was, he says, 'the one and only film that ever gave me nightmares' and these recurred for ten years. His explanation of his reaction to the film is uncharacteristically inarticulate, as if distress is still associated with the memory:

> It gave me nightmares. Not because of the, cause of what it, the implications. It's not a monster or anything like that. Just the implications in this particular film.[51]

So although Ralph's own judgement about his ability to handle horror films was apparently sound and his mother was generally careful in her judgement over what he saw, *her* choice of film caused him some trauma on this occasion. It is not known whether Ralph's mother was aware of the BBFC ban on the film, nor how Ralph came to be admitted as a child by cinemas that officially should have barred him. However, it is very interesting to note that Ralph lays the ultimate authority (and responsibility) for the restriction of his viewing on his mother alone. 'Yeah, my mother shouldn't a let me go and see that', he explains, 'That *really upset me*. I didn't tell my mother. She *should* not really have let me see it.'[52]

This example clearly demonstrates something of the complexity surrounding the regulation of children's cinema attendance and film choice in the 1930s, particularly as it relates to the role played by parents. Ralph's interaction with his mother regarding cinema-going included a parental ban (on gangster films), child-parent consensus (on musicals), negotiation and concession (on horror films) and occasional misjudgements (on *Outward Bound*). Moreover, the case of *Outward Bound* shows that while BBFC bans could be ignored by local councils and local council age restrictions could be circumvented by parents and children, parental intervention was apparently the only really effective form of adult regulation of children's cinema attendance.

The effectiveness of parental regulation could vary a great deal, depending on the individuals concerned. Certainly, once children were old enough to attend the cinema alone there was far more opportunity to go against parental authority, by seeing films which parents would normally object to. Interestingly, oral history interviews often produce some ambivalence regarding parental authority in this respect. Where parental authority is mentioned, it is nearly always maternal authority; indeed, many respondents recall their mother's authority as a very powerful influence in the regulation of their behaviour. Husband and wife Irene and Bernard Letchet explain:

Irene:	Well you see your mother ruled you. You know. If your mother said you didn't, you didn't. And there was no resentment.
Bernard:	No. It was just life. [Laughs]
Irene:	You did what mother SAID.[53]

Nevertheless, once children were old enough to go to the cinema unsupervised, many went to see films their parents would not have sanctioned, usually evading parental regulation rather than openly defying it. This was particularly easy to achieve if the parent was unaware of the films their children saw. Olga Scowen remembers sneaking into A films underage: 'I saw quite a lot of A films when I shouldn't have done', she recalls, 'My mother used to let me go and she didn't know what I was going to see, very often.'[54] Note how Olga explains her actions in terms of her mother's permission – 'my mother used to let me go' – albeit, given in ignorance – 'she didn't know what I was going to see'.

Similarly, Ellen Casey really enjoyed horror pictures and would attend these by asking adult strangers outside the cinema to accompany her and her younger brother past the box office:

Now the frightening films – you had to go in with somebody for these. Now I shouldn't a gone to one but I wanted to see him in *Frankenstein*. *The Mummy's Hand [The Mummy]*, *The Old Dark House* – they were all Boris Karloff. And, eh, I'd only be about 10 then. Nine, 10. *Dracula*, 1931. *Dr Jekyll and Mr Hyde*... I used to run home terrified![55]

From her list, it would appear that Ellen attended such films on a fairly regular basis. When asked if she ever had nightmares, she replies:

Oh yeah, I did. My brother did one night. He was going mad, him... So I thought, 'Oh I daren't tell me mother. She'd stop us going.'

These extracts paint a similar picture to that of Olga Scowen. Ellen's attendance was not sanctioned: 'Now I shouldn't a gone', she says. She was only able to attend because her mother was unaware of the situation. Thus, the feelings she recalls – 'Oh I daren't tell me mother. She'd stop us going' – imply that her mother was ignorant of their attendance, that she certainly would not have approved of it and, particularly, that this parental authority was so significant that it had to be evaded, in order that the clandestine cinema-going could continue. Crucially, parental authority was the only form of cinema regulation which might attract punishment if defied – as in the case of one man in Mayer's study, who recalls as a child 'sneaking to see a horror film against my parents' wishes and returning home so impressed by it that I finished up with a nightmare and a caning in the bargain'.[56]

A complex mixture of autonomy, advice, regulation and subversion is also evident in interviews from Buckingham's television study. He finds that 'children often argued explicitly for the need for parental regulation; and asserted that, if they were parents, they would exert a considerable degree of control over their own children's viewing'.[57] He also notes that 'the strategies that children use in attempting to evade or undermine their parents' authority are diverse and often ingenious'. Nevertheless, he argues, 'despite such attempts at evading parental control, children also looked to their parents for guidance, and largely accepted their right to offer it'.[58]

Contradictions in oral history interviews often reveal something of this grey area between parental authority and children's choices, raising important questions regarding who made the final decisions in the regulation of children's viewing. Beatrice Cooper, who was born in 1921 and grew up in Hendon, North London, recalls being forbidden by her mother to see Mae West films and her implication is that she obeyed this ban:

> Mae West. My mother would never allow me to see Mae West…She was a SEX SYMBOL, you see. So they thought I might be spoiled if I saw her.[59]

However, in the same interview, Beatrice surprisingly reveals a penchant for illicit horror films. When asked about *Frankenstein* (1931), released when Beatrice was 9 or 10 years old, she replies:

> That was – they were good films. I loved those. *King Kong* and things like that…they were the ones I used to, em, you know, skip school for…Yeah, because my mother wouldn't have let me go to see them…*King Kong* – I went to see it on my own. And *Frankenstein*. And *The Bride of Frankenstein*. Mmm… Horrifying. But I loved it. You know [laughs] the more horrifying it was, the more I liked it!

Again, when asked about *The Invisible Man*, she replies, 'Oh I saw that…Yes, yes. Oh that's one I must've got off school for.'

So although Beatrice apparently obeyed her mother's ban on Mae West pictures, she *played truant* in order to see horror films (including at least two BBFC 'horrifics') that would have incurred a similar parental ban – as she says, 'my mother wouldn't have let me go to see them'. This clearly throws into question the effectiveness of parental authority in controlling Beatrice's film choices, and suggests that the more likely regulating influence was Beatrice's own preferences. It therefore appears that, for at least some children, BBFC certification rules were ignored but parental regulation of films was adhered to, so long as it did not conflict with the choice of the ultimate authority: the child.

Another example of childhood truancy and defiance of parental regulation comes from Mayer's study, in which a woman recalls that as a girl in the late 1920s she was forbidden to see 'sex pictures'. But this did not stop her:

> At twelve I wondered *what* sort of films they were that I was never allowed to see, and played truant from school – with another small and curious-minded friend – to see my first 'sex' film. It was of the trials and temptations of a rather blowsy continental actress, and puzzled us for weeks...*Did* men kiss women like that, and *did* babies come unwanted, from such episodes and behaviour? So my curiosity aroused...I sneaked off at 12 – now unescorted – to see all the extravagant and unreal epics of sex and high living I could find.[60]

Clearly, therefore, children tended to experience a complex relationship with parental authority regarding their choice of films. But, as with official attempts at regulation, the ultimate authority frequently seems to have rested with children themselves.

Children as Self-regulators of Film Choice

Having shown the limitations of official and parental attempts to control children's film viewing, the question remains as to how children actually chose the films they watched. Some commentators in the 1930s suggested that children were particularly susceptible to dangerous images in films because they went to see whatever was screened, regardless of its content. Thus, the Edinburgh Enquiry argued:

> There is no effective censorship by them such as is exercised by adult patrons of the theatre, who can, and do, by withdrawing their support, cause an unpopular or poor play to be taken off. On the contrary, it appears that the children's attendance is independent of the kind of pictures shown.[61]

However, evidence from the same enquiry contradicts this view, for when 250 young people aged between 14 and 21 were asked 'Do you go to the same Cinema regularly no matter what pictures are shown?', 224 (90%) replied 'No', explaining that they chose films based on a combination of personal preferences for filmstars and genres, newspaper reviews and the comments of friends.[62]

This pattern is confirmed by evidence from oral history and correspondence, which indicates that many children were regular cinema-goers who, like adults, made deliberate decisions regarding the films they wished to see (or to avoid). These decisions were usually based on preferences for stars and genres and were *informed* decisions, made with extensive reference to sources such as cinema trailers, film reviews, magazines like *Picturegoer* and *Film Weekly*, and word-of-mouth recommendations.

Winnie Lees remembers exercising a great deal of discretion over the films she saw. When her interviewer claims that 'between the wars, people didn't discriminate too much about what films they went to see', she replies: 'Oh I wouldn't agree. You know, that may have applied to some people, but it certainly didn't apply to me.'[63] Winnie subscribed to several film magazines and based her viewing on informed personal preferences. 'I used to read up on films even then and reviews of films and I was quite selective about what I would go and see,' she explains. In this way, Winnie also regulated her viewing by *avoiding* certain films, 'because I didn't fancy them, you know... I only went to see films that either I liked the people in or, you know, for some reason or other'.

The amount of choice available to children was great in many cases, due to the number of cinemas springing up all over the country. Irene Letchet, who was raised in Islington, describes the wide selection of films there: 'Of course, there were more cinemas then, you see... so you had a choice... I mean you were a little bit, um... choosy.'[64] Irene also read film magazines 'avidly', and recalls being influenced by trailers, including one for *The Grapes of Wrath* (1940). She explains, 'I just wouldn't go... to *see* that because, having seen the trailer I thought, Oh no. Don't want to see *that*, you know.'[65]

Many children therefore exercised discretion regarding their viewing, basing their decisions on information and experience. Irene, like other respondents, explains that casting was often a clue as to whether or not a film would be worth attending – not only because of her preferences for particular stars, but also because actors were often associated with certain types of role:

> You went to see your favourite film star... I mean, Clark Gable was ALWAYS Clark Gable, no matter WHAT film he was in!... And Spencer Tracy was always SPENCER TRACY. Oh, or the other ones, you know... it was a regular thing.[66]

Sisters Molly Stevenson and Margaret Young also recall choosing their films carefully, based on genre and casting, and using weekly film magazines as a guide. Like many children, they made a beeline for musicals and comedies, although they emphasise the stars rather than the genres when they list 'the Andy Hardy films, and the Ginger Rogers and Fred Astaires...and the Deanna Durbins'. They particularly liked Shirley Temple, Charlie Chaplin, Laurel and Hardy, and the gangster pictures made by the Dead End Kids. However, they did not like *all* films, as Margaret recalls: 'I think we'd what you'd call a catholic taste in films, except for the Frankenstein monster things, which we just did not like at all.' Molly concurs, 'Yes – and the like of Boris Karloff and people like that.'[67]

Such evidence is very important, for it supports the argument that it was personal preference and self-regulation by children that determined whether they went to see horror films, rather than the regulations of the certification system or parental authority. For not only did children choose the films they *wanted* to see based on their preferences for certain actors, they also used casting (rather than certification) as an indication of films they might prefer to *avoid*. Thus, Molly and Margaret avoided Boris Karloff because of their aversion to horror films. Similarly, when asked about Bela Lugosi films, Kath Browne conflates the star and his main genre, recalling, 'I deliberately didn't go, but my girlfriend, she did like thrillers.'[68] Yet Kath also demonstrates that a strong preference for favourite stars could outweigh her aversion to a genre. When asked 'Did you like the thrillers yourself?', she replies: 'No, not all particularly. I mean, I went to see *Jekyll and Hyde* – but that's cos of Spencer Tracy.'[69]

Evidence of children 'banning' horror films for themselves is also plentiful in Mayer's study. One woman recalls having seen Karloff and Lugosi in *The Black Cat* (1934) when she was 6 years old. 'The whole picture terrified me', she remembers. And, after suffering from nightmares, she decided to avoid Boris Karloff films in future: 'I never went back to see one of his again', she says.[70] Another respondent reported having nightmares after seeing *Dr Jekyll and Mr Hyde* as a girl. Afterwards, she wrote, 'I made a point of not going to see films which were alleged to be frightening.'[71] One last example from Mayer's study is a woman who was frightened as a child by one scene in a short comedy film:

After that, I absolutely refused to go to any film which was an out-and-out horror film – *Frankenstein*, *Dracula* or any creepy murder story. I remember when *King-Kong* came [out], all my chums raved about it, but I refused to go as I thought I would be frightened.[72]

The Birkenhead Cinema Enquiry also contains evidence of children 'banning' frightening films for themselves. When asked 'Do the pictures ever keep you from sleeping afterwards?', the report notes that 'many' children replied 'no', adding that this was because they chose not to watch 'Mystery' or 'Ghostly ones'.[73] One young Birkenhead respondent also explained that they had learned 'never to go and see a mystery picture if you are nerves [nervous]'.[74]

In addition to the horror genre, other favourites and pet hates were deeply felt and are still recalled with great gusto, frequently demonstrating that children's tastes could be as unpredictable and varied as those of adults. Jessie Boyd, who was raised in Lancashire in the 1930s, has very strong memories of her preferences. 'I loved "jungle pictures"', she says, 'I adored costume drama, *hated* cowboy films, but was *riveted* by the original *Dracula* [1931].' She continues:

Knock-about comedy didn't appeal to me...Hates? Shirley Temple – ugh! – sickening, simpering *BRAT*. Films in which the story was interrupted by the characters bursting into what came to me as STUPID songs. Most cartoons, including Popeye.[75]

Ellen Casey also produced a surprising and adamant response when asked about her preferences for films:

I didn't like the Saturday matinee because they was mostly westerns. I didn't like westerns. I *didn't* like westerns. You know, all this *shooting* one another and the Indians. I was terrified. So it was very rare I went to the children's matinee – if it was a western. I didn't like them.[76]

Although Ellen could more easily have afforded the cheaper children's matinees, she chose to go less frequently and attended early evening performances in order to see the films she liked most:

When I could get the money together, I used to always save it till there was a MUSICAL on. Or a ROMANCE. That's what I wanted. Oh I LOVED musicals...I made it my business. I never went when the films were, you know, not my taste or whatever.

Eric Holmes, like Ellen, also chose not to attend matinees, and went to the first house with his mother instead. He explains, 'Saturday mornings were for the children when they would show cowboy films, I only went once because I found it to be very noisy and rowdy.'[77]

There is a great deal of other evidence suggesting that many children chose not to go to matinees, either because they disliked the atmosphere or because, like Ellen Casey, they did not like the types of film exhibited. In New York City, attempts to show 'wholesome' films at children's matinees in 1916 failed because children voted with their feet. On offer were films about animals and a production of *Alice in Wonderland*. But, as a newspaper article explained:

The children would not attend on Saturday morning, nor on succeeding Saturday mornings. They wanted to pay more and see a sensational adult picture thrown on the screen. As one little girl of twelve expressed it: 'We like to see them making love and going off in automobiles.' And a boy explained, 'There won't be any shooting or dynamiting in those kid pictures. What's the use of seeing them?'[78]

Finally, for those who attended the pictures in a 'gang', peer group consultation was another common way of selecting films. Denis Houlston describes how such decisions were reached, as his 'gang' did not simply go to one regular cinema, but chose between all the programmes on offer at various local venues:

So how...did you choose what film to go to? Well often as a youngster, it was the *gang* of you, you know...'What're we going to do tonight then, lads?' 'What have they got on up at the Grand?' 'There's something up at the Arcadia and there's something somewhere else.' 'Oh, that's a *sloppy* one! We don't want to see that!' 'But we want to see Robin Hood.' So, you went with the herd.[79]

The evidence presented therefore strongly suggests that many children negotiated their way around official regulation and parental authority, exercising their own personal choices regarding which films to see with care and considerable forethought, weighing up a variety of factors. Certainly it is erroneous to suggest that they went to see whatever was put in front of them. Winnie Lees' comment is representative of many others, as she recalls, 'I only went to see films that either I liked the people in or, you know, for some reason or other'. Furthermore, unlike the unreliable nature of official and parental regulation, when a *child* chose not to see a film, that film was usually effectively banned. This firm and non-negotiable form of self-regulation is evident in responses to films described above, including curt phrases such as, 'I deliberately didn't go' and 'I just wouldn't go'.[80] As Vera Entwistle explains regarding her choice not to see *North West Passage* (1940): 'I didn't go, because I took that decision that I didn't want to go and see it.'[81]

Children as Censors of Screen Images

The second form of self-regulation exercised by children involved the 'cutting' of film content. For, contrary to common assumption, the 'removal' of unwanted scenes and sections of films was effected not only by film-makers, local councils and the BBFC, but also by children themselves, on an individual basis.

The need for children to censor screen images arose from two main sources. As already discussed, while a large amount of choice was exercised by children, they did not always have control over which films they saw, particularly in the case of younger children. Consequently children may have been subjected to screen images that they did not wish to see. Secondly, those who chose which films they saw could still (intentionally or unintentionally) subject themselves to unwanted images. Dorris Braithwaite remembers as a child in Stockport going 'to see a werewolf one' by accident, when it was screened as a double feature with a Bing Crosby film that she wanted to see. 'And we'd gone to see Bing', she explains, 'And of course, on came the were[wolf] and I *hated* it! I couldn't do with horror stories.'[82]

Frightening images could also occur in quite unexpected places. Although Michael Trewern-Bree was a regular filmgoer, he remembers a silent film of the Good Samaritan story shown at Penzance Pavilion by a local church, which 'frightened the life out of' him.[83] Conversely, many respondents who saw *Frankenstein* (1931) remember feeling not fear of the monster, but sympathy. Tom Walsh recalls: 'For a monster he had a kinda human face. He had a kinda gentleness about him which, eh, maybe detracted from the horror of the film.'[84] Tom Affleck agrees that '*Frankenstein* didn't really frighten...somehow we felt great sympathy for the monster.'[85] Nevertheless, sympathetic feelings could also evoke unwanted emotional responses in children, as described by Ellen Casey:

> And I tell you what broke me heart. You'll never believe this! Broke me heart crying in bed about KING KONG! KING KONG! D'you know with the end where all the planes were going round. And he's firing at him and he's grabbing the planes, you know...[86]

Many children therefore found themselves in a position where they needed to censor film content and this was perhaps particularly true of children who *enjoyed* being frightened by films and who therefore watched pictures on the boundaries of what they could 'handle'. Ellen Casey repeatedly chose to go to see Boris Karloff and other horror films from the age of 9 although they frightened her long after the performance:

> I used to be terrified. I used to run home terrified. I used to run home all the way. And then we didn't have no lighting up the stairs and...we used to get a candle...I remember going up the stairs, me hand shaking like that...Terrified. But them films were really frightening...But I made it my business. I never went when the films were, you know, not my taste or whatever.[87]

As will be shown, children like Ellen who deliberately chose to see films that would terrify them apparently enjoyed the 'ride' of watching as much as they dared, before using 'cutting' techniques and other coping mechanisms to regulate their viewing.

For younger children who were distressed by film content, parents could sometimes intervene and censor the child's viewing by

3. 'The hero is in danger': children absorbed by a matinee film. (Reproduced in Richard Ford, *Children in the Cinema*, London: Allen & Unwin, 1939.)

physically removing them from the cinema. Margaret Young remembers being taken to a silent comedy:

> I think it was a Harold Lloyd film and he got his foot into a spittoon and I got so upset, I cried and cried, and my mother had to take me out, cos I thought, he'll never get his foot out of that spittoon!...and, eh, I was taken out of the picture house.[88]

This is an interesting example, in terms of control over the viewing experience. For although it would appear to be Margaret's mother who resolved the situation, it was Margaret that really initiated her *own* removal, by becoming uncontrollably upset: 'I cried and cried, and my mother *had* to take me out', she explains (my italics). Her crying itself could almost be seen as a form of censorship in that it rendered Margaret unable to see the screen. This might be stretching the point, but there were certainly numerous other techniques used by children to 'cut' unwanted screen images.

Some of the most common 'cutting' techniques involved deliberate blocking of film images by children, who physically impaired their view of the screen by covering their eyes or hiding. Thus, a man in Mayer's study remembered that at 16, he had 'covered [his] face at the sight of Spencer Tracy "changing" in two or three scenes from *Doctor Jekyll and Mr Hyde*'.[89] Meanwhile, a woman born in 1926 recalled: 'Almost the only thing I can remember of my very early film-going experiences is seeing a band of horses thunder across the screen, and burying my head in my mother's arm with a yell because I thought we were going to be trampled to death.'[90] Similarly, when Molly Stevenson was taken to see *I Am A Fugitive From A Chain Gang*, she became upset and deliberately blocked many scenes. She says, 'I remember crying and my head being more or less between my knees most of the time.'[91] Dorris Braithwaite remembers reacting to a frightening scene in *North West Passage* (1940), after a man has been carrying a mysterious bag for some time: 'And then he brought out what was in the bag, and it was a skull!', she laughs. 'I was under the chair! I was absolutely terrified!'[92]

Being 'under my chair' would obviously preclude viewing and was a common form of image censorship for children – albeit a relatively gymnastic one. It could simply entail ducking down behind the seats in front or, sometimes, literally getting under one's own seat. There are numerous examples of this from respondents. Hilda Moss remembers taking evasive action from frightening scenes at children's matinees: 'The serials were very gripping', she explains, 'I was always under the seat if things got too scary.'[93] And Molly Stevenson recalls of one performance: 'the first item was a gangster picture and I spent most of the time under the seat'.[94] Similarly, when asked about *Dr Jekyll and Mr Hyde* (1931), Margaret Walsh laughed and replied, 'Oh, I remember hiding under the seats!'[95] A variation on this technique was to ask a brave companion to monitor the screen image while you blocked it. Vera Entwistle, who enjoyed horror films, performed this function for a more timid friend. She recalls:

I used to like being frightened, you know. Used to go and watch *Frankenstein*. And my friend used to be [makes face and laughs] 'Tell me when he's gone off! Tell me when he's gone off!'[96]

A similar response was noted by a young woman in Mayer's study, who used this strategy when frightened by a mask in a comedy film:

> I got a dreadful shock and looked away from the picture instantly. Mother told me she would tell me when to look again...From then on, if it looked as though there would be anything frightening in the film I would tell whoever was with me to 'tell me when to look again'.[97]

For other children, subtler techniques were required, since they wished to control their viewing without completely negating it. In this sense, the children were aiming to regulate both the screen image and their own emotional reactions to it. David Buckingham has described a number of similar 'coping mechanisms' used by children watching horror films on television, who seek to regulate their responses to the material:

> In some instances...children simply learn to avoid material that they feel they will be unable to cope with, either by refusing to watch it in the first place, or by hiding or leaving the room or turning it off when it gets too much. In other cases, they look to comfort in the form of pillows or toys – or indeed people – to hug; or they attempt to distract themselves with other activities...There is ample evidence here that, in all sorts of ways, children learn to regulate their *own* viewing, and their emotional responses to it.[98]

One technique used by young cinema-goers involved watching a film selectively, through their fingers (a strategy also found by Buckingham among television viewers), allowing the child to discover the outcome of events, while also providing a feeling of relative safety. Joan Howarth recalls using this technique during a werewolf picture. She says, 'I was terrified; hiding my face in my mother's shoulder and peeping, from time to time, through my fingers.'[99]

As has been shown, children were often quite able to assess their own ability to handle screen images, and they selected films accordingly. For those who enjoyed surfing between fear and fun, this often meant choosing films on the borderline and using coping mechanisms to reduce the fear element, and thus enhance their enjoyment, of frightening films. This could also include deliberately avoiding the most frightening images in a given film. Joan Donaghue and her friends did this when she was aged between 7 and 9:

> It seemed that there was never anything we didn't want to see. We went especially to be frightened by Boris Karloff in *The Old Dark House* or *Frankenstein* and we would cling to each other and squeal or shut our eyes. It didn't take much to set us off in those days![100]

Thus, Joan and her friends 'went especially to be frightened' by films, and habitually adopted a number of coping strategies. In addition to cutting images by shutting their eyes, they used the security of viewing in a group, they sought reassurance through mutual physical contact and they apparently found some emotional release by squealing.

Tom Walsh also recalled an ambivalent reaction to frightening screen images. He enjoyed the fear and therefore pushed his own boundaries in terms of coping with frightening film content. He said that he 'loved...horror films', but also noted: 'Children have a strange fascination for horror films. They're afraid of them, but they like them.' When Tom went to see *Dr Jekyll and Mr Hyde* (1931) alone, aged 9 or 10, he found that he had over-reached himself and needed to adopt the kind of coping techniques that Buckingham calls 'psychological strategies', which include 'distracting oneself, seeking comfort' and 'seeking more information':[101]

> I was *terrified* by it! And I remember saying to a man in desperation beside me, a grown up man: 'Is he gonnae turn again?' You know, he used to turn into the monster...I was grabbing this man by the arm...He said, 'I don't know son, you better go and ask him.'...He was being funny. But that was a comfort to me you know...that somebody could make a joke about this horrifying...portrayal.[102]

Children therefore used a number of techniques to 'cut' or otherwise regulate both frightening screen images and their own emotional responses to them. And it was not only fear that prompted children to censor films, for there were three other common targets of child film regulation: news reels, educational films and, the ultimate nightmare, 'sloppy stuff'.

Just as some children cut images and scenes from films, others cut entire sections of the cinema programme that did not interest them. Such 'cuts' might involve going to the toilets, fighting, playing, engaging in other activities or even walking out. As Sheila McWhinnie's account of cinema-going in the Gorbals, Glasgow suggests, this kind of activity could become something of a ritual among children:

> The cinema was a great meeting place for all my class-mates and friends in the district. Before leaving school for the day, we would tell each other which cinema we would be at in the evening... Then while the newsreels were on, we would take this opportunity to walk around the cinema in order to see and be seen.[103]

Thus, whole groups of children could effectively censor the newsreels out of their viewing experience and use the time for a different activity entirely.

Worthy attempts to ply young cinema-goers with educational films could also be subject to censorship by children. As Methodist minister Rev. D.O. Soper told a conference in 1937, these films were often met with catcalls by matinee audiences. 'My experience is that instructional films get what is known in Islington as "the bird" and they get it very quickly', he explained. 'Children do not go to matinees... to be instructed, and the first breath of suspicion that they are there to be instructed calls forth a very vigorous protest.'[104] As an alternative to catcalling, individual children might even walk out of a performance they wished to 'censor'. One 11 year-old girl told the Birmingham Enquiry that she left a cinema because she found the film offensive. She recalled: '"The monster killed the girls' brother and when she found out she threw the cross into the sea and said she did not believe in God. I walked out."'[105]

The biggest target for child censors, however, was neither violence, nor horror, nor newsreels, but love scenes – derided by most children (especially boys) as 'soppy bits' or 'sloppy stuff'. Thus, when Ralph Hart was asked to recall what made a good film for children in the 1930s, he replied: 'Action, action and action... No lovin'. Please [laughs] no lovin'... No what the boys called soppy love.'[106] Probably the toughest censors in this respect were the audiences at children's matinees, where derision for sloppy stuff apparently knew no bounds. If the offending material was brief, the action taken might simply involve shouting the scene down, in order to undermine its atmosphere. As Thomas McGowan explains, 'If you got, eh, men and girls slabbering over each other... they would have catcalls, "Aw – get them off! GET THEM OFF!"'[107] However, longer love scenes initiated more extensive cutting by children, who would then ignore the screen altogether:

> When that was on we used to make our *own* entertainment. We used to run up and down the passages, you know? And annoy the chucker outs! Hide under the seats, eh, do, do all sorts of things, play cowboys, until something *interesting* come on, and then you sat down and watched it.

Cinema managers giving evidence at the 1936 BFI Conference on Films for Elementary School Children described similar censorship practices used at matinees. According to one manager, 'love and sex, of course, bore the children to distraction' and during 'the final reconciliation scenes...they make for the exits before the "sloppiness" gets into its stride.' The same manager concluded:

> An uncensored version of Decameron Nights or Balzac's Droll Stories would do no moral harm at a children's matinee. The kiddies would simply start a private fight or swop cigarette cards or find some other diversion until Mickey Mouse or Hoot Gibson came along with some intelligent entertainment.[108]

So the fact that children regulated their own viewing was recognised by at least some managers. A second manager at the conference confirmed that 'love scenes, even in Westerns, are greeted with derision', and he noted that children at matinees would also censor language they considered inappropriate, by shouting it down:

> Dialogue must be rigorously correct or it meets with instant disapproval. Although the average boy has frequent recourse to his own stock of oaths, he will not tolerate it on the screen. Recently we showed a British Film in which a character called someone a 'swine'. At once a murmur of reproof arose and a firm voice shouted: 'Oi, no swearing!'[109]

This form of censorship among matinee audiences was widespread, with children deliberately cutting elements of films that did not meet with their approval. As sisters Molly Stevenson and Margaret Young explain:

Molly: It was only if there was something terribly exciting on the screen that you would get silence...

Margaret: I mean, if there was any kissing or anything like that, that was [laughs] nobody wanted to know!

Molly: [Laughs] 'Let's have some action! No that kind of action! But action!'[110]

Conclusion

During the 1930s, attempts at both official and parental control over children's film viewing were significantly limited, particularly once children reached the age of independent cinema-going. In particular, the restrictive impact of certification was apparently almost negligible, while that of parental authority seems to have been highly variable and potentially subordinate to the preferences of the child. At the same time, children were often selective in their choices of films and would use a variety of censorship strategies and coping techniques when confronted with unwanted screen images.

There is therefore significant agreement between the evidence presented in this chapter and the conclusions drawn by David Buckingham in his study of children and the self-regulation of television viewing. In the 1930s, as in the 1990s, official regulations were used as a guideline, but were often otherwise ignored; parental regulation tended to diminish as children grew older and could evade it; and while some children avoided material they found unappealing, others actively sought out emotionally challenging images, using a range of mechanisms to help them cope.

Certainly, the relationship between children, parents and official censors seems to have been a complex and interactive one. Children did not entirely resist adult attempts to regulate their viewing, but neither did they passively comply. Despite certification regulations and parental authority, film choices were made by children in the 1930s with reference to a number of sources of information, including reviews and magazines, and tended to reflect their personal preferences and moods as well as the influence of external agencies. While some children deliberately sought the stimulation of horror films, for example, others doggedly avoided them, but in both cases the determining factor seems to have been one of personal choice, rather than adult limitation.

Having said this, it would be wrong to characterise children's viewing as devoid of adult regulation. Younger children in particular often found their film choices limited by adult preference. Many children were also restricted by their parents in terms of choice of venue, time of attendance, or level of supervision. Meanwhile, those who chose to watch films without parental sanction often evaded rather than flagrantly opposed this authority by relying on a lack of parental awareness and it is likely that this was not always a successful strategy. Furthermore, some parental bans on certain types of film seem to have been obeyed, although the reasons for this obedience may have been quite complex. The practice of sneaking into A films with strangers has also been shown to rely on the collusion of adults, including the strangers themselves, cinema staff and magistrates. Finally, while BBFC certificates and labels such as A and H may not have successfully kept many children from attendance, they could still influence their film choices, depending on whether children preferred to avoid such material or to watch it. Buckingham draws similar conclusions regarding official television censorship labels and strategies, such as film classifications and the watershed:

> These definitions were used 'negatively', as a means of warning children off material they might find upsetting; yet they were also used 'positively', as a means of marking out material that might be seen as 'stronger' or more exciting. As Julian Wood has noted, the classification system often has the unintended consequence of identifying 'forbidden fruit' which children then actively seek out.[111]

Overall, traditional histories based on the prohibition/institutions model of censorship have tended to paint a limited if not a misleading picture of the activities surrounding attempts to regulate children's cinema-going in the 1930s. What becomes apparent from a study of individual cinema-going experiences is that children were largely unaffected by the restrictions imposed by official censorship bodies, and that they actively censored their own cinema viewing in various ways based on their individual personalities and preferences. Consequently, the relationship of children with parental and official forms of censorship should not be seen solely or even primarily as a top-down, regulatory, prohibitive model. Instead, it might be better characterised as a complex, interactive process, in which children negotiated, subverted and often circumvented both official organs of censorship and parental authority in order to take an active and leading role in the regulation of their own viewing.

Matinees, Clubs and Children's Cinema Culture

Oh it was great – 'cause the life, the cinema life then, it
was everything!...But, this, this, THIS it caught the
imagination of the kids! You know?[1]

Thomas McGoran, Glasgow matinee-goer

As discussed in Chapter 1, histories of censorship and cinema-going often focus on adults and on issues of class, politics and gender, either ignoring children or subsuming them into adult audience models. However, when the child audience is overlooked or dismissed in this way, important aspects of the puzzle are lost. As has been shown, issues relating specifically to child viewers were of central importance in the evolution of cinema-going and censorship. Moreover, children should not ideally be subsumed into adult audience models, for they had a distinct cinema culture of their own.

In examining the motivations and mechanisms of cinema regulation and the memories of some of the children involved, it becomes apparent that the 'flapdoodle' over children's cinema-going was, at least in part, a response to the massive impact that cinema was having on young lives. Although concerns regarding children and film were in one sense simply the latest incarnation of a recurring debate about children and popular culture, these concerns were by no means groundless; cinema did indeed have a profound influence on many children.

This chapter will explore some of the ways in which children related to cinema in the 1930s and consider the extent to which a distinctive children's cinema culture can be identified. Before doing so, it is important to mention two points of clarification regarding this 'distinctive children's cinema culture'. First, children's cinema-going experiences overlapped with those of adults to some extent, creating similarities that blur the distinction in places. Second, children's cinema culture was by no means homogeneous; individual experiences could vary widely, depending on factors such as age, gender, location, family income, parenting style, frequency of attendance, personality and preferences. Nevertheless, important common features in children's cinema-going are apparent and the multifaceted experience of child spectators can be recognised as significantly different from that of adults.

In examining these themes, spectatorship will be considered in its broadest sense. For, as Judith Mayne explains, 'spectatorship is not just the relationship that occurs between the viewer and the screen, but also and especially how that relationship lives on once the spectator leaves the theater'.[2] Bearing this in mind, children's cinema culture will be explored from several angles: the distinctive ways in which children entered the cinema, behaved during exhibitions and engaged with films after the show; the changing nature of children's matinees, including the shift from raucous free-for-all to organised cinema club; and finally, examples of a few children who managed their own cinemas.

Gaining Entry

Children's cinema-going in the 1930s typically involved weekly attendance at a Saturday matinee (sometimes known as the penny or tuppenny rush or crush) and mid-week attendance at early evening first house performances, with family or friends. Generally speaking, unlike most adults, children needed to seek permission and subsidy in order to attend the cinema, and they had some very creative ways of gaining entry to see a film.

There is some debate as to whether children gained admission to matinee performances with jam jars, but oral evidence does bear this out, especially in rural areas and small towns. In fact, on special occasions, some respondents recall gaining cinema entrance in exchange for things like eggs, potatoes, or packets of tea (generally donated by the cinema to local hospitals) and even rabbit skins.[3] Such payment in kind seems only to have been associated with the attendance of children at matinees and was not part of adult cinema-going.

A more important distinctive in the entry of children to cinemas, however, was that it was frequently illicit. The common practice of children gaining entry to A films with strangers (against BBFC and Home Office recommendations and local authority licensing regulations) has already been detailed in previous chapters. But in addition to this, different methods were used by children to get in to the pictures without paying, variously known as sneaking-, cadging-, bunking- or nicking-in. Thus, one child might buy a ticket and then admit their friends through the back door or toilet window. Ellen Casey, who grew up in Manchester in the 1930s, remembers an unusual variation on this strategy. Her local cinema was covered in corrugated iron and she recalls, 'kids used to run along it with sticks [and] somebody'd slip in' when the attendants came out to investigate.[4] Brigadier J.B. Ryall also used both sneaking-in and soliciting strangers as forms of cinema entry as a boy in London. He explains:

> Normally when we went to the Ionic [cinema] one of us would pay and then having been seated by the usherette would go to the toilet and open the emergency exit doors and let our friends in for free. At any of the cinemas if the films being shewn were 'A' or 'H' then you would wait for a man or couple to come along and say 'Please Mister, here's my money would you please buy me a ticket'.[5]

Thus, children had particular ways of gaining entry to the cinema, including payment in kind and a variety of illicit strategies; and even when they entered by conventional means, most still had to seek both permission and subsidy from adults before they could attend.

Inside the Cinema

The experiences of children within the cinema were also somewhat different from those of adults, particularly in that most characteristic form of children's cinema-going, the Saturday matinee. The atmosphere inside an auditorium during a 1930s children's matinee is often recalled by respondents in very vivid colour and detail, creating an overwhelming impression of noise and excitement, both before and during the screening of films. As Irene Letchet recalls, '*the noise was deafening*, because *everybody screamed* the whole time'.[6] Les Sutton has similar memories of his arrival at a matinee in Manchester. Note his use of the present tense, which animates his account:

> Soon we get to the door and push in the dimly-lit hall and it would appear all seats are taken. The noise is deafening, with shouts – screams from the girls – stamping, fighting here and there, children climbing over and crawling under seats, banging seats down, running up and down the aisles, with a ceaseless chatter going on among the less athletic patrons…We are separated and have to sit on the ends of different forms, but may have an opportunity to sit together later when the criminal element sneak to the dearer seats.[7]

Towards the end of this extract, Les refers to another practice common among children of limited funds, known as 'upping' – buying a ticket for a cheap seat and then moving to a more expensive one. As Irene Letchet recalls, 'it was only ninepence to get in…if you went and sat right in the front. Well if it wasn't too full you could keep nipping back a few rows, you see!'[8] Dickie Alexander also explains: 'We used to buy tickets for the cheap front seats and crawl up under the seats to the dearer back seats. If the usher caught you he would throw you out.'[9]

Before the show started, there were two other important aspects of cinema-going for children: food and comics. Many brought food with them, including oranges, nuts, sweets and sandwiches (which were often eaten on arrival), while others bought sweets and ices at the cinema itself. Of course, adults enjoyed eating at the cinema too, but cinema managers in the 1930s complained that children's matinees produced far more litter, due to the large amount of food consumed. In particular, many tried to phase out the eating of monkey nuts at matinees, as the shells clogged the vacuum cleaners.[10]

Meanwhile, magazines or comics might be read while waiting for the show to begin, sometimes back-copies, distributed by cinema managers to keep their audience relatively quiet and happy. One of

Mayer's respondents (in his 1945 sociological study of cinema-going) recalls her ritual on arrival at the cinema for first-house performances in the 1930s:

> We arrived promptly at 6.30 when the doors opened, and claimed our usual seats. Then, after taking off our coats and hats, we would bring out all kinds of sticky concoctions and chew noisily. When we had become acclimatised, we would read what we considered to be the very best literature – namely the *Wizard*, *Chips*, *Schoolgirls' Own* and *Film Fun*. The show started at 7.[11]

At matinees, once the show began, the noise level would quickly rise to a crescendo, reflecting and increasing excitement in the auditorium. Valentine Tucker attended Saturday matinees in Dagenham from 1934 and she recalls the atmosphere with some animation:

> We stamped our feet and whistled and clapped until our hands were sore and the building shook...they were silent films and it did not matter how much noise we made...We all shouted, 'Look be-ind yer!' when a baddie was creeping up on our hero, and in unison with the pounding of the horses hooves our enthusiastic feet slithered on discarded bread crusts and empty winkle shells, and paddled in pools deposited by those who had used the floor as a lavatory rather than miss out on any of the excitement.[12]

This account evokes the thrilling atmosphere and heightened emotional state often remembered in accounts of children's viewing in the 1930s. Interestingly, in Mayer's study, several respondents recalled having a more pronounced level of emotional involvement with films as children. One woman of 27 noted in 1945:

> I find it easier to control my emotions than in my younger days. I get a lump in my throat during a sad scene, but I can remember sobbing bitterly over a film when I was 10 years old. I also used to scream with laughter at the antics of such comedians as Laurel and Hardy.[13]

Another 20 year-old respondent in 1945 recalled the way in which her emotional responses to films had changed with age since the 1930s:

> My usual reaction to an exciting film was to clench my hands and dig my nails into the palms, I still do react that way but when I used to go the matinees and got excited I used to jump up and down in my seat and it wasn't an unusual thing to hear all the other children shouting out to their particular hero in the film that someone was coming up behind them in an exciting part of the serial.[14]

The physically and vocally expressive nature of children's viewing at matinees was different from that of adults, and it could create problems if it was not curbed when watching films in a generationally mixed environment. One of Mayer's respondents noted: 'my parents decided to take me to an adult show... with many warnings about being quiet and threats that I'd get a pasting if I wasn't'.[15] Meanwhile, another respondent recalled that when she saw *Trader Horn* (1931) in Leicester Square as a child, there was a clash of child and adult viewing practices:

> The first time I saw it, it made a shocking hole in my manners. The black men were swinging across the river on branches, whilst crocodiles snapped at their legs. As one of these men was taking off, I suddenly swung myself out of my seat into the lap of the person, an entire stranger, next to me. I held my feet as high as I could in the air, so as not to be bitten. Ye Gods, what a commotion.[16]

The most unruly behaviour for which matinees became known, however, tended to occur during the more 'boring' elements of the show (anything from educational films or newsreels to prolonged bouts of 'sloppy stuff'), which the audience chose not to watch. There are countless descriptions of unruly behaviour from respondents, including fighting within the cinema, using stink bombs, cap guns and knicker-elastic catapults, and children on balconies dropping missiles such as itching powder and even lighted matches onto the patrons below.[17]

One other form of illicit behaviour within the cinema was smoking (perfectly legitimate for adult patrons, of course) and this is generally remembered by male respondents as having been a communal activity.

Thomas McGoran, who went to the cinema in Glasgow as a child, explains:

> We used to smoke in the pictures. The ushers used to watch us about this, you know? You'd go into a wee shop...and you'd buy the cigarettes at a hapenny, and a match to go with it. Now, strictly speaking it was against the law for shopkeepers to sell children cigarettes but just as nowadays a lot of them did...You'd get into the pictures, you'd strike up your cigarette, you'd have a puff and you'd pass it on to your neighbour! *Everybody'd* have a puff of your cigarette! And if the usher came along, somebody'd say 'Here he's coming!' and it'd be stamped out on the floor. And some would smoke cinammon sticks!...And you could buy that for a hapenny in the shops. And it was a devil of a thing to start burning, but it did. You could smoke it. It tasted absolutely terrible![18]

The nature of children's film viewing in the 1930s was therefore quite distinctive, especially during matinee performances. Notably, there tended to be a high level of emotional involvement with the films, which was often expressed both physically and vocally. Moreover, children's cinema-going could frequently involve illicit activity, from sneaking in through a window, or with an adult stranger, to smoking or other types of unruly behaviour. It was this kind of activity that would come under the scrutiny of those introducing more orderly cinema clubs in the late 1930s.

After the Show

The particular ways in which film impacted on children's culture outside the auditorium included an influence of film on play, imitative behaviour (speech, dress, mannerisms and 'love-making') and the availability of various film-related toys and hobbies.[19] But the most immediate impact of the viewing experience was that many children felt and displayed an afterglow effect; a continuing emotional reaction to films, often expressed through re-enactments on the way home. Agnes Watson attended the cinema in Dalmuir and she recalls this important aspect of her relationship with films:

Cowboy films were…my favourite also adventure films and war films. When we left the cinema we were cowboys too as we galloped along holding imaginary reins and slapping our thighs to make the 'horses' go faster. Then we were the swashbuckling Zorro with our trench coats fastened at the neck only and the sleeves hanging loose, with our wooden sword and our 'cape'.[20]

Thomas McGoran tells a similar story:

When we came out of the cinemas if we'd seen a sort of a cowboy picture, we would all be galloping down the road!…And of course, if we'd seen a Boris Karloff film, you would walk down the road like this [mimes] like monsters! If we'd seen a musical picture, we would all be singing and dancing! But, this, this, THIS it caught the imagination of the kids! You know? That they actually were living the lives that they had seen on the screen just before.[21]

This kind of recollection was also common among Mayer's respondents. One young man remembered that after matinees he 'would organize a meeting at a secluded street corner where a clique of us reproduced certain thrilling scenes from the exciting cowboy and adventure plots just seen'.[22] Similarly, a young woman recalled that, at the age of about 4, 'it was a favourite game, after we came home from the picture house, to play at what we had just seen and we girls had to submit to being tied up, shot at and very thoroughly given a rough time'.[23]

After the initial excitement had worn off, cinema continued to affect children's play, inspiring role-playing games like Cops and Robbers, or Cowboys and Indians, or involving specific characters such as Tarzan or Robin Hood. One of Mayer's respondents recalled:

Mostly we went to see cowboy pictures and when the programme was ended we would dash up the road and betend we where cowboys. We would make masks and lots of other things. Robin Hood pictures.[24]

Similarly, Freddie Martin remembers watching *The Adventures of Robin Hood* in 1938, when he was about 6 years old. Afterwards, he and other local children played at Robin Hood, using 'timber slats' as swords, and 'bamboo canes for bows and arrows', in a tenement hallway, which he says 'became our Sherwood Forest'.[25] One other specific example of film-inspired play comes from Jim Dunsmore, who saw *M* (1931), aged 6. At the climax of this film, a child murderer is identified, chased and caught, when someone pats him on the back, having first chalked the letter M on their hand. Jim recalls: 'For some time after that lots of boys were stealing a piece of chalk at school and doing the same thing to their friends.'[26]

Mayer's respondents were specifically asked to comment on the ways in which films had influenced their play, and many confirmed that they had been very influential indeed.[27] One young woman recalled:

> Films affected our play very much. Our second favourite was a good Western film, with plenty of shooting, fighting and fast riding. After becoming thoroughly worked up about Buck Jones or Ken Maynard, we would enact these films, in versions all our own, after school each day the following week.[28]

Another remembered films inspiring her play with her male cousin:

> If we saw a Red Indian film we plagued our most generous uncle for money to buy bows and arrows. If we saw a gangster film we used to turn the old sofa into a barge and pretend we were sailing down a river with stolen property aboard. Now and again we would 'fight' the cushions, and throw them 'overbroard'![29]

There are many more examples. Some children played film charades, while others played Cowboys and Indians with 'horses' made from 'thick poles about 5 feet long with a piece of string tied at the top end for reins'.[30] Many forms of play were directly inspired by film in this way.

Another common form of cinema-related play, especially among girls, involved dressing up as film stars. Lucinda Allan remembers:

> We borrowed high heeled shoes from our mothers, evening dresses, hats, stoles, furs and make up. Rouge and red red lipstick, which we plastered on our faces. We were Hollywood actresses.[31]

Similarly, one of Mayer's respondents explained: 'we...dressed ourselves up in old evening dresses and high-heeled shoes and tried to copy the manner of our favourite film star [Jean Harlow]'.[32] Another recalled:

> One cousin...and I developed a craze for those musicals starring Dick Powell, Ruby Keeler and Ginger Rogers...We used to hum 'I'll string along with you', 'Honeymoon Hotel' and such, and execute what we fondly hoped to be intricate tap-dancing steps. We would dress up, I remember, and pretend to be glamourous lovelies with scores of good-looking admirers simply swooning at our feet if we so much as gave them a glance. (She was Ginger Rogers and I was Ruby Keeler). Of course it was rather awkward to prevent ourselves tripping over our evening dresses, but as they were only coats tied round our waists with the sleeves, it really didn't matter.[33]

Although film clearly had a huge impact on the games children played in the 1930s, of far more concern to those worried about the impact of cinema on children was the apparent influence of the medium on their day-to-day lives, as they imitated stars' conversation, speech, dress, mannerisms and, in particular, 'love-making'.

Cinema was the 'in' place to go, and became the main topic of conversation among children. So much so that such conversation was banned in some school rooms (as happened with the craze of Pokémon in the late 1990s). Slang such as 'OK' and 'youse guys' was lifted from gangster films and became widely used by children, as were the speech patterns of some other film characters. Angus Bruce from Leith explains: 'We were all quite fluent in "Tarzan Speak" since "Ungawa" covered about every contingency.'[34]

One of Mayer's respondents recalled that he 'imitated...American Slang from films with the "Dead End Kids"'.[35] Another explained how cinema-going affected her speech as a girl in the mid-1930s:

> New words crept into my vocabulary, and I remember clearly that my parents were quite shocked when I first used the word 'scram' before them! I liked to copy expressions used by my favourite actors, and use them often.[36]

The specific concern of watch-dogs and others in this regard was the Americanisation of children's speech by their acquisition of the vocabulary of American slang. Although there may have been little cause for real concern, many children did deliberately adopt this fashionable, new vernacular. One of Mayer's respondents remarked:

> I have been imbued with an intense admiration for America, and most things American. The films I have seen have increased this. Whilst at school, which I left when I was 16, I used as many American slang phrases as I could...Nowadays everyone uses American slang, but when I did it five years ago, it was quite a brave thing to do.[37]

In addition to speech, film characters' mannerisms were also freely imitated. Maurice de la Bertauche saw Charles Laughton in *Mutiny on the Bounty* (1935) when he was about 10 years old. He recalls 'stomping around school, scowling with hands clasped behind my back looking at boys I disliked saying: "Have him lashed Mr Christian!"'[38] Meanwhile, Vera Entwistle could do a mean Bette Davis:

> I was Bette Davis. I were Bette Davis, me, when I come home. My Dad used to say, 'Oh look! Her eyes have come out all organ stops...Put your eyes back, Bette!'[39]

Interestingly, one of the young men in Mayer's study also imitated Bette Davis:

> My particular screen idol is Bette Davies who is adept at mannerisms...I've often caught myself using her mode of speech during a conversation using clipped phrases and highly dramatic movements. Yes. I'm sure this actress has influenced my way of thinking and doing things in everyday life. I have seen most of her films four times over and when she is billed at a local cinema it's a certainty that's where I'll be found most evenings that week.[40]

Meanwhile, some children tried to dress like their favourite stars. Ivy Royal recalled that she and her friends tried to 'copy hairstyles, dress and mannerisms'.[41] Similarly, one of Mayer's respondents explained, 'I don't remember ever acting scenes from films, but I did try to copy mannerisms and expressions of popular stars at the time when I had just started work (16)'. She remembered 'making a copy of a dress worn by Janet Gaynor, for myself, when I was 18'.[42] Another of Mayer's respondents, who was 15 in 1930, noted with some amusement that she too had copied her favourite stars: 'I was often better dressed than before...and my hair looked more cared for and more attractively arranged...and what if I did try to look like Joan Crawford – I tried to look like Norma Shearer too – so it all balanced itself out.'[43]

Copying of film stars' dress and mannerisms, while especially popular with girls, was by no means limited to them, for boys also engaged in this kind of activity. Jim Godbold and his friend enjoyed the gangster films of the early 1930s, including *Little Caesar*, *Public Enemy* and *Scarface*, and he remembers:

> When we went to gangsters [my friend] would really come out, you know, he was aping the gangsters. He'd strike a match on the wall, and that...My friend and me, we bought a black shirt and a white tie because one of the gangsters had this.[44]

The film star most copied by girls in the 1930s, however, appears to have been teenaged musical actress Deanna Durbin.[45] Of course, the term 'teenager' had yet to be coined and, by and large, there were no specific fashions worn by young people, but Durbin apparently started something of a trend in this respect. Beatrice Cooper recalls:

> Deanna Durbin was one that I was keen on. Because...she was the same age as me and we both sang...As her films came out, I got the songs. And, em, sang them...and I *dressed* like her...I think a *lot* of kids if that age,...around 15, 16, eh, because there were no *fashions* for children of that age. No teenagers. You either dressed as a very small child, or you dressed as an adult – sophisticated clothes. You know, there were no teenage clothes at that time. And she brought a new fashion.[46]

One of Mayer's respondents also noted that when she was 13 (and Durbin was 14), she was influenced by Durbin's feature film debut, *Three Smart Girls* (1936):

> It was Deanna whom I have to thank for initiating me into my

first attempt at curling my hair, and breaking away from the previous straight school-girl bob. Of course, my Mother had to be consulted, but she agreed with me that if it was all right for Deanna, then it should be all right for me, so there I was with a centre parting, and curly hair! Another direct influence of films on my life.[47]

Another respondent remarked:

I have always taken a very keen interest in Deanna Durbin's films and I used to copy her hair styles and note the styles of her clothes, mine were never exactly the same but accessories were an easier matter and I nearly always took much more interest in Deanna's wardrobe than that of any other star.[48]

There is therefore ample evidence that some children were influenced in terms of their dress and mannerisms by things they saw at the cinema. More worrying for reformers, though, was the apparent influence of films on the sexual behaviour of young people.

One of the main ways in which film seems to have influenced children in terms of their sexuality involved infatuation with particular stars. Many adults were attracted to film stars too, of course, but for children these crushes were often their first experience of sexual attraction. As Irene Letchet recalls:

We all had...the magazines – the *Picturegoer* and all this sort of thing. And *read* these avidly. And collected postcards of your favourite stars...And under your desk lid, you had your favourite film star...pinned. ...Oh! That was the first sort of man [laughs] you fell in love with.[49]

Some of these attractions were mild and rather fickle, such as that of the respondent who admitted, 'when I was about 15 ...I fell in and out of love with practically the whole of Hollywood's manhood'.[50] Meanwhile, others were quite distressing. One respondent recalled that from the age of 13:

I was experiencing varied emotions as a result of picture-going...Passionate school-girl 'crushes' followed each other as new and handsome men made their appearances on the screen.

Many were the nights I cried myself to sleep because John Howard, Preston Foster or Robert Taylor was so far away.[51]

Similarly, another respondent remembered her first crushes on film stars in the late 1930s as being very painful indeed:

It was in my early teens that I first fell in love – and that was with Jan Kiepura, whom I had seen in *Tell Me Tonight*. Love? Infatuation you would say! And I suppose you are right. But it was heartbreakingly real to me. I was assured by adults that I would soon grow out of that phase. But no! All through my teens I continued falling in love, with one film star after another. And each time was sheer torture – a desperate longing to be made love to by them all...I sincerely hope that other youngsters don't go through such hell.[52]

In some cases, the crush could become something of an obsession. One of Mayer's male respondents recalled that from the age of 13 to the present (aged 18) he had been attracted to British actress Sally Gray. He had seen many of her films, but his devotion did not stop there:

Since then, I've accumulated files of cuttings and data about this one actress. I started a collection of stills from her films and put them in albums. I wrote to her and obtained an autographed photograph, which I had framed and hung on the wall of my bedroom where it still is. From my data I found her birthdate and sent her a birthday present, which she acknowledged, later I sent other and more valuable gifts, and at the time I decided to join up I was saving, to be able to send a gift for Xmas.[53]

Films could also impact adolescent sexuality in less conventional ways, as with one of Mayer's women respondents, who had a crush on Greta Garbo:

When I was 11 years old, I...had my first experience of what were known as 'pashes' or 'crushes' on various film stars. Everyone had a favourite, with Bing Crosby well in the lead...I had no particular favourite, until one night, I saw *Queen Christina*. From then on, I was a Garbo fan.[54]

Meanwhile, another respondent found film images a source of sexual/bondage fantasies from the age of 13:

> I...had no emotional reactions to a love scene...nor to any male hero. In fact the only emotion I remember feeling at this stage was when I saw a girl being badly treated by men. I remember vividly a scene in Laurel and Hardy's *The Bohemian Girl* [1936] where the gypsy girl was being dragged out to be whipped. She was stripped and lashed to a post. Of course, she was saved at the last minute. That scene stimulated me a great deal, & I would enact over & over again in the privacy of my own bedroom any scenes like that, with me playing the heroine, of course I usually altered it so that I was not saved so promptly. My saviour was never the film hero, but the particular boy in my class at school that my imagination had fastened on for the time being. This effect of being excited by a scene of a girl being badly treated went on for a long time, until I was 16, at least, I am sure. It gradually faded, but it can still be reactivated occasionally.[55]

The key area in which films influenced the sexual behaviour of young people, however, was in courting or 'love-making'. As one young woman noted in Mayer's study, 'films definitely *did* make me more receptive to love-making *and* I expected it to be a more experienced job than I would have done had I not seen – on the films – how love should be made!'[56] Again, some youngsters apparently followed Deanna Durbin in this regard. One respondent recalls taking tips from the film *First Love* (1939), when she was 14:

> When I first became interested in boys I enjoyed Deanna's first [screen] love affair with Robert Stack in...*First Love* and used to tell my 'boy-friend of the moment' to note the way Robert Stack held Deanna in his arms and kissed her. ...I've always noted little tricks (which I've put into practice) such as curling my boy-friend's hair in my fingers or stroking his face exactly as I've seen my screen favourites do in their love scenes, one of the first things I noticed was that an actress always closes her eyes when being kissed and I don't need to add that I copied that too.[57]

It is unsurprising that various organisations expressed concern regarding the impact of films on children's sexual behaviour, as this was apparently a genuine area of influence among teenagers. In particular, this helps explain the controversy surrounding pre-code 'sex pictures', which were widely available to many young people (see Chapter 3).

Together with play and imitation, the other key way that films impacted on children's culture outside the cinema was through a range of consumable and collectible items and film-related hobbies. Film merchandising was already underway in the 1930s, and many film-related toys were available. Both Margaret Young and Joanna Matthews remember having paper Shirley Temple dolls with an assortment of paper clothes.[58] Joanna Matthews also recalls that after enjoying *Snow White and the Seven Dwarfs* (1937), she and her sister obtained a music-box Snow White doll and 'almost all of the seven dwarfs...made of felt'.[59] Other toys included miniature viewers and off-cut pieces of real film, depicting favourite stars.

Meanwhile, film magazines were massively popular, particularly with girls, who would regularly read British and sometimes American publications, including *Picturegoer, Film Weekly, Picture Show, Film Pictorial, Photoplay, Movie Magazine* and *Screenland*. Once read and perhaps exchanged, magazine contents were then glued into scrapbooks, used as pin-ups in children's bedrooms, or stuck inside their school desks to be secretly adored.[60] Although some boys read and collected film magazines, they were clearly targeted at girls. For example, *Film Pictorial* was packed with advertising for cosmetics and other gendered products, and it also included romantic fiction, woman-to-woman-style interviews with actresses, and articles with titles such as 'Beauty Tips From the Beautiful'.[61]

The popularity of scrapbooks is very evident in Mayer's study, which shows that this was not merely a private activity. One respondent explained, 'every picture of stars or film extracts etc. we used to cut out and paste in a large scrap book to show our friends'.[62] Film diaries were also kept, as young people maintained a record of the films that they had seen.[63]

Where girls might read film magazines, boys often collected film-related cigarette cards, which had film stills or stars' photographs on one side and information about them on the reverse.[64] Children would pester adult smokers to obtain these cards and would then collect and swap them, as well as gamble for them in a variety of pitch and toss games.

In addition, children could buy birthday cards depicting their favourite stars and film postcards, which were highly collectible. Related hobbies for those who were particularly keen included joining film postcard collectors' clubs, or writing to stars for photographs and autographs, which were available from addresses listed in film magazines.[65] This was a highly interactive activity, in which children related in both co-operative and competitive ways and it could be quite expensive and time-consuming, as is apparent in this example from Mayer's study:

> When I was 13 [in 1938]...I was visiting the movies quite often...& very soon I had 'favourite stars'. The next step, of course, was that I wanted pictures of these stars, so I started taking *Picture Show*. Not content with the slow rate at which my collection was growing, I soon started taking *Picture Goer*, *Film Pictorial*, and *Film Weekly* every week, out of pocket-money given to me by an indulgent granny, who would keep me with any hobby...Very soon I was buying American film books (which I infinitely preferred...) & had a number of pen-friends, all over the world, with whom to exchange film pictures. I got an album, & stuck my best pictures in it. This filled up, & I got another – and another, – etc.[66]

Film musicals particularly seem to have captured children's imaginations in terms of related hobbies and pastimes. One of Mayer's respondents recalls designing dresses, after having seen *Gold-Diggers of Broadway* (1929). 'For weeks afterwards I sketched designs for dresses, all over my books', she wrote, 'and nothing suits me better after seeing a good musical, than to knock off a few sketches of the various dresses or costumes worn and to improve and alter them to suit my own taste.'[67] Meanwhile, other children were inspired to collect sheet music or sing numbers from their favourite musicals, as already described in the case of Deanna Durbin fans. Another respondent recalled:

> A new interest presented itself...in the form of the early musicals...I was taking piano-playing lessons myself, just then,

and the effect of these musical films with their catchy
tunes...caused me to be very discontented with my Daisy
Waltzes etc., that I was learning to play. My mother...promised
me that if I should practise very hard...she would buy me some
music from the films. I now have about 2,000 copies of songs.[68]

Dancing also took off as a result of 1930s musicals, particularly among
adults. For children too young to go to dance halls, this meant using
alternative venues. One respondent recalled how she and some friends
learned to dance when she was 11:

We saw Fred Astaire and Ginger Rogers in *Flying Down to Rio*
and that brought on a dancing craze. We saw every
Rogers–Astaire film...and during lunch-hour breaks at school,
the changing room rang with the strains of the 'Carioca' etc. I
learned to dance and became very proficient.[69]

Overall, there is a wealth of evidence suggesting that cinema-going
influenced children's lives in a number of ways, resulting in what
became a distinctive children's cinema culture. Young people often
required permission and subsidy to attend the cinema and they gained
entry by various illicit methods not generally used by adults,
including asking strangers to buy them tickets, sneaking in without
paying and shifting to dearer seats. They could also sometimes gain
entry by means not available to adults, including paying for matinee
tickets with jam jars or other goods. Once inside the cinema, the
viewing experiences of children were also quite different from those
of adult film-goers, especially during matinee performances, which
were characterised by loud noise, vocal and physical interaction with
film images and a great deal of unruly behaviour. The viewing
experiences of children appear to have been more intense than those
of adults, as evidenced in their emotional responses to films and the
devastating crushes some children had on film stars. And children's
cinema culture also involved a range of activities outside the
auditorium, as films influenced their play, hobbies, speech, dress,
mannerisms and behaviour. The scope of this influence is
demonstrated in one respondent's account of her reaction to Deanna
Durbin's films as a child:

She fairly caught my imagination. She became my first & only screen idol. I collected pictures of her, & articles about her & spent hours sticking them in scrapbooks. I would pay any price within the range of my pocket money for a book, if it had a new picture, however tiny, of her in it. I adored her & my adoration influenced my life a great deal. I wanted to be as much like her as possible, both in my manners & clothes. Whenever I was to get a new dress, I would...ask for a dress like she was wearing. I did my hair as much like her as I could manage. If I found myself in any annoying or aggravating situation, which I previously dealt with by an outburst of temper, I found myself wondering what Deanna would do, & modified my own reactions accordingly. She had far more influence on me than any amount of lectures or rows from parents would have had. I went to all her films, & as often as I could, too...I bought all the records she made & played them over & over again.[70]

It is important to reiterate that adults were also influenced by cinema-going in some of the ways described, but it was the combination of aspects in children's cinema culture that was distinctive – not least the fact that this was a generational group culture, with cinema being a focal point around which children interacted. As one respondent recalled:

It was a recognised thing for all the children I played with to go to the pictures often. They knew the names of all the film stars & their latest films. They went whenever they could get anybody to take them, & they always went together to a children's matinee on a Saturday afternoon.[71]

From Matinees to Cinema Clubs

Having looked at the distinctive nature of children's matinees earlier in this chapter, it is important to recognise and outline the evolution in this type of viewing during the 1930s. Children's matinees had been a feature of cinema-going from at least the turn of the century, enabling managers to cram the auditorium with youngsters during the day on Saturdays, so as to free up the evening performance for adults paying

4. Children outside the Glen Cinema, Paisley, some months before the disaster.
From the 1929 promotional film *Paisley Children's Happy Hunting Ground*
(Old Paisley Society Collection at Scottish Screen Archive).

full price. The content and environment of matinees were of some
concern to various groups during the early decades of cinema, but to
little effect.[72] However, in Britain, one event more than any other
caused people to sit up and take notice, resulting in the more stringent
regulation and organisation of matinee shows from the 1930s
onwards.

On the afternoon of 31 December 1929 there was a matinee show
at the Glen Cinema, Paisley.[73] As with many matinees all over the
country, this was something of a free-for-all, with probably well over
700 children, including toddlers, crammed into an auditorium that
seated about 600 adults. They were watching a western, *Desperado
Dude*, when smoke started coming through the auditorium doors. In
fact, the fumes were from a smouldering film in a tin box, which was
about to be kicked out of the building. But there was a fair amount of
smoke and the children started to panic. The level of supervision in the
auditorium was minimal (one male attendant and a girl selling
chocolate) and they were unable to handle the ensuing stampede.

Because the smoke was emanating from the entrance hall, many children rushed for exits by the stage, which led down a short flight of steps to double doors and then outside. The tragedy began when these stiff double doors were pushed apart and the children in front found not freedom, but an immovable steel gate. In the inevitable crush that followed, 70 children were killed and between 30 and 40 were badly injured. As the *Daily Mail* reported the next day, 'most of the dead children were under 10 years of age, while some were only babies' and some families had lost two or three children.[74]

James Porter was 10 years old when he survived the Paisley disaster. He recalled his memories of that day in an interview for the Scottish Film Archive:

> When the panic started, I got out as quickly as I could, through the front. I saw them filling the trams with children to take them to the hospital. There were 16 children living in my street, and all of them were at the Glen that day. They all died, except me. It was a disaster that need never have happened.[75]

Charles Dorward, the Glen's manager, was charged with culpable homicide. In court he claimed that the gate was unlocked that afternoon, but he admitted that it was often locked during matinees, to stop children sneaking in without paying.[76] He was eventually found Not Guilty, but the Glen was never used as a cinema again.

The Paisley disaster was clearly a shocking, tragic event and its impact on matinee performances in Britain was widespread.[77] The enquiry that followed cited a number of contributory factors, including lack of supervision, avoidance of regulations regarding the number of children present and even the influence of the film being shown.[78] The official report explained:

> While it is impossible to say that attendants in proper numbers would have been able to prevent the panic altogether, it is fair to argue that the rush of children might have been...prevented from developing into the mad rush which occurred...A very exciting film was being shown and excitement would lead to children getting out of hand more easily, and this in itself points to the very great necessity of having an adequate number of attendants present as is required by the regulations.[79]

Immediately after the trial and the publication of the report, the Home Office amended the Cinematograph Act of 1909 to include the phrase:

> Where at any exhibition the majority of the persons attending are under 14 years of age the number of attendants required... shall be such as to enable them effectively to control the movements of the children whilst entering and leaving the premises and to ensure the orderly and safe clearance of the hall in case of emergency.[80]

The Paisley disaster raised the profile of issues relating to children's viewing, motivating a number of local surveys, including those detailed in Chapter 4. Among the first was an enquiry conducted in November and December of 1930 by the Sheffield Juvenile Organisations Committee, which focused specifically on children's matinees in the city.[81] All the Sheffield cinemas that held special matinees or had a majority of children in the audience on a Saturday afternoon were visited: 21 venues in all. The audiences ranged in size from 200 to 1,100 and included children aged mainly between 5 and 14 years old.

Among the priorities of the survey was an assessment of the level of supervision at the matinee performances, but in the wake of the Paisley disaster most cinemas appeared to have addressed this issue. The report noted that generally 'several attendants were on duty... five or six being the usual number', although in one case 'only one male attendant appeared to be present... in addition to girls selling chocolates'.[82] However, the amount of control exercised by these attendants varied widely, from those successfully leading community singing, to 'cases, usually where dull programmes were being shown, [when] a good deal of threatening and shouting had to be employed in order to get tolerable order. In one case the lights were turned up and in another case the film was stopped before lively disturbances among the youthful audience could be quietened.'[83] One unpublished visitor's comment noted: 'Children bored and very noisy throughout the performance. Several fights in the audience.'[84]

Being relatively happy with levels of supervision, the Sheffield survey turned its attention to the types of films being shown at matinees, as these were thought to cause problems of unruly behaviour due to boredom. Concern was expressed about the fact that

5. Sisters Jessie and Edith Anderson escaped from the Glen on the day of the disaster. Jessie is pictured here, centre frame, smiling, with Edith to her left, wearing a beret with a badge on it. From the 1929 promotional film *Paisley Children's Happy Hunting Ground* (Old Paisley Society Collection at Scottish Screen Archive).

6. Hugh Blew, who died in the Glen disaster, is pictured here in profile in the centre foreground, looking left, behind boy with school cap on. From the 1929 promotional film *Paisley Children's Happy Hunting Ground* (Old Paisley Society Collection at Scottish Screen Archive).

nearly all cinemas showed 'the same programme...as was shown the previous evening' (to predominantly adult audiences) and only three of the 21 matinees visited were 'unreservedly praised for being children's performances'.[85] Meanwhile, four others showed films 'reported as being actively harmful for children, depicting night-club and "underworld" life'.[86]

Consequently, the report concluded, 'although the arrangements made for the supervision of the children at cinema matinees in Sheffield are on the whole satisfactory, the quality of the entertainment provided leaves much to be desired'.[87] It recommended that more attention should be given to 'increasing the number of films made suitable for children's performances' and making these 'more readily and cheaply available' to cinemas.[88]

The issues identified in Sheffield were relatively minor when compared to the matinee programmes on offer in Scotland's cinemas at this time. As A certificates were not enforced in Scotland, children could attend any films, regardless of their certificate, whether they were accompanied or not. While this did not represent a vast difference in real terms from the English child's experience (as circumventing A film regulations was commonplace), the situation appeared more dangerous in Scotland, as there were no regulations in place, no matter how ineffectual these may have been. As a result, an intensive investigation took place between January and March 1935, when 211 investigators visited 101 cinemas in 14 Scottish towns in order to assess the nature of children's cinema-going there. They reported:

> Almost all towns confirm the fact that specially advertised matinees for children...are not common. The general practice in Scottish towns is to admit children, accompanied or unaccompanied, at reduced rates in the afternoon and early evening (in some areas, particularly on Saturdays) and to show at these hours, the same programme as for the evening, irrespective of whether the films are 'A' or 'U', with, perhaps, the additional attraction, at the afternoon performance, of an instalment of a serial adventure story, or a cowboy film.[89]

Films being shown at Scottish children's matinees included not only large numbers of questionable A films, such as *The Story of Temple*

7. Unaccompanied children regularly watched A films at matinees in Scotland.
Here an orderly queue awaits entry to the Playhouse Cinema, Inverness.
From *Treasure Island* (1935), a silent promotional film for the Playhouse
(Scottish Screen Archive).

Drake (1933) and *Tarzan and His Mate* (1934), but also 'Horrifics',
including *The Ninth Guest* (1934) and films with suggestive titles,
such as *Cupid in the Rough* and *Love, Honor and Oh, Baby!*.
    Specific anxiety about the programmes at children's matinees,
fuelled by evidence from various studies such as those already
mentioned, led to an interesting shift of focus among reformers during
the 1930s. Essentially, those concerned about matinees gradually
stopped denouncing films that children should *not* see, as it became
clear that these would not go away. Instead, discussion started to
revolve around what children *should* see. Suggested alternatives
included setting aside whole cinemas for children and a campaign grew
up that called for more films to be made specifically for the young
audience. Key events in this regard included conferences run by the
BFI, the Public Morality Council and the Cinema Christian Council
in 1936.[90] Although feature films for children were not made in Britain
until the 1940s, children's productions were a familiar concept, for

Children's Hour provided 'radio for children' every weekday at 5 p.m. from 23 December 1922 (just eight days after the BBC Ltd was first registered).[91]

By the mid-1930s, therefore, the debate was becoming increasingly productive as well as prohibitive in nature, and perhaps the most important change in this regard was a gradual move away from raucous matinees towards orderly, wholesome children's cinema clubs.[92]

The earliest systematic attempt to introduce this kind of 'clean, healthy, entertainment' in Britain was that of Sidney Bernstein in 1928, who started running non-profit-making shows for children in his Granada cinema chain. However, while initially successful, the scheme folded a year later because so few children were coming along. Bernstein blamed lack of co-operation from local schools, but the real problem was that children preferred the exciting programmes on offer at other cinemas, rather than sitting through films chosen with children in mind, such as nature documentaries or a two-hour silent version of *Peter Pan* (1924). Other worthy attempts followed Bernstein's lead, but all ran aground, as young patrons wanted gangsters and monsters, not literary adaptations and educational films.

In America, meanwhile, a viable alternative emerged at the end of the 1920s, when Disney and the National Committee for Better Films joined forces to create Mickey Mouse Clubs. These clubs provided an attractive matinee programme, always including Disney cartoons, a serial episode and a carefully selected feature film. But the key difference, which would influence children's matinees both in America and Britain, was the introduction of various rituals and elements aimed at shaping the character of young cinema-goers and improving the reputation of the cinema itself. These included community singing, saluting the American flag and memorising a club motto:

> I will be a square-shooter in my home, in school, on the playgrounds, or wherever I may be. I will be truthful and honorable and strive always to make myself a better and more useful little citizen. I will respect my elders, help the aged, the helpless and children smaller than myself. In short, I will be a good American.[93]

The Mickey Mouse Club idea soon spread to Britain, where the first club started in 1934 at the Odeon cinema, Worthing. Here, the manager wrote a special song for club members to sing each week, which emulated the American club's motto, encouraging patriotism, good behaviour and impeccable morals, while also promoting loyalty to Odeon cinemas:

> Every Saturday morning, where do we go?
> Getting into mischief? Oh dear, no!
> To the Mickey Mouse Club with our badges on,
> Every Saturday morning at the O – DE – ON!
>
> Play the game, be honest, and every day
> Do our best at home, at school, at play;
> Love of King and Country will always be our song,
> Loyalty is taught us at the O – DE – ON![94]

An Odeon Area Manager was impressed by the Worthing club and the idea was quickly introduced at other cinemas in the Odeon circuit, as well as at some non-Odeon cinemas. Soon after, cinema clubs were organised by many other cinemas across the country, gradually replacing the relatively riotous matinee with its more orderly alternative.

By 1939, most circuits had created new cinema clubs of their own: Mickey Mouse Clubs on the Odeon circuit; Grenadier Clubs at Granada; Chums Clubs on the Union circuit (before it was absorbed by ABC in 1937, which then began ABC Minors Clubs); and Shirley Temple or Pop-Eye Clubs in some Gaumont British cinemas.[95] There were also various individual children's clubs running along similar lines in independent cinemas.

The clubs all boasted the provision of 'suitable' films along with competitions, community singing and other activities, including collections for charity and talks on subjects such as road safety. They were generally well-staffed by numerous adult supervisors and 'responsible' older children, who sometimes formed a committee to help run the club. Using memorised mottos, club songs, badges, rules and codes of conduct, they encouraged children to conform, to behave well and to act as caring and responsible citizens, making it clear to both parents and reformers that the image of children's matinees had changed for good.[96] This philosophy was embodied in the two new verses that were added to the Mickey Mouse Club song in 1937:

Before we cross a busy road, we know it pays
To think of motor cars and look both ways;
If a car's approaching we wait until it's gone,
Safety first they teach us at the O – DE – ON!

For the poor and needy, a gift we'll always share
For other people's troubles have a care.
To the sick and suffering our sympathies belong,
We're taught to think of others at the O – DE – ON![97]

Although children's cinema clubs became increasingly widespread by the end of the 1930s, the less refined children's matinee did persist in some places. John Ford, who attended the tuppenny rush at a Watford flea-pit, known as the Coliseum, remembers the transition that took place after about 1936:

The Gaumont and Odeon cinema chains started their own (sixpenny) children's Saturday morning matinee clubs complete with Uncles and Aunties together with opportunities to do 'good deeds' like saving silver paper for hospitals. The films were sanitised … especially for children, allegedly to counteract the pernicious anti-social content of the more robust fare offered by the Coliseum, which, I regret to say, continued to hold the allegiance of myself and a good many others.[98]

The transition from matinee to children's cinema club was not always smooth and children did not always comply. In particular, cinema managers running the clubs could have a hard time controlling their young audiences. Noise (especially) and subversive behaviour continued, as one manager found when he used a public address system, in order to be heard above the din. He explained:

The very first time I used the newly installed microphone, I opened out with 'Good Morning, Mickeys and Minnies, and how are you to-day?' A boy in the front immediately replied, 'Lousy'.[99]

8. Members of Sidcup Mickey Mouse Club after a performance. (Reproduced in Richard Ford, *Children in the Cinema*, London: Allen & Unwin, 1939.)

Children as Cinema Proprietors and Managers

Finally, in trying to gain a comprehensive view of children's interactions with cinema, it is worth mentioning the fascinating but little-known evidence of children who ran their own cinemas in the 1930s and created all sorts of problems for the authorities. Two examples are detailed below, but this enterprising appropriation of cinema by children for their own ends would certainly benefit from further research.

The Farley Place Kinema, Ramsgate was run by Eddie Oliver between 1931 and 1934 (from the ages of 10 to 13 years). In a letter to the Home Office in 1932, Mr Butler, the Chief Constable for Ramsgate, explained that 11-year-old Oliver had for some time been charging one penny for entrance to film shows in the tiny basement of his parents' shop, twice nightly and on Saturday afternoons.[100] When police made an inspection in August 1932 they found Oliver in sole charge of 49 children aged 3 to 11 years, crammed onto closely-packed benches, in a room measuring 12 ft 4 in by 13 ft 11 in. Electricity cables ran erratically across the room and the projector was attached by a wire to the room's light fitting.

Numerous police inspectors, the Chief Fire Officer, the Chief Constable and the Public Health Department all failed to stop the shows with gentle persuasion. Official routes also proved fruitless. Oliver used no music (so did not require a Music and Dancing Licence) and non-flammable film (so did not require a Cinematograph Licence either). Nor could the police invoke the Children and Young Persons Act of 1933 when it was passed, because although there were as many as 70 children in the basement cinema at any one time, this Act only applied to groups of over 100 children.

Oliver publicised his business with professionally produced handbills and custom printed balloons, which he gave away at performances.[101] His one-hour shows included films such as Charlie Chaplin's *Easy Street* (1917) and popular characters, including Felix the Cat and Rin-Tin-Tin.[102] Inspectors described the small room with one exit and one narrow gangway as a 'death-trap'. They visited the premises every weekend for 18 months, taking cuttings of films being shown for testing, but all were found to be non-flammable.

Eventually, the police stopped the shows by invoking a special clause of the Public Health Act 1890. But 13-year-old Oliver was

Wednesday, January 3, 1934

BOY OF 13 TO RUN PENNY CINEMA AGAIN

He Wants to Get Hall Approved for Shows

16,000 CHILDREN SAW HIS UNDERGROUND FILMS

Eddie Oliver, the thirteen-year-old Ramsgate boy whose underground penny cinema led to his mother being fined, is undaunted by the ban on his enterprise.

"Although my cinema has been closed down," he said yesterday, "I shall start again as soon as I find a hall which is approved by the local authorities. Ever so many people have congratulated me on my shows."

Eddie's mother was summoned at Ramsgate on Monday for contravening the Public Health Act by permitting the shows. A police officer stated that he found seventy children watching the show, which was held in a room, 12 feet by 13 feet, that had only one exit and one gangway. The room was described as a "death-trap."

His Great Ambition

Eddie told a reporter that all his life his ambition had been to become an operator at a big cinema.

"I really started five years ago," he added, "when I bought a magic lantern and gave shows in my bedroom in front of a few friends.

"Then I sold my magic lantern and some of my other toys, including a gramophone which I had won. With the money I bought a small, second-hand projector and started to give shows three years ago.

"More and more children came to see the shows, and 'Eddie Oliver's Penny Pictures' became a regular attraction among the children in the evenings and on Saturday afternoon.

"Every night I used to turn the handle of my projector for two hours."

Takes His Own Films

"Then I started saving up to buy a motor. Eventually I was able to take up to 300 feet of film, and obtained a new projector. I now have two projectors.

"I saved up every penny and bought my own camera, which has enabled me to take pictures of local events and show them.

"Since I started, more than 16,000 children and a number of adults have paid to see my shows. I have bought many films, as well as those which I took myself.

"Once, when a local cinema was showing a silent film and it broke down, the operator ran to my house and asked me to mend it, as they had no cement."

Eddie Oliver, the enterprising thirteen - year - old Ramsgate boy, with his cinema apparatus.

9.   Media attention for young Ramsgate cinema entrepreneur Eddie Oliver in the *Daily Mirror*, 3 January 1934.

undaunted. Thanks to press coverage, he was presented with a new talkie projector worth £135 during a visit to Gaumont British Studios and he vowed to find suitable premises to establish a much bigger cinema business in the near future.[103] Importantly, the Farley Place Kinema was not an isolated case. Chief Constable Butler wrote that he knew of two similar cinemas in Ramsgate alone, plus many more across the country.[104]

A second interesting example is that of 13-year-old Alfred Warminger from Norwich, who set up a cinema for children in a converted woodshed behind the Globe Inn (where his father was the publican) in 1934. Warminger used non-flammable films just as Oliver did. He had an audience of 150 children and a few adults on his first night and made a profit of £70 in eight months of trading. At 14 years old he left school and, in addition to running his original venue, he established the new 350-seat Enterprise Cinema in Norwich, with financial backing from his father.[105]

Conclusion

Although historians have tended to portray the cinema audience as a relatively unified entity (split only by class or gender), the evidence provided in this chapter strongly suggests that in interwar Britain, children established and fostered their own, somewhat subversive, cinema culture, involving activities and rituals both inside and outside the cinema.

Miriam Hansen and Judith Mayne have both suggested that the cinema was used by groups such as women, immigrants and gay and lesbian viewers, as an 'alternative public sphere' – a place where they could indulge more freely in voyeurism and active spectatorship than they could in other environments.[106] In the same way, I would argue that during a period when home, school and even leisure activities (such as uniformed youth movements) were strong on discipline, the cinema was colonised by children as an alternative public sphere, which offered liberating escapism through films and a warm, dark, virtually adult-free environment for engaging in 'wild' and subversive behaviour.

By using illicit or conventional means of entry and by establishing rituals for matinee viewing, children were able to assert a sense of ownership and control over a public space – the cinema – which was unavailable to them elsewhere. And the consequent popularity of this cultural form can easily be demonstrated, not only in the numbers of children going to the cinema, but also in the many ways in which they allowed film to penetrate and permeate their lives.

The popularity of children's cinema-going, the influence of films, the sense of autonomy among children and the unruly behaviour associated with matinees all represented a direct threat to the virtual monopoly of established youth organisations and other 'healthy' pastimes, as is evident in the comments of one of Mayer's respondents:

> I have become so interested in films, that my ordinary life has completely changed. For instance, before going to the films I would go as often as 6 times a week to the Young Men's Christian Association (I joined at the age of 14), each Sunday I went cycling with my pals, and occasionally went for walks. This has all stopped with a terrific Halt. No longer do I go 6 times a week to the club, or each Sunday go cycling and walking. Sunday evening means pictures to me.[107]

It is therefore unsurprising, given the impact of cinema on children's culture, that real concern was expressed by some adults, especially those from groups traditionally associated with the socialisation of the young, including women's organisations, schools, churches and youth movements.

As a result, over the 1930s, children's cinema culture came under increasing scrutiny and surveillance, culminating in attempts at cultural control, including the establishment of new cinema clubs. Debates surrounding young people and cinema-going gradually became more productive and less prohibitive in nature – no longer simply denouncing the medium, but suggesting and producing alternative modes of viewing for children. From this point, organised clubs, 'suitable' films and separate cinemas for children increasingly became a means of defining and regulating the body of the child film-goer, attempting to dissociate the child viewer from 'adult' films and providing them instead with a sanitised cinema-going experience of approved films within a controlled environment.

7

Children and Cinema: Control and Resistance

Everybody is talking about the movies, about what is wrong with them, what is right with them; whether they are moral or immoral. There are many who say they are the one and just as many who say they are the other, and in between there are those who say they are both and those who say they are neither...

Alice Miller Mitchell, *Children and Movies* (Chicago, 1929)

Fears about the social effects of new media have recurred for over two centuries and the debates they generate nearly always revolve primarily around the potential impact of these new media on children. Despite thousands of research projects, conferences and other enquiries (most of which find the medium in question to be intrinsically benign), such debates persist today, with recent controversies surrounding children's use of mobile phones, computer games and the Internet. Whenever a shocking incident occurs involving young people, the immediate reaction is often to blame the latest forms of popular culture, however tenuous this link might be – as in the bogus scapegoating of *Child's Play 3* in the James Bulger murder case, or neo-Nazi websites, television, film and the music of 'shock rocker' Marilyn Manson after the Columbine High School Massacre.[1]

In his 2001 article 'Reservoirs of Dogma: An Archaeology of Popular Anxieties', Graham Murdock called for more detailed historical research into these fears and their associated debates:

> If we are to develop a more comprehensive analysis of the interplay between popular media and everyday thinking, feeling and behaviour, and to argue convincingly for expressive diversity in film, television and the new media, we need to challenge popular fears. Retracing the intellectual and political history that has formed them is a necessary first step.[2]

This book has sought to retrace some of that history, to contribute to academic understanding of the nature and impact of recurring debates surrounding children and media usage by exploring one key example – the controversy surrounding children and cinema in the 1930s – from a number of different perspectives. A wide range of evidence and approaches from a number of disciplines have been utilised to examine the ways in which children in 1930s Britain interacted with attempts to control their viewing. And the issue has been approached from numerous points of view, including those of moral watch-dogs, enquiry committees, the Home Office, the press, censorship boards, local authorities, cinema managers, film-makers and children themselves, in order to consider not only what happened, but how and why it happened.

In particular, the focus has been on mechanisms used to try to control or contain children's viewing, along with an assessment of the extent to which these mechanisms were successful. This aspect of the 1930s debate has important ramifications for all debates surrounding children and popular culture. For, despite the attempts of the BBFC and others to limit the access of young people to films, many children were essentially the regulators of their own viewing in the 1930s, as they frequently subverted or circumvented the largely ineffectual mechanisms of official cinema regulation. This supports evidence from other research which suggests that while regulations aimed at limiting children's access to new media may create a false sense of control that allays certain fears, in reality children frequently evade such attempts at regulation.

One question has emerged that might be applied to all kinds of debates about young people and popular culture: were those who called for increased regulation and changes to film production in the 1930s aiming to protect children, or to control them? As has been shown, the arena of cinema was often one of complex power-play between children and a range of adults, including parents, reformers, censors, film-makers, politicians and the press. David Buckingham has identified similar power-play in debates about children and television and he argues that 'television viewing is merely part of the broader struggle for power and control between parents and children'.[3] Similarly, concern expressed about children's cinema-going often seems to have been less about film images than it was about a perceived loss of control over the culture and behaviour of children. The anxiety expressed in the 1930s by teachers, parents, churches and youth organisations therefore reinforces the suggestion made by Bazalgette and Buckingham that, in debates about children and new entertainment media, 'the threat which has been posed by each successive technological development...has derived from the fact that they seem to offer less and less control for adults'.[4]

One of the other main issues at the heart of this book has been the question of whether or not the controversy surrounding children's cinema-going in 1930s Britain constituted a moral panic. Certainly, there was a great deal of debate which had a fundamental influence on the development of cinema regulation and censorship in Britain and elsewhere, but this was not a moral panic in the classic sense, for a number of reasons. First, the reaction of various bodies to the medium of cinema in the 1930s was neither sudden nor rapid, for the subject had already been discussed for over three decades by 1930. Second, the reaction was not wholly hostile. Issues were often discussed in a complex, thoughtful manner, displaying a range of agenda, different methodologies and rhetorical strategies and reaching very different (often positive) conclusions. Meanwhile, the key establishments of church, education and the media were by no means uniformly opposed to children's cinema-going; they displayed a great deal of ambivalence and difference of opinion as to the medium's potential and any possible threat it might pose. Finally, the reactions that emerged were neither groundless nor irrational, for there was apparently genuine cause for concern.

Cinema was the first mass medium to be distributed simultaneously to audiences of millions and by the 1930s, with the advent of talking films, it experienced massive growth and huge popularity with young people (the first generation to be fundamentally influenced by so-called mass culture). Before the Hays Code was applied in 1934, significant numbers of films explored taboo subjects on the edges of conventional morality and existing regulations proved ineffective at restricting the access of children to such material. Furthermore, cinema posed a potential challenge to the influences of home, school, church and youth group; it spawned a distinct children's cinema culture involving alternative role models, an ambiguous moral code, a new learning environment and a largely unregulated arena of play. So it is hardly surprising that parental, religious, educational and youth organisations should have considered it a potentially dangerous phenomenon. Ultimately, therefore, the controversy surrounding children and the cinema in 1930s Britain was too gradual, complex and varied to be described as a classic moral panic.

Nevertheless, the consequences of debates about young people's viewing in the 1930s were substantial and these may be split into two overlapping categories: restrictive and productive. Restrictive consequences included the growth of official film censorship and cinema regulation practices in Britain. It was concern regarding the impact of the medium on children that drove the development of censorship in Britain (and elsewhere) before 1930 and, after the coming of talkies, further concern led to the creation of new restrictions, such as 'horrific' labels and H certificates, all of which were introduced with children in mind.

Meanwhile, productive consequences of the debate were numerous. In particular, the 1930s saw the introduction of organised, supervised children's cinema clubs, which aimed to replace the more raucous, largely unsupervised matinees that were seen as a central problem. Other creative ideas aimed at solving the 'problem' of children's cinema-going included the establishment of special children's cinemas and the promotion of films made specifically for young audiences. In Britain, this culminated in the production of films specifically for children from 1943 and, from 1951, the creation of a new, pan-industry production agency known as the Children's Film Foundation, which took on the task of making 'suitable' films for children in Britain for the next 30 years.[5]

But this was not the end of the debate about children and screen images, as it would re-emerge even more strongly from the 1950s and 1960s, when high levels of screen sex and violence and the advent of

10. A Saturday matinee queue in Plaistow, east London, 1937 (British Film
    Institute).

television and video gave children greater access to 'unsuitable'
material than ever before. Subsequently, controversies about all kinds
of new media have followed in quick succession, with recent targets
including playground text-messaging and Internet chatrooms.[6]

It therefore seems inevitable that when popular new entertainment
media, such as virtual reality, emerge in the future, the primary
concern will continue to focus, as it did in the 1930s, on the impact of
these new technologies on children. Some will target each new form as
a scapegoat for apparent increases in juvenile delinquency and some
will argue that the new media technology poses a direct threat to
children and, therefore, society. Given the inevitability of this debate,
one key question remains: is such concern motivated by a desire to
protect children, or to control them?

Appendix 1

T.P. O'Connor's 43 Rules of the BBFC

1. Indecorous, ambiguous and irreverent titles and sub-titles.
2. Cruelty to animals.
3. The irreverent treatment of sacred subjects.
4. Drunken scenes carried to excess.
5. Vulgar accessories in the staging.
6. The *modus operandi* of criminals.
7. Cruelty to young infants and excessive cruelty and torture to adults, especially women.
8. Unnecessary exhibition of underclothing.
9. The exhibition of profuse bleeding.
10. Nude figures.
11. Offensive vulgarity, and impropriety in conduct and dress.
12. Indecorous dancing.
13. Excessively passionate love scenes.
14. Bathing scenes passing the limits of propriety.
15. References to controversial politics.
16. Relations of Capital and Labour.
17. Scenes tending to disparage public characters and institutions.
18. Realistic horrors of warfare.
19. Scenes and incidents calculated to afford information to the enemy.
20. Incidents having a tendency to disparage our Allies.
21. Scenes holding up the King's uniform to contempt or ridicule.
22. Subjects dealing with India, in which British officers are seen in an odious light, and otherwise attempting to suggest the

disloyalty of Native States or bringing into disrepute British prestige in the Empire.

23. The exploitation of tragic incidents of the war.
24. Gruesome murders and strangulation scenes.
25. Executions.
26. The effects of vitriol throwing.
27. The drug habit, e.g. opium, morphia, cocaine, etc.
28. Subjects dealing with White Slave traffic.
29. Subjects dealing with the premeditated seduction of girls.
30. 'First night' scenes.
31. Scenes suggestive of immorality.
32. Indelicate sexual situations.
33. Situations accentuating delicate marital relations.
34. Men and women in bed together.
35. Illicit sexual relationships.
36. Prostitution and procuration.
37. Incidents indicating the actual perpetration of criminal assaults on women.
38. Scenes depicting the effect of venereal diseases, inherited or acquired.
39. Incidents suggestive of incestuous relations.
40. Themes and references relative to 'race suicide'.
41. Confinements.
42. Scenes laid in disorderly houses.
43. Materialization of the conventional figure of Christ.

Source: National Council of Public Morals, *The Cinema: Its Present Position and Future Possibilities* (London, 1917).

Appendix 2

BBFC Codified Grounds for Censorship, 1926

Religious
1. The materialised figure of Christ.
2. Irreverent quotations of religious texts.
3. Travesties of familiar Biblical quotations and well-known hymns.
4. Titles to which objection would be taken by religious organisations.
5. Travesty and mockery of religious services.
6. Holy vessels amidst incongruous surroundings, or shown used in a way which would be looked upon as desecration.
7. Comic treatment of incidents connected with death.
8. Painful insistence of realism in death bed scenes.

Political
1. Lampoons of the institution of monarchy.
2. Propaganda against monarchy and attacks on royal dynasties.
3. Unauthorised use of royal and university arms.
4. Themes which are likely to wound the just susceptibilities of our allies.
5. White men in state of degradation amidst native surroundings.
6. American law officers making arrests in this country.
7. Inflammatory sub-titles and Bolshevist propaganda.
8. Equivocal situations between white girls and men of other races.

Military
1. Officers in British regiments shown in a disgraceful light.
2. Horrors in warfare and realistic scenes of massacre.

Social
1. The improper use of the names of well-known British institutions.
2. Incidents which reflect a mistaken conception of the police forces in this country in the administration of justice.
3. Sub-titles in the nature of swearing, and expressions regarded as objectionable in this country.
4. Painful hospital scenes.
5. Scenes in lunatic asylums and particularly in padded cells.
6. Workhouse officials shown in an offensive light.
7. Girls and women in a state of intoxication.
8. Orgy scenes.
9. Subjects which are suitable only for scientific or professional audiences.
10. Suggestive, indecorous and semi-nude dancing.
11. Nude and semi-nude figures, both in actuality and shadowgraph.
12. Girls' clothes pulled off, leaving them in scanty undergarments.
13. Men leering at exposure of women's undergarments.
14. Abortion.
15. Criminal assault on girls.
16. Scenes in and connected with houses of ill repute.
17. Bargain cast for a human life which is to be terminated by murder.
18. Marital infidelity and collusive divorce.
19. Children following the example of a drunken and dissolute father.
20. Dangerous mischief easily imitated by children.
21. Subjects dealing with venereal disease.

Questions of Sex
1. The use of the phrase 'sex-appeal' in sub-titles.
2. Themes indicative of habitual immorality.
3. Women in alluring or provocative attitudes.
4. Procuration.
5. Degrading exhibitions of animal passion.
6. Passionate and unrestrained embraces.
7. Incidents intended to show clearly that an outrage has been perpetrated.
8. Lecherous old men.

9. White slave traffic.
10. Innuendoes with a direct indecent tendency.
11. Indecorous bathroom scenes.
12. Extenuation of a woman sacrificing her honour for money on the plea of some laudable object.
13. Female vamps.
14. Indecent wall decorations.
15. Men and women in bed together.

Crime
1. Hanging, realistic or comic.
2. Executions and incidents connected therewith.
3. Objectionable prison scenes.
4. Methods of crime open to imitation.
5. Stories in which the criminal element is predominant.
6. Crime committed and condoned for an ostensibly good reason.
7. 'Crook' films in which sympathy is enlisted for the criminals.
8. 'Third degree' scenes.
9. Opium dens.
10. Scenes of, traffic in and distribution of illicit drugs.
11. The drugging and ruining of young girls.
12. Attempted suicide by asphyxiation.
13. Breaking bottles on men's heads.

Cruelty
1. Cruel treatment of children.
2. Cruelty to animals.
3. Brutal fights carried to excess, including gouging of eyes, clawing of faces and throttling.
4. Knuckle fights.
5. Girls and women fighting.
6. Realistic scenes of torture.

Source: BBFC Annual Report 1926, pp. 5–8.

Appendix 3

List of 'Don'ts and Be Carefuls', adopted by California Association for guidance of producers, 8 June 1927

Resolved, That those things which are included in the following list shall not appear in pictures produced by the members of this Association, irrespective of the manner in which they are treated:

1. Pointed profanity – by either title or lip – this includes the words 'God', 'Lord', 'Jesus', 'Christ' (unless they be used reverently in connection with proper religious ceremonies), 'hell', 'damn', 'Gawd', and every other profane and vulgar expression however it may be spelled;
2. Any licentious or suggestive nudity – in fact or in silhouette; and any lecherous or licentious notice thereof by other characters in the picture;
3. The illegal traffic in drugs;
4. Any inference of sex perversion;
5. White slavery;
6. Miscegenation (sex relationships between the white and black races);
7. Sex hygiene and venereal diseases;
8. Scenes of actual childbirth – in fact or in silhouette;
9. Children's sex organs;
10. Ridicule of the clergy;
11. Willful offense to any nation, race or creed:

And be it further *Resolved,* That special care be exercised in the manner in which the following subjects are treated, to the end that vulgarity and suggestiveness may be eliminated and that good taste may be emphasized:

1. The use of the flag;
2. International relations (avoiding picturizing in an unfavorable light another country's religion, history, institutions, prominent people, and citizenry);
3. Arson;
4. The use of firearms;
5. Theft, robbery, safe-cracking, and dynamiting of trains, mines, buildings, etc. (having in mind the effect which a too-detailed description of these may have upon the moron);
6. Brutality and possible gruesomeness;
7. Technique of committing murder by whatever method;
8. Methods of smuggling;
9. Third-degree methods;
10. Actual hangings or electrocutions as legal punishment for crime;
11. Sympathy for criminals;
12. Attitude toward public characters and institutions;
13. Sedition;
14. Apparent cruelty to children and animals;
15. Branding of people or animals;
16. The sale of women, or of a woman selling her virtue;
17. Rape or attempted rape;
18. First night scenes;
19. Man and woman in bed together;
20. Deliberate seduction of girls;
21. The institution of marriage;
22. Surgical operations;
23. The use of drugs;
24. Titles or scenes having to do with the law enforcement or law-enforcing officers;
25. Excessive or lustful kissing, particularly when one character or the other is a 'heavy":

Resolved, That the execution of the purposes of this resolution is a fair trade practice.

Source: Raymond Moley, *The Hays Office* (New York, 1945), pp. 240–41.

Appendix 4

**Films classified as 'Horrific' or certified 'H' by the BBFC
1933–40**

1933   *The Ghoul*
        The Invisible Man
        King Kong
        Vampire (Vampyr)
        The Vampire Bat

1934   *The House of Doom*
        The Medium
        The Ninth Guest
        The Son of Kong
        The Tell Tale Heart

1935   *The Bride of Frankenstein*
        The Hands of Orlac
        The Mark of the Vampire
        The Night on the Lonely Mountain
        The Raven
        The Werewolf of London

1936   *The Devil Doll*
        The Man Who Changed His Mind

1937   *The Thirteenth Chair*

1938   *I Accuse (J'Accuse)*

1939   *The Cat and the Canary* (Cut 1943 version was 'A')
        Boy Slaves
        A Child is Born
        The Dark Eyes of London
        The Gorilla
        Hell's Kitchen
        The Man They Could Not Hang
        The Monster Walks
        On Borrowed Time ('A' from July 1945)
        The Return of Doctor X
        The Son of Frankenstein

1940   NONE

Source: James C. Robertson, *The British Board of Film Censors: Film Censorship in Britain, 1896–1950* (London, 1985), p. 183.

Appendix 5

Members of the Edinburgh Cinema Enquiry Committee

Boys' Brigade (Edinburgh)	Colonel W.C.C. Sinclair, D.S.O., T.D.*
Boys' Brigade (Leith)	Peter B.W. Smith R. Borthwick M.A., B.Sc.*
Boys' Club Union	C.J. Tait, B.Sc.*
Boy Scouts Association	Colonel R.S. Harding Rev. W. Burnett, B.D.*
Catholic Enquiry Office	Miss George
Church Lads' Brigade	John Blamire
Church of Scotland (Edinburgh Presbytery)	Rev. J. Maxwell Blair, M.A. Isaac J. Cowie
Education Committee	Councillor Thomas Paris*
Educational Institute of Scotland	Miss Henderson, L.L.A., F.E.I.S.* Miss Muir, J.P., F.E.I.S.* Sam Hamilton, M.A.* Miss Janet Renwick, F.E.I.S. George Cowe, M.A., F.E.I.S.*

Edinburgh Diocesan Social Service Board	E.W.M. Balfour-Melville, M.A.*
Girls' Association	Miss Stanford Miss P. Brown
Girls' Club Union	Miss Craw Miss Gee
Girls' Friendly Society	Miss D. Gunn
Girl Guides	Mrs Porter Miss Dalmahoy*
Girls' Guildry	Mrs Middleton Miss E. Irvine
Howard League	Miss Turnbull Miss Crawford
Juvenile Organisations Committee	Miss M.G. Cowan, O.B.E., M.A.* The Hon. Lady Hope, O.B.E., J.P.*
Mothers' Union	Mrs Gardyne
National Council of Women (Edinburgh)	Miss H.M. Blair Miss Troup Miss E. De La Cour, O.B.E., J.P.
National Vigilance Association	Miss K.M. Stewart Mrs Cadell
Roman Catholic Church	The Rt Rev. Monseigneur M'Gettigan*
Scottish Council for Research in Education	R.R. Rusk, M.A., B.A., Ph.D.*
Scottish Temperance Alliance	Thomas Murray
St Vincent De Paul Society	R. Davidson, B.Com.
Women Citizens Association	Mrs M'Call* Mrs Burt* Miss Macgregor*

Women Citizens Association	Mrs Makepeace
(Junior Section)	Mrs Anderson
Y.W.C.A. of Great Britain	Miss D. Crerar
Y.W.C.A. of Scotland	Miss Kemp
Co-opted	J.R. Peddie, M.A., D.Litt* Very Rev. J. Harry Miller, C.B.E., D.D* Mrs Alice M. Ross, M.A.* Mrs Bruce* Mrs Griffith Thomas J. Mackie, M.A., D.Sc., F.R.S.E.* D.S.W. Pentland* Rev. W. Ross, B.D.*
Honorary Secretaries	Miss M. Gunn Miss Martin Stewart

* Members of Executive Committee

Composition of the Edinburgh Cinema Enquiry Committee
1931–33

	General Committee	%	Executive Committee	%	Proportional Representation*
Total members	57	100	25	100	44%
Men	22	39	15	60	68%
Women	35	61	10	40	29%
Married women (Mrs)	12	21	5	20	42%
Single women (Miss)	23	40	5	20	22%
Clergy	5	9	4	16	80%
Graduates	15	26	14	56	93%
Education organisations	7	12	6	24	86%
Religious organisations	9	16	2	8	22%
Youth organisations	22	39	7	28	32%
Women's organisations	11	19	3	12	27%
Social/moral campaigners	7	12	1	4	14%

* Proportion of general committee members of each category on executive committee

Source: Compiled from data in John Mackie (ed.), *The Edinburgh Cinema Enquiry: Being an investigation conducted into the influence of the film on school children and adolescents in the city* (Edinburgh, 1933).

Notes and References

Chapter 1

1. David Buckingham, *Children Talking Television: The Making of Television Literacy* (London, 1993), p. 7. See also Ellen Wartella and Byron Reeves, 'Historical Trends in Research on Children and the Media: 1900-1960', *Journal of Communication*, 35, 2 (Spring 1985), pp. 119–20.

2. Examples regarding Columbine from one edition of a British newspaper are: 'All American Monsters', 'Sick Lyrics of Marilyn Manson', 'Hitler-Worshipping Fanatics Linked by a Web of Hate' and 'Outsiders, A Gun Culture and a Dangerous Diet of TV Death and Destruction', *Daily Record*, 22 April 1999, pp. 1 & 6–9.

3. Graham Murdock, 'Reservoirs of Dogma: An Archaeology of Popular Anxieties', in Martin Barker and Julian Petley (eds), *Ill Effects: The Media/Violence Debate*, 2e (London, 2001), p. 153.

4. Annette Kuhn, *An Everyday Magic: Cinema and Cultural Memory* (London, 2002). Amongst a wide range of other source material, *An Everyday Magic* draws on the memories of respondents contacted through the Cinema Culture in 1930s Britain project, many of whom were children in the 1930s.

5. Dean Rapp, 'The British Salvation Army, the Early Film Industry and Working Class Adolescents, 1897–1918', *Twentieth Century British History*, 7, 2 (1996), pp. 157–88; David Fowler, 'Teenage Consumers? Young wage earners and leisure in Manchester, 1919–1939', in A. Davies & S. Fielding (eds), *Workers' Worlds: Cultures and Communities in Manchester and Salford, 1880–1939* (Manchester, 1992), pp. 133–55.

6. Anton Kaes, 'The Debate About Cinema: Charting a Controversy 1909–1929', *New German Critique*, 40 (Winter 1987), pp. 7–33. David Welch, *Propaganda & the German Cinema 1933–1945* (Oxford, 1985). Gary D. Stark, 'Cinema, Society and the State: Policing the Film Industry in Imperial Germany', in Gary D. Stark and Bede Karl Lackner (eds), *Essays on Culture and Society in Modern Germany* (Arlington, 1982), pp. 122–66.

7. Richard Stites, *Russian Popular Culture: Entertainment and Society Since 1900* (Cambridge, 1992), pp. 54–63, 85–7 & 124–6, *passim*.

8. See also Garth Jowett & James Linton, *Movies As Mass Communication* (London, 1980); Daniel J. Czitrom, *Media and the American Mind: From Morse to McLuhan* (Chapel Hill, 1982); Carmen Luke, *Constructing the Child Viewer: A History of the American Discourse on Television and Children 1950–1980* (New York, 1990), pp. 35–42.

9. Garth Jowett, Ian Jarvie and Kathryn H. Fuller, *Children and the Movies: Media Influence and the Payne Fund Controversy* (Cambridge, 1996), p. i.

10. Richard deCordova, 'Ethnography and Exhibition: The Child Audience, the Hays Office and Saturday Matinees', *Camera Obscura* (May 1990), p. 103. One useful book which has since looked at issues relating to youth and cinema during the silent period in America is Kathryn H. Fuller, *At the Picture Show: Small-Town Audiences and the Creation of Movie Fan Culture* (London, 1996).

11. See Wartella & Reeves, 'Historical Trends', pp. 118–33; Buckingham, *Children Talking Television*; David Buckingham, *Children and Television: An Overview of the Research* (BFI Mimeo, London, 1987); Cary Bazalgette & David Buckingham (eds), *In Front of the Children: Screen Entertainment and Young Audiences* (London, 1995).

12. Buckingham, *Children and Television*, p. 2.

13. For example, see Barker and Petley (eds), *Ill Effects*. A few recent scares have received more detailed treatment, as in Martin Barker's *A Haunt of Fears: The Strange History of the British Horror Comics Campaign* (London, 1984).

14. Simon Rowson, 'Statistical Survey of the Cinema Industry in Great Britain in 1934', *Journal of the Royal Statistical Society*, 99 (1936), p. 70.

15. Jeffrey Richards, *The Age of the Dream Palace: Cinema and Society in Britain 1930–1939* (London, 1984), p. 3.

16. Peter Stead, *Film and the Working Class: The feature film in British and American Society* (London, 1989), p. 46.

17. Wartella & Reeves, 'Historical Trends', pp. 124–5.

18. Michael Mitterauer, *A History of Youth* (Oxford, 1992), pp. 1–4. See also William Kessen, 'The Child and Other Cultural Inventions', in Frank S. Kessel and Alexander W. Siegel (eds), *The Child and Other Cultural Inventions* (New York, 1983), pp. 26–47

19. Examples include Harry Hendrick, 'Constructions and Reconstructions of British Childhood: An Interpretive Survey, 1800 to the Present' and Allison James and Alan Prout, 'A New Paradigm for the Sociology of Childhood', both in Allison James and Alan Prout (eds), *Constructing and Reconstructing Childhood: Contemporary Issues in the Sociological Study of Childhood*, 2e (London, 1997).

20. British Film Institute Special Collections (hereafter BFI) – London County Council (LCC) Verbatim Reports 1929–1930: Proceedings of conference between the LCC Theatres and Music Halls Committee and the BBFC, on the Attendance of Unaccompanied Children at Exhibitions of A Films, 6 November 1929.

21. Public Record Office (hereafter PRO) – HO45/17036: Films for children 1932–1937, letter from CEA to Home Office, 30 January 1934.

22. *News Chronicle*, 2 and 3 February 1934.

23. Where evidence from children is included (either from contemporary reports and surveys, or oral history interviews and correspondence), original spelling and grammar have been preserved and the term [*sic*] has not been used.

24.   Richards, *Dream Palace*, p. 89.

25.   Peter Horsfield, 'Moral panic or moral action? The appropriation of moral panics in the exercise of social control' (http://vic.uca.org.au/ecrp/panics.html).

26.   Kenneth Thompson, *Moral Panics* (London, 1998), p. ix.

27.   Thompson, *Moral Panics*, p. 72.

28.   Philip Jenkins, *Intimate Enemies: Moral Panics in Contemporary Great Britain* (New York, 1992), p. 10.

29.   Thompson, *Moral Panics*, pp. 19–20.

30.   For an overview of developments in oral history, see Penny Summerfield, 'Culture and Composure: Creating Narratives of the Gendered Self in Oral History Interviews', *Cultural and Social History*, 1 (2004), pp. 65–93.

31.   Martin A. Conway, *Autobiographical Memory: An Introduction* (Milton Keynes, 1990), pp. 11–14.

32.   Kuhn, *An Everyday Magic*, p. 9. This entire book is a fascinating study on the issue of cultural memory and cinema.

33.   Paul Thompson, *The Voice of the Past*, 2e (Oxford, 1988), p. 132.

34.   Catherine Lumby, 'No Kidding: Paedophilia and Popular Culture', *Continuum: Journal of Media and Cultural Studies*, 12, 1 (1998), p. 52.

Chapter 2

1.   This overview of early cinema regulation owes much to the work of others, particularly Neville March Hunnings, Annette Kuhn, Rachael Low, Jeffrey Richards and James Robertson.

2.   W.S.M. Knight, 'Kinematograph Shows: Do They Require Licences?', *Kinematograph and Lantern Weekly*, 2 (25 February 1909), 1143.

3.   H. Mark Gosser, 'The *Bazar de la Charité* Fire: The Reality, the Aftermath, the Telling', *Film History*, 10, 1 (1998), pp. 70–89.

4.   See Hunnings, *Film Censors*, p. 41n.

5.   Mutascopes were like eleborate flick-books: cards fastened to a large, rotating wheel which gave the impression of moving pictures when watched through a peepshow-style viewer.

6.   James C. Robertson, *The Hidden Cinema: British Film Censorship in Action, 1913–1972* (London, 1989), p. 1.

7.   Walter Reynolds, *Kinematograph and Lantern Weekly* (11 February 1909).

8.   Cited in Hunnings, *Film Censors*, p. 49.

9.   Hunnings, *Film Censors*, pp. 49–51.

10.   *Bioscope*, 7 December 1911, p. 675.

11.   PRO–HO45/10551, 'Re. Censorship of Kinematograph Films', deputation document presented to the Home Office, 13 November 1912.

12.   Hunnings, *Film Censors*, p. 57; James C. Robertson, *The British Board of Film Censors: Film Censorship in Britain, 1896–1950* (London, 1985), p. 7; Annette Kuhn, *Cinema, Censorship and Sexuality 1909–1925* (London, 1988), p. 25.

13.   See Kuhn, *Cinema, Censorship*.

14.   Robertson, *BBFC*, pp. 20–21.

15.   T.P. O'Connor, *The Principles of Film Censorship* (London, 1923).

16.   *Bioscope*, 13 March 1913, p. 780.

17.   *Bioscope*, 27 March 1913, p. 995.

18.   PRO–HO45/10811/312397/1: Conference of local authorities, 14 April 1916.

19.   PRO–HO158/17, circular 264, 149, 16 May 1916.

20.   Cited in Hunnings, *Film Censors*, p. 63.

21.   BBFC Annual Report 1919, pp. 3–4.

22.   BBFC Annual Report 1929, p. 1.

23.   BBFC Annual Report 1921, p. 9.

24.   Rachael Low, *The History of the British Film, 1918–1929* (London, 1971), p.60.

25.   BBFC Annual Report 1926, pp. 5–8.

26.   PRO–HO45/10551, 'Re. Censorship of Kinematograph Films', deputation document presented to the Home Office, 13 November 1912.

27.   PRO–HO45/10551/163175/52: Leaflet issued by BBFC, January 1913.

28.   Robertson, *BBFC*, p. 8; Kuhn, *Cinema, Censorship*, p. 22.

29.   Low, *British Film 1918–1929*, p.57.

30.   Hunnings, *Film Censors*, p. 140.

31.   PRO–HO45/22906: Censorship: powers of BBFC and local authorities 1923–1929. However, the Home Office files suggest that this 'progress' still represented widely varying opinions and levels of compliance across the country.

32.   Kuhn, *Cinema, Censorship*, pp. 21, 27, 121, 133, 152.

33.   Dr Humbert, 'Effect of Cinematograph on the Mental and Moral Well-Being of Children: A Report to the Child Welfare Committee of the League of Nations, Geneva, May 1926', in W.M. Seabury, *Motion Picture Problems: The Cinema and the League of Nations* (New York, 1929), pp. 324–5.

34.   BBFC Annual Report 1926.

35.   Low, *British Film 1918–1929*, p. 58.

36.   Much has been written on the history of film censorship in America. For a thorough treatment, see Gregory D. Black, *Hollywood Censored: Morality Codes, Catholics, and the Movies* (Cambridge, 1994). For briefer overviews, see Anthony Slide, *'Banned in the USA': British Films in the United States and Their Censorship, 1933–1960* (London, 1998) and Ruth Vasey, *The World According to Hollywood 1918–1939* (Exeter, 1997).

37.   Vasey, *The World According to Hollywood*, p. 4.

38.   Black, *Hollywood Censored*, p. 18.

39.   Cited in Black, *Hollywood Censored*, p. 10.

40.   Ibid., p. 12.

41.   Ibid., p. 11.

42.   Ibid., p. 9.

43.   Ibid., p. 11.

44.   Ibid., pp. 12–13; Daniel J. Czitrom, *Media and the American Mind: From Morse to McLuhan* (Chapel Hill, 1982), p. 47.

45.   Cited in Black, *Hollywood Censored*, p. 15.

46.   Black, *Hollywood Censored*, p. 15.

47.   Ibid., p. 12.

48.   National Council of Public Morals (NCPM), *The Cinema: Its Present Position and Future Possibilities* (London, 1917), p. 323.

49.   Ibid., p. 324.

50.   Ibid.

51. Humbert, 'Geneva 1926', pp. 304–5.
52. Ibid., pp. 326–7.
53. Vasey, *The World According to Hollywood*, p. 5.
54. Cited in Black, *Hollywood Censored*, p. 38.
55. Ibid., p. 40.
56. Vasey, *The World According to Hollywood*, p. 5.
57. NCPM, *The Cinema*, pp. 313–31; Humbert, 'Geneva 1926', pp. 265–335.
58. Humbert, 'Geneva 1926', pp. 305–6; Gary D. Stark, 'Cinema, Society and the State: Policing the Film Industry in Imperial Germany', in Gary D. Stark and Bede Karl Lackner (eds), *Essays on Culture and Society in Modern Germany* (Arlington, 1982), p. 137.
59. Humbert, 'Geneva 1926', p. 302.
60. Ibid., pp. 302–3.
61. NCPM, *The Cinema*, pp. 328–9; Humbert, 'Geneva 1926', pp. 292–4 & 303.
62. Humbert, 'Geneva 1926', pp. 298–9.
63. Ibid., p. 298.
64. Ibid., pp. 315–16.
65. Ibid., p. 317.
66. Ibid., p. 314. My italics.
67. Ibid., p. 312. My italics.
68. Ibid., p. 303–16; NCPM, *The Cinema*, pp. 328–9.
69. Humbert, 'Geneva 1926', pp. 315 & 322.
70. Ibid., p. 315.
71. Ibid., p. 313.
72. NCPM, *The Cinema*, p. 331.
73. For more detail, see Stark, 'Cinema, Society', pp. 133–9.
74. Cited in Stark, 'Cinema, Society', p. 134.
75. Ibid., p. 133.
76. Hunnings, *Film Censors*, pp. 338–44.
77. Cited in Hunnings, *Film Censors*, p. 340.
78. Ibid.
79. Humbert, 'Geneva 1926', pp. 278–9.
80. Translation of an *arrêté* cited in Hunnings, *Film Censors*, p. 338.
81. Humbert, 'Geneva 1926', p. 274.
82. Hunnings, *Film Censors*, pp. 316–17.
83. Humbert, 'Geneva 1926', p. 297.
84. Ibid., pp. 276 & 296–7.
85. Ibid., pp. 321–2.
86. Hunnings, *Film Censors*, p. 316.
87. Ibid. p. 316–17. My italics.
88. Ibid., p. 363.
89. Humbert, 'Geneva 1926', p. 292; Hunnings, *Film Censors*, p. 394.
90. Humbert, 'Geneva 1926', pp. 299–300.

Chapter 3

1. BBFC Annual Report 1928, p. 9.

2.   Margaret Dickinson and Sarah Street, *Cinema and State: The Film Industry and the Government 1927–84* (London, 1985), p. 40.

3.   BBFC Annual Reports 1928, pp. 9–10, and 1931, p. 10.

4.   BBFC Annual Report 1928, p. 10. By 1931, the BBFC noted 'most of the cinemas...have now been wired for auditory films' and there was no need, 'as was the case last year, to issue a silent and auditory version of the majority of...feature films'. BBFC Annual Report 1931, p. 5.

5.   BBFC Annual Reports 1929, p. 8, and 1932, p. 8.

6.   *Evening Standard*, 22 October 1931. My italics.

7.   BBFC Annual Reports 1921, pp. 9–10; 1923, p. 6; and 1925.

8.   BBFC Annual Report 1925, p. 8.

9.   BBFC Annual Report 1929, p. 9.

10.   *Evening News*, 18 November 1932.

11.   Overall, the evidence points towards a watershed in film content from 1934, but there is some debate regarding the balance of continuity and change around this date. Richard Maltby, '*Baby Face*, or How Joe Breen Made Barbara Stanwyck Atone for Causing the Wall Street Crash', in Annette Kuhn and Jackie Stacey (eds), *Screen Histories: A Screen Reader* (Oxford, 1998), p. 166; Ruth Vasey, *The World According to Hollywood 1918–1939* (Exeter, 1997), pp. 100–31; Gregory D. Black, *Hollywood Censored: Morality Codes, Catholics, and the Movies* (Cambridge, 1994), p. 191; Thomas Doherty, *Pre-Code Hollywood: Sex, Immorality and Insurrection in American Cinema* (New York, 1999), pp. 2 & 8–11.

12.   BBFC Annual Report 1928, p. 8.

13.   Black, *Hollywood Censored*, p. 110.

14.   Despite the generally poor characterisation and treatment of women in most gangster films, they were also popular with some girls. See Cinema Culture in 1930s Britain (hereafter CCINTB 92–1: Margaret Young; 92–2: Molly Stevenson; and 95–182: Ellen Casey; also J. P. Mayer, *British Cinemas and Their Audiences: Sociological Studies* (London, 1948), pp. 35, 83 & 109.

15.   CCINTB 95–214: Jim Godbold, interview, 6 July 1995.

16.   Birmingham Cinema Enquiry Committee, *Report of Investigations, April 1930–May 1931* (Birmingham, 1931), p. 8.

17.   Ibid., pp. 14 & 17.

18.   Birkenhead Vigilance Committee, *The Cinema and the Child: A Report of Investigations, June–October 1931* (Birkenhead, 1931), p. 15.

19.   John Mackie (ed.), *The Edinburgh Cinema Enquiry: Being an investigation conducted into the influence of the film on school children and adolescents in the city* (Edinburgh, 1933), pp.15–16.

20.   Mackie, *Edinburgh Cinema Enquiry*, p. 17.

21.   Cited in Black, *Hollywood Censored*, p. 109.

22.   Black, *Hollywood Censored*, p. 110.

23.   Letter from James Wingate, cited in Black, *Hollywood Censored*, p. 115.

24.   *Motion Picture Herald*, 1 August 1931.

25.   Black, *Hollywood Censored*, p. 123.

26.   Ibid., p. 129.

27.   Ibid., p. 131.

28.   BFI: BBFC Scenarios, 1932, No.94 – *When the Gangs Came to London*.

29.   James C. Robertson, *The British Board of Film Censors: Film Censorship in Britain, 1896–1950* (London, 1985), pp.78–9.

30.   Cited in Vasey, *World According to Hollywood*, p. 114.

31.   BBFC Annual Reports 1921, p. 10; 1923, p. 6; 1925, p. 9.

32.   See Maltby, '*Baby Face*', pp. 164–83.

33.   *Variety*, 2 February 1932, 6. For more on this issue, see Doherty, *Pre-Code Hollywood*, pp. 120–5

34.   BBFC Annual Report 1929, p. 10. See also 1932, p. 17.

35.   BBFC Annual Report 1931, pp. 9–10.

36.   Ibid.

37.   Vasey, *World According to Hollywood*, p. 124.

38.   'Deadline for Film Dirt', *Variety*, 13 June 1933, I, 36.

39.   CCINTB 95–34: Denis Houlston, interview, 26 April 1995.

40.   Ibid.

41.   Cited in Black, *Hollywood Censored*, p. 72.

42.   CCINTB 95–208: Beatrice Cooper, interview, 27 November 1995.

43.   Cited in Maltby, '*Baby Face*', p. 183.

44.   Cited in Black, *Hollywood Censored*, p. 61.

45.   Mariann Hoffmann, 'Children and the Cinema', in International Educational Cinematographic Institute, *The Social Aspects of the Cinema* (Rome, c.1930), p. 123.

46.   Ibid.

47.   Cited in John Walker (ed.), *Halliwell's Film and Video Guide*, 13 edn (London, 1997), p. 47.

48.   *Variety*, 18 July 1933, 3.

49.   Roy Kinnard, *Horror in Silent Films: A Filmography, 1896–1929* (London, 1995), pp. 1–5. See also S.S. Prawer, *Caligari's Children: The Film as Tale of Terror* (Oxford, 1980), p. 9.

50.   CCINTB 92–11a: Tom Walsh, interview, 27 January 1995.

51.   CCINTB 95–87: Joan F. Donoghue, correspondence, 11 February 1995.

52.   For example, the subversive anarchy of Marx Brothers' comedies, *Cocoanuts* (1929), *Animal Crackers* (1930), *Horse Feathers* (1932) and *Duck Soup* (1933), and the voyeuristic eroticism of Busby Berkeley musicals, *The Kid From Spain* (1932), *Night World* (1932) and *Gold Diggers of 1933* (1933).

53.   For details, see Frank Walsh, *Sin & Censorship: The Catholic Church and the Motion Picture Industry* (Cambridge, 1994) and Black, *Hollywood Censored*.

54.   Cited in Black, *Hollywood Censored*, pp. 167–8.

55.   Ibid., p. 159.

56.   Anthony Slide, *'Banned in the USA': British Films in the United States and Their Censorship, 1933–1960* (London, 1998), p. 4.

57.   Doherty, *Pre-Code Hollywood*, pp. 10–11.

58.   Cited in Black, *Hollywood Censored*, p. 175.

59.   Black, *Hollywood Censored*, pp. 178–80.

60.   Cited in Black, *Hollywood Censored*, p. 190.

61.   Ibid., p. 191.

62.   Jeffrey Richards, *The Age of the Dream Palace: Cinema and Society in Britain 1930–1939* (London, 1984), p. 109.

63.   PRO–HO45/10551/163175/52: Leaflet issued by BBFC, January 1913.

64.   Rachael Low, *The History of the British Film, 1929–1939: Film Making in 1930s Britain* (London, 1985), p. 58.

65.   PRO–HO45/14731: Children and the cinema 1929–1932. This file includes the questionnaire and circular, compiled results and many individual responses.

66.   Ibid; PRO–HO45/15207: Film Censorship in the UK 19 May 1932–26 May 1933.

67.   Its secondary function was to address issues relating to 'non-commercial films and private cinema performances', PRO–HO45/17036: Films for children, 1932–1937.

68.   PRO–HO45/15208: FCCC, 1931–1933.

69.   Beckenham not only banned films passed by the BBFC, they also reclassified U films as As, including the horror comedy *The Gorilla* (1938), which they famously described as 'too full of growls' for children.

70.   Tom Johnson, *Censored Screams: The British Ban on Hollywood Horror in the Thirties* (London, 1997), p. 18.

71.   PRO–HO45/15207: Film Censorship in the UK 19 May 1932–26 May 1933; PRO–HO45/17036: Films for children, 1932–1937.

72.   *Kinematograph Weekly*, 12 April 1934, p. 18; *Today's Cinema*, 5 February 1937.

73.   PRO–HO45/15206: Film Censorship in the UK 18 September 1931–30 April 1932.

74.   *Kinematograph Weekly*, 21 April 1932, p. 25.

75.   PRO–HO45/17036: Films for children, 1932–1937.

76.   Ibid.

77.   BBFC Annual Report 1932.

78.   PRO–HO45/17036: Films for children, 1932–1937.

79.   BBFC Annual Report 1930, p. 11.

80.   PRO–HO45/17036: Films for children, 1932–1937.

81.   Under Secretary of State, Home Office, *Children and 'A' Films: [A letter to] the Clerk to the Licensing Authority, under the Cinematograph Act 1909, 6 March 1933* (London, HMSO, 1934).

82.   This had already been tried in Birmingham. See PRO–HO45/17036: Films for children, 1932–1937; PRO–HO45/15208: FCCC, 1931–1933.

83.   See *Today's Cinema*, 23 December 1932; *Daily Film Renter*, 24 December 1932; *Belfast News-Letter*, 29 December 1932.

84.   PRO–HO45/17036: Films for children, 1932–1937 – letter from Ministry of Home Affairs, Stormont, dated 24 February 1933.

85.   BFI – LCC Verbatim Reports 1929–1930: Proceedings of conference between LCC Theatres and Music Halls Committee and BBFC, on the Attendance of Unaccompanied Children at Exhibitions of A Films, 6 November 1929.

86.   BFI – BBFC Verbatim Reports 1932–1935; PRO–HO45/17036: Films for children, 1932–1937.

87.   BFI – Press Books & Clippings Files: *Frankenstein* (1931).

88.   For examples, see Chapter 5.

89.   PRO–HO45/15208: FCCC, 1931–1933.

90.   BFI Special Collections – BBFC Verbatim Reports 1932–1935: Proceedings of the National Conference on Problems Connected with the Cinema, convened by the Birmingham Cinema Enquiry Committee, 27 February 1932; *Kinematograph Weekly*, 28 January 1932, p. 21.

91.   PRO–HO45/15208: FCCC, 1931–1933.

92.   Ibid.

93.   Ibid.

94.   BFI – BBFC Verbatim Reports 1932–1935; PRO–HO45/17036: Films for children, 1932–1937.

95.   BFI – LCC Verbatim Reports 1929–1930.

96.   BFI – BBFC Verbatim Reports 1930–1931; PRO–HO45/15208: FCCC, 1931–1933.

97.   BFI – LCC Verbatim Reports 1929–1930.

98.   BFI Special Collections – BBFC Verbatim Reports 1932–1935; *Kinematograph Weekly*, 28 January 1932, p. 21.

99.   BFI Special Collections – BBFC Verbatim Reports 1932–1935.

100.   Neville March Hunnings, *Film Censors and the Law* (London, 1967), p. 142.

101.   *Today's Cinema*, 22 November & 20 December 1935; 2 November 1936; 12 January 1937; *The Cinema*, 6 January 1937.

102.   *Today's Cinema*, 2 November 1936.

103.   Hunnings, *Film Censors*, p. 142.

104.   PRO–HO45/17036: Films for children, 1932–1937.

105.   *Today's Cinema*, 26 April 1937.

106.   BFI Special Collections – Censorship Folder, Verbatim Reports 1930–1938. This was widely reported – see *The Times*, 17 February 1937; *Morning Post*, 17 February 1937; *Manchester Guardian*, 18 February 1937.

107.   *Today's Cinema*, 9 June 1937.

108.   Black, *Hollywood Censored*, p. 199.

109.   Cited in Black, *Hollywood Censored*, p. 238.

110.   BBFC Annual Report 1935, p. 1.

111.   PRO–HO45/24945: FCCC 1934–1951.

112.   Doherty, *Pre-Code Hollywood*, p. 1.

113.   For more details, see Black, *Hollywood Censored*, pp. 275–80.

114.   The initial series was *Dead End* (1937), *Crime School* (1938), *Angels With Dirty Faces* (1938), *They Made Me a Criminal* (1939), *Hell's Kitchen* (1939) and *The Angels Wash Their Faces* (1939).

115.   For more analysis, see Annette Kuhn, *An Everyday Magic: Cinema and Cultural Memory* (London, 2002), pp. 66–97.

116.   For discussion of these wider trends, see Allison James and Alan Prout (eds), *Constructing and Reconstructing Childhood: Contemporary Issues in the Sociological Study of Childhood*, 2e (London, 1997); Frank S. Kessel and Alexander W. Siegel (eds), *The Child and Other Cultural Inventions* (New York, 1983); Harry Hendrick, *Children, Childhood & English Society 1880–1990* (Cambridge, 1997).

117.   BFI Special Collections – Censorship Folder, Verbatim Reports 1930–1938.

118.   PRO–HO45/21118: Admission of children to cinemas 1937–1947.

119.   Ibid.

Chapter 4

1.   National Council of Public Morals, *The Cinema: Its Present Position and Future Possibilities – being the report and chief evidence taken by the Cinema Commission of Inquiry, instituted by the National Council of Public Morals* (London, 1917), p. vii. My italics.

2.   Ibid., pp. x & 332.

3.   Ibid., p. xlvii. My italics.

4.   Ibid., pp. xxxvii–xxxviii.

5.   For examples of 1920s surveys in America, see Richard deCordova, 'Ethnography and Exhibition: The Child Audience, the Hays Office and Saturday Matinees', *Camera Obscura* (May 1990), p. 104n.

6.   International reports include: International Educational Cinematographic Institute, *The Social Aspects of the Cinema* (Rome, c.1930); International Institute of Educational Cinematography, *The International Congress of Educational and Instructional Cinematography, Rome 1934* (Rome, 1934); League of Nations Child Welfare Committee, Twelfth Session, April 27th, 1936, *Recreational Aspects of Cinematography* (Geneva, 1936); League of Nations Advisory Committee on Social Questions, *The Recreational Cinema and the Young* (Geneva, 1938); International Institute of Intellectual Co-operation, *The Cinema and the Public: Preliminary Results of an International Enquiry* (Paris, 1940); see also W. M. Seabury, *Motion Picture Problems: The Cinema and the League of Nations* (New York, 1929).

7.   For a detailed overview, see Garth Jowett, Ian Jarvie and Kathryn Fuller, *Children and the Movies: Media Influence and the Payne Fund Controversy* (Cambridge, 1996).

8.   For full details see Bibliography, under Payne Fund Studies. There was also an unpublished volume, P.G. Cressey and F.M. Thrasher, *Boys, Movies and City Streets* (New York, 1933), several drafts of which are reprinted in Jowett et al., *Children and the Movies*.

9.   Published reports include: Commission on Educational and Cultural Films, *The Film in National Life: Being the report of an enquiry conducted by the Commission into the service which the cinematograph may render to education and social progress* (London, 1932); Corporation of Glasgow Education Department, Sub-committee on Visual Education, *The Film in the Classroom* (Glasgow, November, 1933); Erith Education Committee, *The Effect of War Films on Child Opinion: Report of an Investigation, Erith, 1935* (Erith, 1935); British Film Institute, *The Cinema and Education: A Summary of the Reports Issued by Various Local Education Authorities in Great Britain, by A. A. Denholme* (London, 1937); Scunthorpe Grammar School, *An Enquiry into the Cinema-Going Habits and Tastes of the Pupils of Scunthorpe Grammar School, November, 1938* (Scunthorpe, 1938). Cinema enquiries were also conducted by the Catholic Church in Britain and in cities such as Bristol and Barnsley. See BFI – Censorship Folder, Verbatim Reports 1930–1938.

10.   Notably, the Sheffield study published by A.D.K. Owen, 'Cinema Matinees for Children', *Social Service Review* (July 1931), pp. 141–4, and the BFI's *Report of the Conference on Films for Elementary School Children, November 20–21, 1936* (London, 1937).

11.   Rachael Low, *The History of the British Film, 1929–1939: Film Making in 1930s Britain* (London, 1985), p. 59.

12.   Eventually, the BCEC became known as the National Cinema Inquiry Committee.

13.   Birmingham Cinema Enquiry Committee, *Report of Investigations, April 1930–May 1931* (Birmingham, 1931), p. 3.

14.   For example, see BBFC Verbatim Reports 1930–1931: Proceedings of a meeting convened by the BCEC, 'Cinema and its Influence Today', 7 November 1930. Also BBFC Verbatim Reports 1932–1935: Proceedings of the National Conference on

Problems Connected with the Cinema, convened by the Birmingham Cinema Enquiry Committee, 27 February 1932; Some Observations on the National Conference of 27 February 1932 (anon.); Proceedings of a meeting between the Home Secretary, Rt. Hon. Sir Herbert Samuel, and a deputation from the Birmingham Conference on Film Censorship, 6 April 1932. See also Richards, 'Cinema and cinema-going', pp. 43–8, and *Dream Palace*, pp. 57–60.

15. Birkenhead Vigilance Committee, *The Cinema and the Child: A Report of Investigations, June–October 1931* (Birkenhead, 1931), p. 3.

16. Ibid.

17. Ibid., pp. 22–3.

18. F.H. Spencer, *School Children and the Cinema: London County Council Education Committee* (London, 1932), p. 1.

19. BFI – LCC Verbatim Reports 1929–1930: Proceedings of LCC meeting (18 June 1929), re: Report of the Theatres and Music Halls Committee, 'Cinematograph Exhibitions – Attendance of Unaccompanied Children at Exhibitions of A films', 8 May & 12 June 1929.

20. Ibid.

21. Ibid.

22. Spencer, *School Children and the Cinema*, p. 1.

23. John Mackie (ed.), *The Edinburgh Cinema Enquiry: Being an investigation conducted into the influence of the film on school children and adolescents in the city* (Edinburgh, 1933), p. 5.

24. This number soon increased to 27 – see Appendix 5.

25. Mackie, *Edinburgh Cinema Enquiry*, pp. 5–6.

26. Ibid., pp. 11–12.

27. Ibid., p. 30.

28. Ibid., pp. 33 & 40.

29. Ibid., p. 49.

30. Jeffrey Richards, *The Age of the Dream Palace: Cinema and Society in Britain 1930–1939* (London, 1984), p. 67.

31. BFI – BBFC Verbatim Reports 1930–1931: Proceedings of meeting between the BBFC and a deputation from the London Public Morality Council, 3 April 1930. My italics.

32. BFI – BBFC Verbatim Reports 1930–1931: Proceedings of a meeting convened by the BCEC, 'Cinema and its Influence Today', 7 November 1930, p. 24. My italics.

33. Richards, Jeffrey, 'The Cinema and Cinema-going in Birmingham in the 1930s', in J. Walton and J. Walvin (eds), *Leisure in Britain 1780–1939* (Manchester, 1983), p. 46.

34. *News Chronicle*, 21 July 1936.

35. For the impact of church conversion and Sunday opening in 1930s Birmingham, see Richards, 'Cinema and Cinema-going', pp. 39–43.

36. Spencer, *School Children and the Cinema*, p. 1.

37. Ibid.

38. Ibid., pp. 3–4.

39. Ibid., pp. 4–5.

40. Ibid., p. 6.

41. Ibid.

42.   Ibid., p. 4. See Chapter 5 for further evidence.

43.   BFI Censorship Folder – Verbatim Reports 1930–1938: Proceedings of a conference, 'Children and Films', held under the auspices of the Cinema Christian Council and the Public Morality Council, 16 February 1937, p. 33.

44.   Spencer, *School Children and the Cinema*, pp. 4–5.

45.   Ibid.

46.   Ibid., p. 5.

47.   Ibid., pp. 5–6.

48.   Ibid., p. 5.

49.   Ibid., p. 6.

50.   Ibid.

51.   Mackie, *Edinburgh Cinema Enquiry*, p. 5.

52.   Ibid., p. 11.

53.   Ibid., p. 6.

54.   Ibid., p. 13.

55.   Ibid., p. 14.

56.   Ibid., p. 32.

57.   Ibid., p. 41.

58.   Ibid., pp. 46–7.

59.   Ibid., p. 45.

60.   Ibid., p. 37.

61.   Ibid., p. 39.

62.   Ibid., p. 7.

63.   Ibid., p.11.

64.   Ibid., p. 7.

65.   Ibid., p. 11.

66.   BCEC, *Report of Investigations*, p. 3.

67.   Ibid.

68.   Ibid., p. 4.

69.   Ibid., p. 3.

70.   BVC, *Cinema and the Child*, p. 3.

71.   BCEC, *Report of Investigations*, p. 5.

72.   Ibid., p. 10.

73.   The phrase 'or children you know' was used in the BCEC questionnaire only.

74.   BCEC, *Report of Investigations*, p. 12.

75.   Mackie, *Edinburgh Cinema Enquiry*, p. 35.

76.   BCEC, *Report of Investigations*, pp. 12–13.

77.   Ibid., p. 13.

78.   Ibid., pp. 13–15.

79.   Ibid., pp. 16–17.

80.   Ibid.

81.   Robert Hodge and David Tripp, *Children and Television: A Semiotic Approach* (Cambridge, 1986).

82.   BVC, *Cinema and the Child*, p. 16.

83.   Ibid., pp. 11–12.

84.   BCEC, *Report of Investigations*, p. 16.

85.   Enquiry by the West Midland Auxiliary Movement, reported in *Times Educational Supplement*, 11 December 1926.

86.   Kenneth Thompson, *Moral Panics* (London, 1998), pp. 19–20.

87.   Spencer, *School Children and the Cinema*, p. 3.

88.   BFI Censorship Folder – Verbatim Reports 1930–1938: Proceedings of a conference, 'Children and Films', held under the auspices of the Cinema Christian Council and the Public Morality Council, 16 February 1937, p. 3.

89.   Ibid., pp. 2–3.

90.   Ibid., pp. 17–19.

91.   Ibid., p. 12.

92.   *Morning Post*, 1 September 1937.

93.   *News Chronicle*, 15 January 1938.

94.   *Daily Express*, 10 January 1938.

95.   *News Chronicle*, 6 April 1937.

96.   *Glasgow Herald*, 13 April 1935.

97.   *Today's Cinema*, 16 April 1935.

98.   *Today's Cinema*, 4 November 1936.

99.   *Newcastle Evening Chronicle*, 10 December 1937.

100.   *Glasgow Herald*, 13 April 1935.

101.   *Newcastle Evening Chronicle*, 10 December 1937.

102.   *The Cinema*, 30 December 1936.

103.   The conference report was published as: British Film Institute, *Report of the Conference on Films for Elementary School Children, November 20–21, 1936* (London, 1937).

104.   *Grimsby Daily Telegraph*, 23 November 1936.

105.   *Sheffield Independent*, 24 November 1936.

106.   *The Birmingham Mail*, 3 June 1931. For another example relating to the 1936 BFI conference, see the *Nottingham Guardian*, 23 November 1936.

107.   *Daily Film Renter*, 15 July 1936.

108.   Thompson, *Moral Panics*, p. 9.

Chapter 5

1.   BFI – BBFC Verbatim Reports 1930–1931: Proceedings of a Private Cinema Conference convened by the London Public Morality Council, 12 January 1931, p. 14.

2.   For example, Robertson identifies four levels of censorship: the BBFC, local authorities, 'extra-parliamentary critics and would-be social reformers' and 'the production companies themselves'. James C. Robertson, *The Hidden Cinema: British Film Censorship in Action, 1913–1972* (London, 1989), p. 3.

3.   Annette Kuhn, *Cinema, Censorship and Sexuality 1909–1925* (London, 1988), pp. 3–4.

4.   Ibid., p. 127.

5.   Ibid., p. 129.

6.   See David Buckingham, *Moving Images: Understanding Children's Emotional Responses to Television* (Manchester, 1996); David Buckingham, *Children and Television: An Overview of the Research* (London, BFI Mimeo, 1987); David Buckingham, *Children Talking Television: The Making of Television Literacy* (London, 1993); Robert Hodge & David Tripp, *Children and Television: A Semiotic*

Approach (Cambridge, 1986); Barie Gunter & Jill McAleer, *Children and Television: The One-Eyed Monster?* (London, 1990).

7.   For examples, see John Tulloch, *Television Drama: Agency, Audience and Myth* (London, 1990).

8.   Gunter & McAleer, *Children and Television*, p. 157.

9.   Buckingham, *Moving Images*, p. 254.

10.   Ibid., pp. 303–7.

11.   CCINTB 95–110: Betty Verdant, correspondence, 19 February 1995.

12.   CCINTB 95–48: Brigadier J.B. Ryall CBE, correspondence, 8 February 1995.

13.   CCINTB 95–81: Bernard Goodsall, correspondence, 10 February 1995.

14.   CCINTB 95–60: Olive M. Johnson, correspondence, 14 February 1995.

15.   SFA–8/41: Bill Grant, interview, 7 December 1981.

16.   CCINTB 95–34: A. Denis Houlston, interview, 26 April 1995.

17.   CCINTB 95–190: Olga Scowen, interview, 6 July 1995.

18.   *The Times*, 16 & 18 April 1932; *Justice of the Peace*, 30 April 1932.

19.   Tom Johnson, *Censored Screams: The British Ban on Hollywood Horror in the Thirties*, (London, 1997), p. 30.

20.   Ibid., p. 81.

21.   *Daily Express*, 17 February 1937.

22.   *Today's Cinema*, 28 January 1937.

23.   CCINTB 95–121: James F. Barton, correspondence, 27 February 1995.

24.   Leslie Halliwell, *Seats in All Parts: Half a Lifetime at the Movies* (London, 1985), p. 64.

25.   CCINTB 95–182: Ellen Casey, interview, 31 May 1995.

26.   See CCINTB 95–33: Les Sutton, extract from his own writings, p. 114; CCINTB 95–201: Raphael 'Ralph' Hart, interviews, 24 July & 27 November 1995; CCINTB 95–208: Beatrice Cooper, interview, 27 November 1995.

27.   CCINTB 95–119: Mr A.M. Peary, correspondence, 21 February 1995.

28.   Richard Gordon in Foreword to Johnson, *Censored Screams*, p. xiii.

29.   Ibid., p. xiv.

30.   CCINTB 95–202: Anthony Venis, interview, 11 July 1995.

31.   Richard Gordon in Foreword to Johnson, *Censored Screams*, p. xiv.

32.   CCINTB 95–195: Eileen Barnett, interview, 18 July 1995. My italics.

33.   SFA–8/45: Winnie Lees, interview, 14 June 1983.

34.   Bruce Peter, *100 Years of Glasgow's Amazing Cinemas* (Edinburgh, 1996), pp. 128–9.

35.   CCINTB 95–51: Vera Entwistle, questionnaire.

36.   CCINTB 95–182: Ellen Casey, interview, 31 May 1995; CCINTB 95–121: James F. Barton, correspondence, 27 February 1995.

37.   CCINTB 95–96: Bob Surtees, correspondence, 6 February 1995.

38.   CCINTB 95–39: Mr J Murray, interview, 9 May 1995.

39.   Buckingham, *Moving Images*, p. 83.

40.   CCINTB 92–4: Sheila McWhinnie, questionnaire 92–4–3d.

41.   CCINTB 92–11b: Margaret Walsh, interview, 27 January 1995.

42.   CCINTB 92–2: Molly Stevenson, interview, 5 December 1994.

43.   CCINTB 95–91: Joan Howarth, correspondence, 3 February 1995.

44.   J.P. Mayer, *British Cinemas and Their Audiences: Sociological Studies* (London, 1948), p. 99.

45.   CCINTB 95–33: Les Sutton, extract from his own writings, p. 112.
46.   CCINTB 95–93: Jessie Boyd, correspondence, 5 February 1995.
47.   CCINTB 95–77: Mrs M. Schneiderman, correspondence, 10 February 1995.
48.   CCINTB 95–201: Raphael 'Ralph' Hart, interview, 24 July 1995.
49.   CCINTB 95–201: Raphael 'Ralph' Hart, interviews, 24 July & 27 November 1995.
50.   Robertson, *Hidden Camera*, p. 40.
51.   CCINTB 95–201: Raphael 'Ralph' Hart, interview, 24 July 1995.
52.   CCINTB 95–201: Raphael 'Ralph' Hart, interview, 27 November 1995.
53.   CCINTB 95–207a & 95–207b: Irene and Bernard Letchet, interview, 21 July 1995.
54.   CCINTB 95–190: Olga Scowen, interview, 6 July 1995.
55.   CCINTB 95–182: Ellen Casey, interview, 31 May 1995.
56.   Mayer, *British Cinemas*, p. 104.
57.   Buckingham, *Moving Images*, p. 256.
58.   Ibid., p. 257.
59.   CCINTB 95–208: Beatrice Cooper, interview, 27 November 1995.
60.   Mayer, *British Cinemas*, p. 97.
61.   John Mackie (ed.), *The Edinburgh Cinema Enquiry* (Edinburgh, 1933), p. 11.
62.   Ibid., p. 31.
63.   SFA–8/45: Winnie Lees, interview, 14 June 1983.
64.   CCINTB 95–207a: Irene Letchet, interview, 21 July 1995.
65.   CCINTB 95–207a: Irene Letchet, interview, 23 November 1995.
66.   CCINTB 95–207a: Irene Letchet, interview, 21 July 1995.
67.   CCINTB 92–1&2: Margaret Young & Molly Stevenson, interview, 20 February 1995.
68.   CCINTB 95–38–26: Multiple interview, 11 May 1995.
69.   CCINTB 95–44: Kath Browne, interview, 1 June 1995.
70.   Mayer, *British Cinemas*, p. 56.
71.   Ibid., p. 63.
72.   Ibid., p. 87.
73.   Birkenhead Vigilance Committee, *The Cinema and the Child: A Report of Investigations, June–October 1931* (Birkenhead, 1931), p. 11.
74.   Ibid., p. 16.
75.   CCINTB 95–93: Jessie Boyd, correspondence, 5 February 1995.
76.   CCINTB 95–182: Ellen Casey, interview, 31 May 1995.
77.   CCINTB 95–108: Eric Holmes, correspondence, 20 February 1995.
78.   Cited in Richard deCordova, 'Ethnography and Exhibition: The Child Audience, the Hays Office and Saturday Matinees', *Camera Obscura* (May 1990), p. 99.
79.   CCINTB 95–34: A. Denis Houlston, interview, 26 April 1995.
80.   CCINTB 95–207a: Irene Letchet, interview, 23 November 1995; CCINTB 95–38–26: Multiple interview, 11 May 1995.
81.   CCINTB 95–38–26: Multiple interview, 11 May 1995.
82.   CCINTB 95–38: Dorris Braithwaite, interview, 11 May 1995.
83.   CCINTB 95–209: Michael Trewern-Bree, correspondence, 20 July 1995.
84.   CCINTB 92–11a: Tom Walsh, interview, 25 November 1994.
85.   CCINTB 92–16: Tom Affleck, recollections 92–16–3c.
86.   CCINTB 95–182: Ellen Casey, interview, 31 May 1995.

87.   Ibid.
88.   CCINTB 92–1: Margaret Young, interview, 5 December 1994.
89.   Mayer, *British Cinemas*, p. 41.
90.   Ibid., p. 64.
91.   CCINTB 92–2: Molly Stevenson, interview, 5 December 1994.
92.   CCINTB 95–38: Dorris Braithwaite, interview, 11 May 1995.
93.   CCINTB 95–135: Hilda Moss, correspondence, February 1995.
94.   CCINTB 92–2: Molly Stevenson, correspondence, 23 December 1992.
95.   CCINTB 92–11b: Margaret Walsh, interview, 27 January 1995.
96.   CCINTB 95–36: Norman Wild, interview, 13 June 1995 – Vera Entwistle interpreting.
97.   Mayer, *British Cinema*, p. 87.
98.   Buckingham, *Moving Images*, pp. 129–30.
99.   CCINTB 95–91: Joan Howarth, correspondence, 3 February 1995.
100. CCINTB 95–87: Joan F. Donoghue, correspondence, 11 February 1995.
101. Buckingham, *Moving Images*, p. 307.
102. CCINTB 92–11a: Tom Walsh, interview, 27 January 1995.
103. CCINTB 92–4: Sheila McWhinnie, questionnaire.
104. BFI Censorship Folder – Verbatim Reports 1930–1938: Proceedings of a conference, 'Children and Films', held under the auspices of the Cinema Christian Council and the Public Morality Council, 16 February 1937, p. 17.
105. Birmingham Cinema Enquiry Committee, *Report of Investigations, April 1930–May 1931* (Birmingham, 1931), p. 19.
106. CCINTB 95–201: Raphael 'Ralph' Hart, interview, 24 July 1995.
107. CCINTB 92–9: Thomas McGoran, interview, 30 November 1994.
108. British Film Institute, *Report of the Conference on Films for Elementary School Children, November 20–21, 1936* (London, 1937), p. 32.
109. Ibid.
110. CCINTB 92–1&2: Margaret Young & Molly Stevenson, interview, 5 December 1994.
111. Buckingham, *Moving Images*, pp. 255–6.

Chapter 6

1.   CCINTB 92–9: Thomas McGoran, interview, 20 November 1994.
2.   Judith Mayne, *Cinema and Spectatorship* (London, 1993), pp. 1–3.
3.   There is a range of evidence for such payment in kind, but the rather unusual example of rabbit skins is from CCINTB 95–127, Phyllis Bennett, interview, 27 November 1995.
4.   CCINTB 95–182: Ellen Casey, interview, 31 May 1995.
5.   CCINTB 95–48: Brigadier J.B. Ryall, letter, 8 February 1995.
6.   CCINTB 95–207a: Irene Letchet, interview, 21 July 1995.
7.   CCINTB 95–33 Les Sutton, book extracts.
8.   CCINTB 95–207a: Irene Letchet, interview, 21 July 1995.
9.   NMS: Dickie Alexander (1932) – Piershill.
10. Richard Ford, *Children in the Cinema* (London, 1939), pp. 44–6.

11. J.P. Mayer, *British Cinemas and Their Audiences: Sociological Studies* (London, 1948), p. 64.

12. CCINTB 95–98: Valentine Tucker, letter, 6 February 1995.

13. Mayer, *British Cinemas*, p. 30.

14. Ibid., p. 41.

15. Ibid., p. 37.

16. Ibid., p. 62.

17. CCINTB 95–209: Michael Trewern-Bree, letter, 20 July 1995.

18. CCINTB 92–9: Thomas McGoran, interview, 20 November 1994.

19. For other examples see Annette Kuhn, *An Everyday Magic: Cinema and Cultural Memory* (London, 2002), pp. 100–37.

20. NMS: Agnes Watson, Dalmuir.

21. CCINTB 92–9: Thomas McGoran, interview, 20 November 1994.

22. Mayer, *British Cinemas*, p. 104.

23. Ibid., pp. 55–6.

24. Ibid., p. 31.

25. NMS: Freddie Martin, letter, 7 October 1999.

26. NMS: Jim Dunsmore, Edinburgh.

27. The specific question was: 'How did films influence your play and other activities?' Mayer, *British Cinemas*, p. 14.

28. Ibid., p. 50.

29. Ibid., p. 109.

30. Ibid., pp. 41 and 114–15.

31. NMS: Lucinda Allan, Grantown-on-Spey.

32. Mayer, *British Cinemas*, p. 56.

33. Ibid., p. 65.

34. NMS: Angus Bruce, letter, 30 September 1999.

35. Mayer, *British Cinemas*, p. 36.

36. Ibid., p. 50.

37. Ibid., p. 129.

38. CCINTB 95–92: Maurice F. Dela Bertauche, letter, 6 February 1995.

39. CCINTB 95–36: Vera Entwistle, in interview with Norman Wild, 13 June 1995.

40. Mayer, *British Cinemas*, p. 104.

41. CCINTB 95–299: Ivy Royal, letter, 21 September 1995.

42. Mayer, *British Cinemas*, pp. 30–1.

43. Ibid., pp. 97–8.

44. CCINTB 95–214: Jim Godbold, interview, 17 October 1995.

45. For other examples of Durbin's influence see Kuhn, *Everyday Magic*, pp. 114–20.

46. CCINTB 95–208: Beatrice Cooper, interview, 27 November 1995.

47. Mayer, *British Cinemas*, p. 83.

48. Ibid., p. 42.

49. CCINTB 95–207a: Irene Letchet, interview, 21 July 1995.

50. Mayer, *British Cinemas*, p. 65.

51. Ibid., p. 51.

52. Ibid., pp. 83–4.

53. Ibid., p. 54.

54.   Ibid., p. 46.

55.   Ibid., p. 89.

56.   Ibid., p. 98.

57.   Ibid., p. 42.

58.   CCINTB 92–1: Margaret Young, interview, 5 December 1994.

59.   Joanna Matthews, born 15 March 1929, Cumberland. Personal correspondence with author, 7 January 2003.

60.   See for example, CCINTB 95–216–8&9: Scrapbooks of cuttings from 1930s film magazines.

61.   *Film Pictorial*, 30 September 1933, p. 23. See Kuhn, *Everyday Magic*, pp. 123–8.

62.   Mayer, *British Cinemas*, p. 41. See also pp. 44 & 83.

63.   See, for example, CCINTB 92–1–20c: Margaret Young, ms diary, 1930s–1940s. Also Mayer, *British Cinemas*, p. 83.

64.   See, for example, CCINTB 92–1–20a: Collection of 1930s cigarette cards.

65.   For examples see CCINTB 95–34–25,26 & 27: *The Golden Album of Film Stars – Picturegoer* collectors' albums of early 1930s signed postcard photographs; CCINTB 95–34–28: Collection of 159 *Picturegoer* Postcard Club cards; CCINTB 95–34–29a–q: Letters and photographs in response to fan mail, early 1930s; CCINTB 96–3–3: Scrapbook of 1930s film star photographs.

66.   Mayer, *British Cinemas*, p. 128.

67.   Ibid., p. 46.

68.   Ibid., p. 45.

69.   Ibid., p. 47.

70.   Ibid., p. 90.

71.   Ibid., p. 85.

72.   See Terry Staples, *All Pals Together: The Story of Children's Cinema* (Edinburgh, 1997), pp. 1–28; and Richard deCordova, 'Ethnography and Exhibition: The Child Audience, the Hays Office and Saturday Matinees', *Camera Obscura* (May 1990), pp. 90–107.

73.   The official report was published as: Major T.H. Crozier (H.M. Chief Inspector of Explosives), *Report to the Right Honourable Secretary of State for Scotland on the Circumstances attending the Loss of Life at the Glen Cinema, Paisley, on the 31st December, 1929* (HMSO, 1930).

74.   *Daily Mail*, 1 January 1930, p. 1.

75.   SFA – 8/35: Interview with James Porter (b.1919), April 1981.

76.   *The Times*, 1 & 2 May 1930.

77.   For numerous examples see PRO–HO45/15166: Control of cinematograph theatres after Paisley inquiry 1930–1933.

78.   Section 121 of the Children Act 1908 stated that if any entertainment for young people attracted more than 100 children and the venue included stairs, the provider of that entertainment must employ enough adult attendants to prevent overcrowding and to safeguard the welfare of the children involved. Crozier, *Report*, p. 14.

79.   Crozier, *Report*, p. 9.

80.   This amendment aimed to reinforce the 1908 Children Act, cited in Note 78. It was effective from 1 July 1930; a circular was sent out to all licensing authorities to inform them on 19 June 1930 and it was widely reported in the press. PRO–HO45/15166: Control of cinematograph theatres after Paisley inquiry 1930–1933.

81.   PRO–HO45/14731: Children and the cinema 1929–1932; see also the published report, A.D.K. Owen, 'Cinema Matinees for Children', *Social Service Review* (July 1931), pp. 141–4.

82.   Owen, 'Cinema Matinees', p. 142.

83.   Ibid.

84.   PRO–HO45/14731: Children and the cinema 1929–1932.

85.   Owen, 'Cinema Matinees', p. 142.

86.   Ibid., p. 143.

87.   PRO–HO45/14731: Children and the cinema 1929–1932.

88.   Owen, 'Cinema Matinees', p. 144.

89.   PRO–HO45/17036: Films for children 1932–1937.

90.   See British Film Institute, *Report of the Conference on Films for Elementary School Children, November 20–21, 1936* (London, 1937); PRO–HO45/17036: Films for children 1932–1937; and British Film Institute, *Suggested Programmes for Children's Matinees* (London, 1937).

91.   David Oswell, 'Early Children's Broadcasting in Britain: Programming for a Liberal Democracy', *Historical Journal of Film, Radio and Television*, 18, 3 (1998), pp. 375 & 382.

92.   For a contemporary overview of this movement, and other 'productive' approaches, see Ford, *Children in the Cinema*.

93.   Cited in Staples, *All Pals Together*, p. 52.

94.   Ibid., p. 53.

95.   Ford, *Children in the Cinema*, p. 162.

96.   For the philosophy of the Odeon clubs, see Odeon Theatres Limited, *Odeon National Cinema Club for Boys and Girls: Aims and Objects* (Birmingham, no date: 194?).

97.   Cited in Staples, *All Pals Together*, p. 60.

98.   CCINTB 95–141: John Ford, letter, 13 February 1995.

99.   Cited in Ford, *Children in the Cinema*, p. 157.

100.   PRO–HO45/16327: Unsuitable premises for children's cinema exhibitions 1932–1935. Letter dated 20 August 1932.

101.   Ibid. See also *Daily Sketch*, 4 January 1934.

102.   PRO–HO45/16327: Farley Palace Kinema handbill from 1932.

103.   *The Daily Mirror*, 3 January 1934; *Daily Mail*, 2 & 3 January 1934; *Daily Sketch*, 4 January 1934; *Manchester Guardian*, 2 January 1934.

104.   PRO–HO45/16327: Letter dated 8 January 1934 and *passim*.

105.   *Daily Mirror*, 17 September 1934; *Today's Cinema*, 18 September 1934; *Daily Mail*, 18 September 1934; *News Chronicle*, 18 September 1934.

106.   Miriam Hansen, *Babel and Babylon: Spectatorship in American Silent Film* (London, 1991); Mayne, *Cinema and Spectatorship*, p. 67.

107.   Mayer, *British Cinemas*, p. 118.

Chapter 7

1.   For example, see 'All American Monsters', 'Sick Lyrics of Marilyn Manson', 'Hitler-Worshipping Fanatics Linked by a Web of Hate' and 'Outisders, A Gun Culture and a Dangerous Diet of TV Death and Destruction', *Daily Record*, 22 April

1999, pp. 1 & 6–9; see also Martin Barker and Julian Petley (eds), *Ill Effects: The Media/Violence Debate*, 2e (London, 2001), pp. 23 & 27–46.

2.   Graham Murdock, 'Reservoirs of Dogma: An Archaeology of Popular Anxieties', in Barker & Petley (eds), *Ill Effects*, p. 153.

3.   David Buckingham, *Moving Images: Understanding Children's Emotional Responses to Television* (Manchester, 1996), p. 257.

4.   Cary Bazalgette and David Buckingham (eds), *In Front of the Children: Screen Entertainment and Young Audiences* (London, 1995), p. 3.

5.   For more detail on these developments see Terry Staples, *All Pals Together: The Story of Children's Cinema* (Edinburgh, 1997).

6.   For example, see Meridian Tonight, 'Children and the Internet', 10 July 2001 (http://www.meridian.tv.co.uk/pdf_files/consumer/sortedchildinternet.pdf); or 'Chat Danger – Parent's Guide' (http://www.chatdanger.com/parents/main.htm).

Bibliography

Unpublished Primary Sources

Oral History and Correspondence Archives

Cinema Culture in 1930s Britain, Institute For Cultural Research (CCINTB), Lancaster University
While all files in this archive were examined, only those considered directly relevant are listed below. Numbers refer to individual respondents whose files may include interview transcripts, questionnaires and correspondence. Dates of birth are listed as (known) or [estimated]. Geographical locations, where listed, refer to the place in which respondents lived as children. All interviews were conducted by Valentina Bold.

CCINTB 92–1   Margaret Young (24 November 1925) – Glasgow
CCINTB 92–2   Molly Stevenson (17 June 1923) – Glasgow
CCINTB 92–3   Marjorie Cunningham (21 July 1930) – Cowcaddens, Glasgow
CCINTB 92–4   Sheila McWhinnie (19 November 1919) – Gorbals, Glasgow
CCINTB 92–9   Thomas McGoran (22 November 1927) – Glasgow
CCINTB 92–11a   Tom Walsh (1922) – Glasgow
CCINTB 92–11b   Margaret Walsh (29 August 1928) – Glasgow
CCINTB 92–16   Tom Affleck [1924] – Lesmahagow, Lanarkshire
CCINTB 92–35   A. Murrie (1928) – Hamilton, Lanarkshire
CCINTB 95–32   Annie Wright (November 1919) – Manchester
CCINTB 95–33   Les Sutton (3 March 1922) – Ardwick, Manchester
CCINTB 95–34   A. Denis Houlston (20 Feb 1917) – Levenshulme, Manchester
CCINTB 95–36   Norman Wild (23 August 1926) – Bolton
CCINTB 95–38   Doris Braithwaite (1922) – Stockport

CCINTB 95–39	Mr J. Murray (November 1920) – Bury, Greater Manchester
CCINTB 95–44	Kath Browne (1921) – Bolton
CCINTB 95–48	Brigadier J.B. Ryall, C.B.E. (1922) – Golders Green, London
CCINTB 95–51	Vera Entwistle (1 December 1926) – Bolton
CCINTB 95–54	Mr S.H. Beadle (1915) – Beckenham/Penge, London
CCINTB 95–55	J. Charles Hall (1927) – Battersea, London
CCINTB 95–60	Olive M. Johnson (1922) – Exeter
CCINTB 95–66	Beryl M. Down [1929] – Welsh mining valley
CCINTB 95–77	Mrs M. Schneiderman (1931) – London
CCINTB 95–81	Bernard Goodsall [pre-1925] – Essex
CCINTB 95–83	Mr W. Ward (1923) – Manchester
CCINTB 95–87	Joan F. Donoghue (1923)
CCINTB 95–91	Joan Howarth
CCINTB 95–92	Maurice F. Dela Bertauche (1925)
CCINTB 95–93	Jessie Boyd (30 November 1922) – Middleton, Lancashire
CCINTB 95–96	Bob Surtees (1922) – South Shields
CCINTB 95–98	Valentine Tucker (1925) – Dagenham, London
CCINTB 95–100	Lewis Howells (1923) – Blaenavon, Gwent
CCINTB 95–108	Eric Holmes – East End of London
CCINTB 95–110	Betty Verdant
CCINTB 95–119	Mr A.M. Peary (1925) – North London
CCINTB 95–121	James F. Barton (1923) – Sheffield
CCINTB 95–127	Phyllis Bennett – Norwich
CCINTB 95–135	Hilda Moss (1927) – Welsh valley
CCINTB 95–141	John Ford (1923) – Watford
CCINTB 95–175	Arthur Orrell (29 March 1920) – Farnworth/Bolton
CCINTB 95–182	Ellen Casey (1921) – Manchester
CCINTB 95–190	Olga Scowen (4 December 1918) – Harrow, London
CCINTB 95–195	Eileen Barnett (1924) – North London
CCINTB 95–201	Raphael 'Ralph' Hart (1921) – Golders Green, London
CCINTB 95–202	Anthony Venis (1924) – Wembley, London
CCINTB 95–207a	Irene Letchet (1923) – Islington, London
CCINTB 95–207b	Bernard Letchet (15 February 1926) – Finchley, London
CCINTB 95–208	Beatrice Cooper (1921) – Hendon, London
CCINTB 95–209	Michael Trewern-Bree [1920s] – Penzance, Cornwall
CCINTB 95–214	E. Jim Godbold (1918) – Stowmarket, Suffolk
CCINTB 95–230	Sam Reilly (1932) – Dennistoun, Glasgow
CCINTB 95–232	Raymond Aspden (1923) – Blackburn
CCINTB 95–233	M. Coia
CCINTB 95–272	Zonia Ives (1926) – Great Yarmouth
CCINTB 95–276	Eric Williams (1925) – Great Yarmouth
CCINTB 95–279	J.G. Leggett (1921) – Great Yarmouth
CCINTB 95–299	Ivy Royal (17 November 1921) – Norwich
CCINTB 95–304	Lilian Wilkinson – Norwich
CCINTB 95–316	Barbara Duncan (1927) – Norwich
CCINTB 95–318	Dulcie Chapman [1927] – Littleport, Cambs
CCINTB 95–322	Mr E.F. Prew (1932) – Ipswich
CCINTB 95–325	Mrs Zena Jesney [1919] – London

CCINTB 95–334   Irene Woollestone (30 August 1912) – Norwich
CCINTB 95–337   Mrs T. Mather (4 July 1934) – Stretford, Lancs
CCINTB 95–338   Mr N. Wright (19 March 1920) – Manchester
CCINTB 95–341   Mr W. Ashton (28 August 1923) – Rostrevor, County Down

Memorabilia and donations

CCINTB 92–1–20a   Collection of 1930s cigarette cards
CCINTB 92–1–20c   Margaret Young ms diary 1930s–1940s
CCINTB 95–216–8&9   Scrapbooks of cuttings from 1930s film magazines
CCINTB 95–34–25,26&27 *The Golden Album of Film Stars* – *Picturegoer* collectors' albums of early 1930s signed postcard photographs
CCINTB 95–34–28   Collection of 159 *Picturegoer* Postcard Club cards
CCINTB 95–34–29a–q   Letters and photographs in response to fan mail, early 1930s
CCINTB 96–3–3   Scrapbook of 1930s film star photographs

Oral History Collection, Scottish Film Archive, Glasgow
Unless otherwise stated, interviewer was Janet McBain, Curator of Scottish Film Archive. Includes file number, (date of birth) where known and [date of interview].

8/5   George Singleton (born c.1899) – Manager and owner of Singleton's cinemas from the 1920s [9 December 1977]
8/8   Robert Douglas – Projectionist [21 March 1978]
8/10   Mr J.K.S. Poole (b.1911) – Owner of the Cameo, Edinburgh [24 May 1978]
8/11   Peter Armour – Owner and manager of the Picture House, Campbelltown [24 July 1978]
8/12   James 'Jimmy' Nairn – Manager, film-maker, since 1918 [19 September 1978]
8/17   Bill Ramsay – Manager of Victoria Cinema, Dundee [21 June 1979]
8/18   Robert Gavin and Robert Scott – Former managers of ABC cinemas, West of Scotland [12 December 1979]
8/28   George Miller – Projectionist and manager [29 July 1980]
8/29   J.B. Barclay – Co-founder of Scottish Evacuation Film Scheme, 1939, relating its history for the National Library of Scotland [29 January 1980]
8/30   J.B. Barclay – Co-founder of Saturday morning cinema shows for Edinburgh school children 1932–8, relating their history for the National Library of Scotland [1980]
8/35   James Porter (b.1919) and William Stirling (b.1922) – Survivors of the Glen Cinema Disaster in Paisley, 31 December 1929 [April 1981]
8/39   Ken Smith – Manager, and Charlie Brownlie – Projectionist, of the Odeon Cinema, Eglinton Toll, Glasgow [24 October 1981]
8/40   Oscar Baillie (b.1909) – Manager for Gaumont British and George Green Ltd. [12 November 1981]

8/41   Bill Grant (b.1909) – Employee, Paramount Film Renters [7 December 1981]

8/42   'Chick' Ellis (b.1891) – Film renter & sales manager for Fox & Warner Bros. [5 March 1982]

8/45   Winnie Lees (b.1914) – Film critic, *Sunday Mail*, 1950–83 [14 June 1983]

8/46   Johnny Mulhearn (b.1911) – Spool boy, projectionist [20 June 1983]

8/47   George Kemp (b.1913) – Exhibitor [28 June 1983]

8/48   John Boll – Spool boy and projectionist [4 July 1983]

8/49   Alex Frutin (b. pre-1903) – Exhibitor and theatre owner [7 July 1983]

8/50   Alec Davidson – Projectionist; started cinema work 1927 [4 August 1983]

8/51   Bessie McCue *née* Fury – Usherette at the Royal, Glasgow, c.1930–46 [8 August 1983]

8/52   Mrs Smillie – BB children's matinee member [10 August 1983]

8/53   Mrs Stevenson (b.1903) – Attender of children's matinees, 1909–11 [10 August 1983]

8/54   Bert Mcguffie (b.1896) – Attender of Wellington Palace, Gorbals, Glasgow, c.1908 [17 August 1983]

8/55   Katie Smith (b.1910) and Jack Smith – Cinema-goers since c.1914 [September 1983]

8/57   Richard Telfer – Cinema organist, Edinburgh 1932–50 [2 November 1983]

8/58   Alex Hamill – Chocolate Boy (aged 14) and Spool Boy (aged 15) during the 1930s and projectionist after World War Two [8 November 1983]

8/64   Vess Hudson – Manager and owner, interviewed with his sister and their film-going friend [6 December 1984]

8/65   Jack Brown – Manager for Rank, from the 1930s [14 December 1984]

8/66   Willie Tennant – Cinema pianist, c.1927–30 [c.1985]

8/67   Mrs Jenny Chapman (b.1910) – Daughter of a cinema owner in Kirriemuir, 1913–20 [27 March 1985]

8/68   Mrs Peggy McBride – Manageress, La Scala, Edinburgh, 1923–? [27 March 1985]

8/69   Mrs Mary Robertson – Attender of children's matinees in Glasgow, c.1918 [November 1985]

8/70   Mrs Peg Howie – Manageress of the Kinema, Newmills, interviewed with her son, Frank [26 March 1986]

8/71   Graham Salmon – Former secretary of Cinematograph Exhibitors' Association, interviewed with his sister, Catherine [3 April 1986]

8/79   Sandy Campbell – Projectionist, Cupar and Dunfermline [4 August 1987]

5/7/97   David Gouk – Former Pathe film distributor and member of the Glasgow Cinema Club, interviewed by unknown party for the People's Palace Museum, Glasgow [6 November 1975]

5/7/314 Norman Woolstenhulme – Former cinema manager and film distributor; interviewers Catriona Finlayson & Matthew Hume [1 February 1996]

5/7/315 Derek Cameron – Owner and manager of Dominion Cinema, Edinburgh; interviewers Catriona Finlayson and Matthew Hume [16 January 1996]

5/7/316   Charlie Hamill – Projectionist for Paragon, Gorbals, Glasgow, from
c.1930; interviewers Catriona Finlayson and Matthew Hume [c.1995–6]
5/7/319   Grahame Wear – Manager, Odeon Cinema, Clerk Street, Edinburgh;
interviewers Catriona Finlayson and Matthew Hume [21 December
1995]

**'Going to the Pictures' Project, Scottish Life Archive, National Museums of
Scotland, Edinburgh**
All the material in this collection was examined; that considered directly relevant
is listed below. Individual correspondents' files include letters and other materials.
Dates of birth are listed as either (known) or [estimated]. Geographical locations,
where listed, refer to the place in which respondents lived as children.

Dickie Alexander (1932) – Piershill
Lucinda Allan [1923] – Grantown-on-Spey
George Anderson
Elspeth Beaton – Glasgow
Angus Bruce – Leith
Molly Buchanan (1930) – Glasgow
Joan Connelly [1929]
Mary Cook (1915) – Dundee
William Cooper [1925] – Aberdeen
Mabel Cunningham (1920) – Dennistoun, Glasgow
Jim Douglas (1933) – Fife
May Dunn (1931) – Glasgow
Jim Dunsmore [1925] – Edinburgh
John Finnie [1928] – Innerleithen, Edinburgh
Hazel Galloway
Catherine Jarvis (1905)
J.D. MacDonald [1925] – Thurso
Freddie Martin [1932] – Glasgow
Mathilda Roberts [1918] – Edinburgh
Agnes Watson – Dalmuir
Walter Watt (November 1924)
John Williamson (1929)
Ann Young (1938) – Townhead, Glasgow

Other Archives

Public Record Office, Kew
HO45/10551/163175: Film Censorship 1912–1914
HO45/10811/312397/1: Conference of local authorities, 14 April 1916
HO45/11008/272403: CHILDREN – child attendance at cinematograph 1915–1917
HO45/12969: Children and the cinema 1919–1928
HO45/139/6: PORTFOLIO – no.12 BBFC
HO45/14731: Children and the cinema 1929–1932
HO45/15166: Control of cinematograph theatres after Paisley inquiry 1930–1933
HO45/15175: Cinematograph regulations, miscellaneous, 1930–1933

HO45/15206: Film Censorship in the UK 18 September 1931–30 April 1932
HO45/15207: Film Censorship in the UK 19 May 1932–26 May 1933
HO45/15208: Film Censorship Consultative Committee 1931–1933
HO45/16327: Unsuitable premises for children's cinema exhibitions 1932–1935
HO45/17036: Films for children [children and 'A' Films] 1932–1937
HO45/18047: CHILDREN – children taking part in entertainments 1933–1939
HO45/20876: Cinema operators: age and qualifications 1915–1947
HO45/21118: Admission of children to cinemas 1937–1947
HO45/21310: CHANNEL ISLANDS – admission of children to cinemas 1947
HO45/22906: Censorship: powers of BBFC and local authorities 1923–1929
HO45/24084: BBFC legal position and work of the board 1926–1950
HO45/24945: Film Censorship Consultative Committee 1934–1951
MEPO2/1528: METROPOLITAN POLICE – BBFC, Inception and functions
   1913

Special Collections, British Film Institute, London
BBFC Verbatim Reports 1930–1931 and 1932–1935
Censorship Folder – Verbatim Reports 1930–1938
London County Council Verbatim Reports 1929–1930
BFI Clippings Collection 1935–1940
Bernstein Collection
Ivor Montagu Collection
BBFC Scenarios 1930–1939
Snow White and the Seven Dwarfs Collection
Press books and clippings files

Special Collections, Margaret Herrick Library, Beverly Hills, California
Production Code Administration (Hays Office) Files
Press Books and Clippings Files
A. Arnold Gillespie Collection
Bud Barsky Collection
Biography Collections
Metro Goldwyn Mayer Script Collection

Published Primary Sources

Allen, Lady Allen of Hurtwood (July 1946), 'Children and the Cinema', reprinted
   from *The Fortnightly Review*.
Bell, Oliver (1938), *An Exposé of the Principles of British Organisation of
   Children's Recreational Films, to be given in Geneva to the Child Welfare
   Commission of the League of Nations* (London).
Bell, Oliver (1939), *Sociological Aspects of the Cinema* (London).
Birkenhead Vigilance Committee (1931), *The Cinema and the Child: A Report of
   Investigations, June–October 1931* (Birkenhead).
Birmingham Cinema Enquiry Committee (1931), *Report of Investigations, April
   1930–May 1931* (Birmingham).

Blumer, Herbert (ed.), 'The Motion Picture Autobiographies' and 'Private Monograph on Movies and Sex', reprinted in Garth S. Jowett, Ian C. Jarvie and Kathryn H. Fuller (1996), *Children and the Movies: Media Influence and the Payne Fund Controversy* (Cambridge), pp. 242–80.

British Film Institute (1937), *Report of the Conference on Films for Elementary School Children, November 20–21, 1936* (London).

British Film Institute (1937), *Suggested Programmes for Children's Matinees* (London, BFI).

British Film Institute (1937), *The Cinema and Education: A Summary of the Reports Issued by Various Local Education Authorities in Great Britain, by A.A. Denholme* (London).

British Film Institute (1943), *The Film in National Life: Proceedings of a Conference held by the BFI in Exeter, April 1943* (London).

British Film Institute and Motion Picture Association of America (c. 1950), *Delinquent Children: A World Problem* (London).

Browning, H.E. and Sorrell, A.A. (1954), 'Cinemas and Cinema-going in Great Britain', *Journal of the Royal Statistical Society*, Series A, Part 2, pp. 133–70.

Burnett, R.G. and Martell, E.D. (1932), *The Devil's Camera: Menace of a Film-ridden World* (London).

Commission on Educational and Cultural Films (1932) *The Film in National Life: Being the report of an enquiry conducted by the Commission into the service which the cinematograph may render to education and social progress* (London).

Comstock, Anthony (1967), *Traps For The Young* (1883), edited by Robert Bremner (Cambridge, Mass.).

Corporation of Glasgow Education Department, Sub-committee on Visual Education (1933), *The Film in the Classroom* (November).

Cressey, Paul G. (1938), 'The Motion Picture Experience as Modified by Social Background and Personality', *American Sociological Review*, 3 (August), pp. 516–25, reprinted in Garth S. Jowett, Ian C. Jarvie and Kathryn H. Fuller (1996), *Children and the Movies: Media Influence and the Payne Fund Controversy* (Cambridge), pp. 336–45.

Crozier, Major T.H. (H.M. Chief Inspector of Explosives) (1930) *Report to the Right Honourable Secretary of State for Scotland on the Circumstances attending the Loss of Life at the Glen Cinema, Paisley, on the 31st December, 1929* (London: HMSO).

Erith Education Committee (1935), *The Effect of War Films on Child Opinion: Report of an Investigation, Erith, 1935* (Erith).

Film Lovers Annual, The (1932) (London).

Ford, Richard (1939), *Children in the Cinema* (London).

Forman, Henry James (1933), *Our Movie-Made Children* (New York).

Greiner, Grace, 'Children and the Cinema' (1954), *Christus Rex* (July), pp. 252–60.

Humbert, Dr, 'Effect of Cinematograph on the Mental and Moral Well-Being of Children: A report to the Child Welfare Committee of the League of Nations, Geneva, May 1926', in W.M. Seabury (1929), *Motion Picture Problems: The Cinema and the League of Nations* (New York), pp. 265–355.

Hunter, William (1932), *Scrutiny of Cinema* (London).

Interim Report of the Joint Committee on Eyestrain in Cinemas (1919) (London).

International Educational Cinematographic Institute (c.1930), *The Social Aspects of the Cinema* (Rome).

International Institute of Educational Cinematography (1934), *The International Congress of Educational and Instructional Cinematography, Rome 1934* (Rome).

International Institute of Intellectual Co-operation (1940), *The Cinema and the Public: Preliminary Results of an International Enquiry* (Paris).

Juvenile Organisations Committee of the Board of Education (1920), *Report on Juvenile Delinquency* (London).

League of Nations Advisory Committee on Social Questions (1938), *The Recreational Cinema and the Young* (Geneva).

League of Nations Child Welfare Committee, Twelfth Session, April 27th, 1936 (1936), *Recreational Aspects of Cinematography* (Geneva).

London County Council (1951), *London Children and the Cinema* (London).

Mackie, John (ed.) (1933), *The Edinburgh Cinema Enquiry: Being an investigation conducted into the influence of the film on school children and adolescents in the city* (Edinburgh).

Mayer, J.P. (1948), *British Cinemas and Their Audiences: Sociological Studies* (London).

Middlesbrough Head Teachers' Association (1946), *Children and the Cinema: Report on an investigation carried out in June 1946* (Middlesbrough).

Mitchell, Alice Miller (1929), *Children and Movies* (Chicago).

National Council of Public Morals (1917), *The Cinema: Its Present Position and Future Possibilities – being the report and chief evidence taken by the Cinema Commission of Inquiry, instituted by the National Council of Public Morals* (London).

National Council on Freedom from Censorship (1933), *What Shocked the Censors: A Complete Record of Cuts in Motion Film Ordered by New York State Censors, 1/32–3/33* (New York).

National Under Fourteens Council (1947), *Those Saturday Morning Cinema Clubs: Report on the cinema clubs in the London County Council Area* (London).

Newnham, John K., 'Film Censors', in Clarence Winchester (ed.) (1933), *The World Film Encyclopedia: A Universal Screen Guide* (London), pp. 13–17.

Odeon Theatres Limited (194?), *Odeon National Cinema Club for Boys and Girls: Aims and Objects* (Birmingham).

Owen, A.D.K., 'Cinema Matinees for Children' (1931), *Social Service Review* (July), pp. 141–4.

Payne Fund Studies, the
– Blumer, H. (1933), *Movies and Conduct* (New York).
– Blumer, H. and Hauser, P.M. (1935), *Movies, Delinquency and Crime* (New York).
– Charters, W.W. (1933), *Motion Pictures and Youth: A Summary* (New York).
– Cressey, P.G. and Thrasher, F.M. (1933), *Boys, Movies and City Streets* (New York).

- Dale, E. (1935), *Children's Attendance at Motion Pictures* (New York).
- Dale, E. (1935), *The Content of Motion Pictures* (New York).
- Dysinger, W.S. and Ruckmick, C.A. (1933), *The Emotional Responses of Children to the Motion Picture Situation* (New York).
- Holaday, P.W. (1933), *Getting Ideas from the Movies* (New York).
- Margrave, Seton (ed.) (1935), *Meet the Film Stars 1934–1935* (London).
- May, M.A. and Shuttleworth F.K. (1933), *The Social Conduct and Attitudes of Movie Fans* (New York).
- Peters, C.C. (1933), *Motion Pictures and Standards of Morality* (New York).
- Peterson, R.C. and Thurstone, L.L. (1933), *Motion Pictures and the Social Attitudes of Children* (New York).
- Renshaw, S., Miller, V.L. and Marquis, D. (1933), *Children's Sleep* (New York).

Perlman, William J. (ed.) (1936), *The Movies on Trial: The Views and Opinions of Outstanding Personalities Anent Screen Entertainment Past and Present* (New York).

Picture Show Annual for 1933, The (1933), (London).

Rook, Clarence, 'Hooligan London' in *Edwardian London* (1933), Vol.3 (1st edn 1902) (London).

Rowson, Simon (1936), 'Statistical Survey of the Cinema Industry in Great Britain in 1934' *Journal of the Royal Statistical Society*, 99, pp. 67–129.

Scottish Film Council (c.1955), *21 Years of the Scottish Film Council 1934–1955* (Glasgow).

Scunthorpe Grammar School (1938), *An Enquiry into the Cinema-Going Habits and Tastes of the Pupils of Scunthorpe Grammar School, November, 1938* (Scunthorpe).

Seabury, William Marston (1929), *The Public and the Motion Picture Industry* (New York).

Seabury, William Marston (1929), *Motion Picture Problems: The Cinema and the League of Nations* (New York).

Spencer, F.H. (1932), *School Children and the Cinema: London County Council Education Committee* (London).

Tavistock Institute of Human Relations (1947), *Report of an appraisal of children's road safety films, conducted for Petroleum Films Bureau* (London).

Under Secretary of State, Home Office (1934), *Children and 'A' Films: [A letter to] the Clerk to the Licensing Authority, under the Cinematograph Act 1909, 6 March 1933* (London: HMSO).

Ward, J.C. (1949), *Children and the Cinema: An inquiry made by the Social Survey in October 1948 for a Departmental Committee appointed by the Home Secretary, the Secretary of State for Scotland and the Minister of Education* (London).

Watts, Stephen (ed.) (1938), *Stars and Films of 1938* (London: Daily Express Publications).

Wheare, K.C. (1950), *Report of the Departmental Committee on Children and the Cinema* (London).

Newspapers and Periodicals

Answers
Belfast News-Letter
Bioscope
Birmingham Gazette
Birmingham Mail
Birmingham Post
Box Office
Bristol Evening Post
Catholic Film News
Catholic Herald
Cinematograph Times
Daily Express
Daily Film Renter
Daily Mail
Daily Mirror
Daily News
Daily Sketch
Daily Telegraph
Education
Enfield Gazette
Evening News
Evening Standard
Film Daily
Film Pictorial
Film Weekly
Glasgow Herald
Grimsby Daily Telegraph
Guardian
Harrison's Reports
Hendon Times
Hollywood Reporter
Hollywood Spectator
Illustrated London News
Justice of the Peace
Kinematograph and Lantern Weekly
Leeds Mercury
Leicestershire Mercury

Linlithgowshire Gazette
Liverpool Daily Post
Manchester Guardian
Methodist Recorder
Monthly Film Bulletin of the BFI
Morning Post
Motion Picture Daily
Motion Picture Herald
New York Herald Tribune
New York Journal
New York Post
New York Sun
New York Times
New Zealand Herald
Newcastle Evening Chronicle
News Chronicle
News of the World
Nottingham Guardian
Observer
The People
Photoplay
Picturegoer
Sheffield Independent
Showman's Trade Review
Sight and Sound
Stage
Star
Sunday Graphic
Sutherland Echo
Times
Times Educational Supplement
Today's Cinema (The Cinema)
Variety
Variety Daily
Weekly Scotsman
Wolverhampton Express & Star
Yorkshire Evening News

Secondary Sources

Agajanian, Rowena (1998), '"Just For Kids?" Saturday Morning Cinema and Britain's Children's Film Foundation in the 1960s', *Historical Journal of Film, Radio and Television*, 18, 3, pp. 395–409.

Anderson, James A. (1981), 'Research on Children and Television: A Critique',

Journal of Broadcasting, 25, pp. 395–400.

Anderson, James A., Meyer, Timothy P. and Hexamer, Anne, 'An Examination of the Assumptions Underlying Telecommunications Social Policies Treating Children as a Specialized Audience', in M. Burgoon (ed.) (1982), *Communication Year Book 5* (New Brunswick), pp. 369–84.

Ang, I. (1991), *Desperately Seeking the Audience* (London).

Aries, Philippe (1960), *Centuries of Childhood* (Harmondsworth).

Barker, Martin (1984), *A Haunt of Fears: The Strange History of the British Horror Comics Campaign* (London).

Barker, Martin (1989), *Comics: Ideology, Power and the Critics* (Manchester).

Barker, Martin and Petley, Julian (eds) (2001), *Ill Effects: The Media/Violence Debate*, 2e (London).

Barr, Charles (ed.) (1986), *All Our Yesterdays: 90 Years of British Cinema* (London).

Bazalgette, Cary and Buckingham, David (eds) (1995), *In Front of the Children: Screen Entertainment and Young Audiences* (London).

Bernstein, Matthew (ed.) (1999), *Controlling Hollywood: Censorship and Regulation in the Studio Era* (New Brunswick).

Black, Gregory D. (1989), 'Hollywood Censored: The Production Code Administration and the Hollywood Film Industry, 1930–1940', *Film History*, 3, 3, pp. 167–89.

Black, Gregory D. (1994), *Hollywood Censored: Morality Codes, Catholics, and the Movies* (Cambridge).

Brownlow, Kevin (1990), *Behind the Mask of Innocence: Sex, Violence, Prejudice, Crime – Films of Social Conscience in the Silent Era* (Berkeley).

Buckingham, David (1987), *Children and Television: An Overview of the Research* (London: BFI Mimeo).

Buckingham, David (1993), *Children Talking Television: The Making of Television Literacy* (London).

Buckingham, David (1996), *Moving Images: Understanding Children's Emotional Responses to Television* (Manchester).

Buckingham, David, Davis, Hannah, Jones, Ken and Kelley, Peter (1999), *Children's Television in Britain: History, Discourse and Policy* (London).

Campbell, Beatrix (1995), 'Moral Panic', *Index on Censorship*, 24, 2, pp. 57–61.

Chanan, Michael (1980), *The Dream that Kicks: The Prehistory and Early Years of Cinema in Britain* (London).

Chen, Milton, 'Six Myths About Television and Children', in Everette E. Dennis and Edward C. Pease (eds) (1996), *Children and the Media* (London), pp. 77–85.

Clarens, Carlos (1977), 'The Hollywood G-Man, 1934–45', *Film Comment*, 13, 3, pp. 10–16.

Clifford, Brian R., Gunter, Barie and McAleer, Jill (1995), *Television and Children: Program Evaluation, Comprehension and Impact* (New Jersey).

Connell, Ian, 'Fabulous Powers: Blaming the Media', in Len Masterman (ed.) (1986), *Television Mythologies: Stars, Shows and Signs*, 2e (London), pp. 88–93.

Conway, Martin A. (1990), *Autobiographical Memory: An Introduction* (Milton Keynes).

Cooke, Lez, 'British Cinema: From Cottage Industry to Mass Entertainment', in Clive Bloom (ed.) (1993), *Literature and Culture in Modern Britain, Volume 1: 1900–29* (London), pp. 167–88.

Cullingford, Cedric (1984), *Children and Television* (Aldershot).

Curran, James and Porter, Vincent (eds) (1983), *British Cinema History* (London).

Czitrom, Daniel J. (1982), *Media and the American Mind: From Morse to McLuhan* (Chapel Hill).

Davies, P. & Neve, B. (eds) (1981), *Cinema, Politics & Society in America* (Manchester).

deCordova, Richard (1990), 'Ethnography and Exhibition: The Child Audience, the Hays Office and Saturday Matinees, *Camera Obscura* (May), pp. 90–107.

Dickinson, Margaret and Street, Sarah (1985), *Cinema and State: The Film Industry and the Government 1927–84* (London).

Doherty, Thomas (1999), *Pre-Code Hollywood: Sex, Immorality and Insurrection in American Cinema* (New York).

Drotner, Kirsten (1988), *English Children and their Magazines, 1751–1945* (London).

Eckert, Charles, 'Shirley Temple and the House of Rockerfeller', in Christine Gledhill (ed.) (1991), *Stardom: Industry of Desire* (London), pp. 60–73.

Elkin, F., and Handel, G. (1972), *The Child and Society: The Process of Socialization* (New York) (1st edn 1960).

Eysenck, H. J. and Nias, D. K. B. (1978), *Sex, Violence and the Media* (London).

Federal Trade Commission (2000), *Marketing Violent Entertainment To Children: A Review Of Self-Regulation And Industry Practices In The Motion Picture, Music Recording & Electronic Game Industries* (www.ftc.gov/opa/2000/09/youthviol.htm – published September, most recently viewed May 2004).

Fowler, David, 'Teenage Consumers? Young wage-earners and leisure in Manchester, 1919–1939', in A. Davies and S. Fielding (eds) (1992), *Workers' Worlds: Cultures and Communities in Manchester and Salford, 1880–1939* (Manchester).

Frayling, Christopher (1996), *Nightmare: The Birth of Horror* (London).

Fuller, Kathryn H. (1996), *At the Picture Show: Small-Town Audiences and the Creation of Movie Fan Culture* (London).

Gianetti, L. and Eyman, S. (1991), *Flashback: A Brief History of Film* (New Jersey)

Glancy, H. Mark (1992), 'MGM Film Grosses, 1924–1948: The Eddie Mannix Ledger', *Historical Journal of Film, Radio and Television*, 12, 2, pp. 127–44.

Glancy, H. Mark (1999), *When Hollywood Loved Britain: The Hollywood 'British' Film 1939–45* (Manchester).

Gordon, Colin (ed.) (1980), *Power/Knowledge: Selected Interviews and Other Writings 1972–1977 by Michel Foucault* (Hemel Hempstead).

Gosser, H. Mark (1998), 'The *Bazar de la Charité* Fire: The Reality, the Aftermath, the Telling', *Film History*, 10, 1, pp. 70–89.

Gunter, Barie and McAleer, Jill (1990), *Television and Children: The One-Eyed Monster?* (London).

Gunter, Barie and McAleer, Jill (1997), *Television and Children*, 2e (London).

Hall, Stuart and Jefferson, Tony (eds) (1976), *Resistance Through Rituals: Youth Subcultures in Post-war Britain* (London).

Halliwell, Leslie (1985), *Seats in All Parts: Half a Lifetime at the Movies* (London).

Hansen, Miriam (1991), *Babel and Babylon: Spectatorship in American Silent Film* (London).

Harrison, Brian (1973), 'For Church, Queen and Family: The Girls' Friendly Society 1874–1920', *Past and Present*, 61, pp. 107–38.

Hartley, John (1998), '"When Your Child Grows Up Too Fast": Juvenation and the Boundaries of the Social in the News Media', *Continuum*, 12, 1, pp. 9–30.

Hendrick, Harry (1997), *Children, Childhood & English Society 1880–1990* (Cambridge).

Hiley, Nicholas (1999), '"Let's Go to the Pictures": The British Cinema Audience in the 1920s and 1930s,' *Journal of Popular British Cinema*, 2, pp. 39–53.

Hodge, Robert and Tripp, David (1986), *Children and Television: A Semiotic Approach* (Cambridge).

Hoikkala, T., Rahkonen, O., Tigerstedt C. and Tuormaa, J. (1987), 'Wait a Minute Mr Postman! – Some Critical Remarks on Neil Postman's Childhood Theory', *Acta Sociologica*, 30, 1, pp. 87–99.

Howitt, Dennis and Cumberbatch, Guy (1975), *Mass Media, Violence and Society* (London).

Humphries, Stephen (1995), *Hooligans or Rebels? An Oral History of Working Class Childhood and Youth 1889–1939* (Oxford) (1st edn 1981).

Hunnings, Neville March (1967), *Film Censors and the Law* (London).

Jacobs, Lea (1991), *The Wages of Sin: Censorship and the Fallen Woman Film 1928–1942* (London).

James, Allison and Prout, Alan (eds) (1997), *Constructing and Reconstructing Childhood: Contemporary Issues in the Sociological Study of Childhood*, 2e (London).

Jenkins, Philip (1992), *Intimate Enemies: Moral Panics in Contemporary Great Britain* (New York).

Johnson, Tom (1997), *Censored Screams: The British Ban on Hollywood Horror in the Thirties* (London).

Jowett, Garth S. and Linton, J.M. (1980), *Movies as Mass Communication* (London).

Jowett, Garth S., Jarvie, Ian C. and Fuller, Kathryn H. (1996), *Children and the Movies: Media Influence and the Payne Fund Controversy* (Cambridge).

Kaes, Anton (1987), 'The Debate About Cinema: Charting a Controversy 1909–1929', *New German Critique*, 40 (Winter), pp. 7–33.

Kellerman, Jonathan (1999), *Savage Spawn: Reflections on Violent Children* (New York).

Kessel, Frank S. and Siegel, Alexander W. (eds) (1983), *The Child and Other Cultural Inventions* (New York).

Kift, Dagmar (1996), *The Victorian Music Hall: Culture, Class and Conflict* (Cambridge).

Kinder, Marsha (1991), *Playing with Power in Movies, Television and Video Games: From Muppet Babies to Teenage Mutant Ninja Turtles* (Oxford).

Kinnard, Roy (1995), *Horror in Silent Films: A Filmography, 1896–1929* (London).

Kuhn, Annette (1988), *Cinema, Censorship and Sexuality 1909–1925* (London:).

Kuhn, Annette and Stacey, Jackie (eds) (1998), *Screen Histories: A Screen Reader* (Oxford).

Kuhn, Annette (1999), 'Memories of Cinema-Going in the 1930s', *Journal of Popular British Cinema*, 2, pp. 100–20.

Kuhn, Annette (2002), *An Everyday Magic: Cinema and Cultural Memory* (London).

Larsen, Otto N. (ed.) (1968), *Violence and the Mass Media* (London).

Lewis, Sian (2000), 'Local Authorities and the Control of Film Exhibition in Britain in the Interwar Period', *Journal of Popular British Cinema*, 3, pp. 113–20.

Low, Rachael and Manvell, Roger (1948), *The History of the British Film, 1896–1906* (London).

Low, Rachael (1949), *The History of the British Film, 1906–1914* (London).

Low, Rachael (1950), *The History of the British Film, 1914–1918* (London).

Low, Rachael (1971), *The History of the British Film, 1918–1929* (London).

Low, Rachael (1985), *The History of the British Film, 1929–1939: Film Making in 1930s Britain* (London).

Lucie-Smith, Edward (1997), 'Eros & Innocence', *Index on Censorship*, 26, 2, pp. 139–44.

Luke, Carmen (1990), *Constructing the Child Viewer: A History of the American Discourse on Television and Children 1950–1980* (New York).

Lumby, Catharine (1998), 'No Kidding: Paedophilia and Popular Culture', *Continuum*, 12, 1, pp. 47–54.

McPherson, Don (ed.) (1980), *Traditions of Independence: British Cinema in the Thirties* (London).

May, Lary (1980), *Screening Out the Past: The Birth of Mass Culture and the Motion Picture Industry* (Oxford).

May, Margaret (1973), 'Innocence and Experience: the Evolution of the Concept of Juvenile Delinquency in the Mid-Nineteenth Century', *Victorian Studies*, 17, 1 (September), pp. 7–29.

Mayne, Judith (1993), *Cinema and Spectatorship* (London).

Melling, P.H., 'The mind of the mob: Hollywood and popular culture in the 1930s', in P. Davies and B. Neve (eds) (1981), *Cinema, Politics and Society in America* (Manchester), pp. 19–39.

Miles, Peter and Smith, Malcolm (1987), *Cinema, Literature and Society: Elite and Mass Culture in Interwar Britain* (London).

Miller, Frank (1994), *Censored Hollywood: Sex, Sin and Violence on Screen* (Atlanta).

Mitterauer, Michael (1992), *A History of Youth* (Oxford).

Moley, Raymond (1945), *The Hays Office* (New York).

Monaco, Paul (1976), *Cinema and Society: France and Germany During the Twenties* (New York).

Murdock, Graham and McCron, Robin (1979), 'The Television and Delinquency Debate', *Screen Education*, 30 (Spring), pp. 51–67.

Murphy, Robert (1989), *Realism and Tinsel: Cinema and Society in Britain, 1939–1948* (London).

Murphy, Robert (ed.) (1997), *The British Cinema Book* (London).

Musgrove, Frank (1964), *Youth and the Social Order* (London).

Neville, Richard (1970), *Play Power* (London).

Oswell, David (1998), 'Early Children's Broadcasting in Britain: Programming for a Liberal Democracy', *Historical Journal of Film, Radio and Television*, 18, 3, pp. 375–93.

Peter, Bruce (1996), *100 Years of Glasgow's Amazing Cinemas* (Edinburgh).

Philips, Baxter (1975), *Cut: The Unseen Cinema* (London).

Prawer, S. S. (1980), *Caligari's Children: The Film as Tale of Terror* (Oxford).

Prince, Stephen (ed.) (2000), *Screening Violence* (New Jersey).

Pronay, Nicholas, 'The First Reality: Film Censorship in Liberal England', in K.R.M. Short (ed.) (1981), *Feature Films as History* (London), pp. 113–37.

Pronay, Nicholas, 'The Political Censorship of Films in Britain', in N. Pronay and D. Spring (eds) (1982), *Propaganda, Politics and Film, 1918–45* (London).

Rapp, Dean (1996), 'The British Salvation Army, the Early Film Industry and Working Class Adolescents, 1897–1918', *Twentieth Century British History*, 7, 2, pp. 157–88.

Reader, Keith (1981), *Cultures on Celluloid* (London).

Richards, Jeffrey (1973) *Visions of Yesterday* (London).

Richards, Jeffrey (1981), 'The British Board of Film Censors and Content Control in the 1930s: Images of Britain', *Historical Journal of Film, Radio and Television*, 1, 2, pp. 95–116.

Richards, Jeffrey (1982), 'The British Board of Film Censors and Content Control in the 1930s: Foreign Affairs', *Historical Journal of Film, Radio and Television*, 2, 1, pp. 39–48.

Richards, Jeffrey, 'The Cinema and Cinema-going in Birmingham in the 1930s', in J. Walton and J. Walvin (eds) (1983), *Leisure in Britain 1780–1939* (Manchester), pp. 31–52.

Richards, Jeffrey and Aldgate, A. (1983), *Best of British: Cinema and Society 1930–70* (Oxford).

Richards, Jeffrey (1984), *The Age of the Dream Palace: Cinema and Society in Britain 1930–1939* (London).

Richards, Jeffrey and Sheridan, Dorothy (eds) (1987), *Mass Observation at the Movies* (London).

Richards, Jeffrey (ed.) (1998), *The Unknown 1930s: An Alternative History of the British Cinema 1929–1939* (London).

Ridgewell, Stephen (1996), 'The People's Amusement: Cinema and Cinema-going in 1930s Britain', *The Historian*, 52, pp.18–21.

Robertson, James C. (1982), 'British Film Censorship Goes to War', *Historical Journal of Film, Radio and Television*, 2, 1, pp. 49–64.

Robertson, James C. (1985), *The British Board of Film Censors: Film Censorship in Britain, 1896–1950* (London).

Robertson, James C. (1989), *The Hidden Cinema: British Film Censorship in Action, 1913–1972* (London).

Rose, Jacqueline, 'Peter Pan and the Commercialisation of the Child', in Tony Bennett (ed.) (1990), *Popular Fiction, Technology, Ideology, Production, Reading* (London), pp. 413–25.

Rowland, William (1983), *The Politics of TV Violence: Policy Uses of Communication Research* (London).

Sarris, Andrew (1977), 'Big Funerals: The Hollywood Gangster, 1927–1933', *Film*

Comment, 13, 3, pp. 6–9.

Satcher, David (Surgeon General) (2000), *Youth Violence: A Report of the Surgeon General* (http://www.surgeongeneral.gov/library/youthviolence/report.html – most recently viewed May 2004).

Schultze, Quentin J., Anker, Roy M., et al. (1991), *Dancing in the Dark: Youth, Popular Culture, and the Electronic Media* (Grand Rapids, MI).

Sedgwick, John (1998), 'Cinema-going Preferences in Britain in the 1930s', in Jeffrey Richards (ed.), *The Unknown 1930s: An Alternative History of the British Cinema 1929–1939* (London), pp. 1–35.

Sedgwick, John (1998), 'Film 'Hits' and 'Misses' in Mid-1930s Britain', *Historical Journal of Film, Radio and Television*, 18, 3, pp. 333–51.

Sedgwick, John (1999), 'The Comparative Popularity of Stars in Mid-1930s Britain', *Journal of Popular British Cinema*, 2, pp. 121–7.

Shaw, Colin (1999), *Deciding What We Watch: Taste, Decency, and Media Ethics in the UK and the USA* (Oxford).

Shindler, Colin (1996), *Hollywood in Crisis: Cinema and American Society 1929–1939* (London).

Slide, Anthony (1998), *'Banned in the USA': British Films in the United States and Their Censorship, 1933–1960* (London).

Springhall, John (1977), *Youth, Empire and Society: British Youth Movements, 1883–1940* (London).

Springhall, John (1986), *Coming of Age: Adolescence in Britain 1860–1960* (Dublin).

Springhall, John (1998), *Youth, Popular Culture and Moral Panics: Penny Gaffs to Gangsta Rap, 1830–1996* (Basingstoke).

Staples, Terry (1997), *All Pals Together: The Story of Children's Cinema* (Edinburgh).

Stark, Gary D. and Lackner, Bede Karl (eds) (1982), *Essays on Culture and Society in Modern Germany* (Arlington)

Stead, Peter (1989), *Film and the Working Class: The Feature Film in British and American Society* (London).

Steadman, Raymond Williams (1977), *The Serials: Suspense and Drama by Instalment*, 2e (Oklahoma).

Stickland, Irina (1973), *The Voices of Children 1700–1914* (Oxford).

Summerfield, Penny (2004), 'Culture and Composure: Creating Narratives of the Gendered Self in Oral History Interviews', *Cultural and Social History*, 1, pp. 65–93.

Sutton, David (2000), *A Chorus of Raspberries: British Film Comedy 1929–1939* (Exeter).

Thompson, Kenneth (1998), *Moral Panics* (London).

Tucker, Nicholas (1977), *What Is a Child?* (London).

Tulloch, John (1990), *Television Drama: Agency, Audience and Myth* (London).

Turner, Graeme (1988), *Film as Social Practice* (London).

Vasey, Ruth (1997), *The World According to Hollywood 1918–1939* (Exeter).

Vaughn, Stephen (1990), 'Morality and Entertainment: The Origins of the Motion Picture Production Code', *Journal of American History*, 77, 1, pp. 39–65.

Walvin, James (1982), *A Child's World: A Social History of English Childhood 1800–1914* (Harmondsworth).

Walvin, James, 'Children's Pleasures', in J. Walton and James Walvin (eds) (1983), *Leisure in Britain, 1780–1939* (Manchester).

Wartella, Ellen and Reeves, Byron (1985), 'Historical Trends in Research on Children and the Media: 1900–1960', *Journal of Communication*, 35, 2 (Spring), pp. 118–33.

Waters, Harry, 'What TV Does to Kids', reprinted in James Monaco (ed.) (1978), *Media Culture* (New York), pp. 241–61.

Winick, Mariann Pezzella and Winick, Charles (1979), *The Television Experience: What Children See* (London).

Youngblood, Denise J. (1992), *Movies for the Masses: Popular Cinema and Soviet Society in the 1920s* (Cambridge).

Zelizer, Viviana A. (1985), *Pricing the Priceless Child: The Changing Social Value of Children* (New York).

Zinman, David (1973), *Saturday Afternoon at the Bijou* (New York).

Index